DEVELOPING LANGUAGE AND LITERACY in the English National Curriculum

DEVELOPING LANGUAGE AND LITERACY

in the English National Curriculum

edited by Bridie Raban-Bisby

University of Melbourne, Institute of Education

with Greg Brooks

National Foundation for Educational Research

and Sheila Wolfendale

University of East London

In collaboration with the

UNITED KINGDOM READING ASSOCIATION

Trentham Books/UKRA

First published in 1995 by Trentham Books Limited

Trentham Books Limited
Westview House
734 London Road
Oakhill
Stoke-on-Trent
Staffordshire
England ST4 5NP

British Cataloguing in Publication Data
A catalogue record for this book is available from the British Library.

ISBN: 1 85856 036 5

Designed and typeset by Trentham Print Design Ltd., Chester and printed in Great Britain by Bemrose Shafron Ltd., Chester.

Contents

Introduction

SECTION 1: ENGLISH IN A NATIONAL CURRICULUM

Chapter 1 3
Literacy and policy
Graham Frater

Chapter 2 19
Some current initiatives in language and literacy education in Australia
Paul Brock

Chapter 3 41
National Curriculum English
Brian Cox

Chapter 4 51
The state of English in the state of England
Bridie Raban-Bisby

SECTION 2: ISSUES OF PRACTICE

Chapter 5 69
What's happening to knowledge about language (KAL) in the primary years?
Michael Lockwood

Chapter 6 81
Teaching phonological skills to reception age children
Jonathan Solity

Chapter 7 99
Young early readers: a preliminary report of the development of a group of children who were able to read fluently before Key Stage 1
Rhona Stainthorp and Diana Hughes

Chapter 8 115
Strategies for curriculum diversity and decentralisation, professional autonomy and quality outcomes: the experience of post-compulsory English education in the Australian Capital Territory
Jacqueline Manuel

SECTION 3: ASSESSING ENGLISH

Chapter 9 135
Reading standards: a Key Stage 1 study
Julia Davies and Ivy Brember

Chapter 10 147
Profiling pupil achievement in language and literacy: current issues and trends
Gerry Shiel and Patrick Forde

Chapter 11 161
Assessing reading in secondary schools: a Romanian perspective
Roxana Mihail

SECTION 4: FAMILY LITERACY

Chapter 12 179
Family literacy: ownership, evaluation and accountability
Anne Bentley, Margaret Cook and Colin Harrison

Chapter 13 189
Parents' contribution to children's literacy learning
Jo Weinberger

Chapter 14 203
Connections and negotiations: early literacy learning at home and school
Kathryn Kohl

Chapter 15 211
Families matter: adults reading aloud to children at home and at school and its implications for language education
Julie Spreadbury

Chapter 16 227
The ALBSU family literacy initiative
Annabel Hemstedt

Chapter 17 239
Hackney PACT, home reading programmes and family literacy
Roger Hancock

Chapter 18 251
The '99 by 99' Campaign: the pledge for literacy
Charlie Griffiths

Introduction

Since the Education Reform Act in 1988, schools in England and Wales have been experiencing the introduction and implementation of a traditional subject-based National Curriculum, seen as an entitlement for all pupils.

The subject which has attracted the most controversy has been English. During the early days the working group, chaired by Professor Brian Cox, experienced some problems of membership and clearly found the task complicated and demanding. With the introduction of the new curriculum planned for the beginning of the school year in 1989, only the papers for Key Stage 1 (5 to 7 year olds) were available. The rest of the curriculum for Key Stages 2, 3 and 4 became available subsequently. Only beyond this time was it possible to test the English curriculum in practice. However, the government had already decided to rewrite the English Order, stressing and emphasising certain aspects at the expense of others.

How and why these choices are relevant, how and why they are made and who makes them are questions that continue to shroud the English curriculum across time. Graham Frater's informed analysis of what counts as English and why this is hotly contested gives us an insight into some of the tensions and pressures evident to the present day.

Professor Brian Cox takes up the story of his work in constructing the National Curriculum for English with his working group at the end of the 1980s. He alerts us to the difficulties, both intellectual and political in designing a curriculum which was ultimately largely welcomed by the profession. This was a tribute to his unceasing efforts to pay regard to both what was required and what was reflected in best practice. What has happened subsequently is described by Professor Cox and he alerts us to some of the realities of political interference with the curriculum and underlines the loss of influence which has been the hallmark of the teaching profession in recent years.

In contrast, Paul Brock from Australia gives us a glimpse of professionally driven curriculum development. He describes in detail the process and the outcomes of his own work as one of a group of government advisers drawn from the profession of English teachers at all levels. There are valuable insights here into the ways in which academics and teachers are integrated into the iterative work of curriculum design. There are some important conclusions concerning the definition of literacy and the entitlement of all pupils in Australia.

As the English National Curriculum has been subjected to rewrites and consultations over a two year period, advantage has been taken of the need to 'slim down' the whole National Curriculum to achieve the changes demanded by government at the beginning of the decade. Evaluation of the implementation of the Cox version of the English National Curriculum (Raban et al., 1994) was completely undermined and hijacked by misleading and determined government interference. Here the discourse of the documents which contain various versions of the rewritten English National Curriculum over time is analysed and evaluated. The comparison and contrast bear witness to the underlying value systems which have been clashing with the professional debate which has been developed and refined during the last twenty-five years. This paper finishes with an analysis of the new English National Curriculum which was published in January 1995 and implemented in all schools from September 1995. While damage has been done and much has been lost during the last five years, perhaps there is room for teachers to reassert their sense of ownership over a curriculum development which has unfortunately and deliberately left them de-skilled and confused.

Section 2 papers address issues of practice which are in direct response to concerns over the implementation of the new curriculum for English. Top of this particular agenda is the teaching of grammar and the teaching of reading.

Michael Lockwood's paper tracks the elusive progress of Knowledge about Language through the National Curriculum and primary teachers' responses to this aspect of English. He highlights the range of support which teachers require to implement this part of their work and how an over-emphasis on Standard English is swamping a more appropriate focus on language in use and the ways in which language functions. Teachers are keen to address issues of language description but not at the cost of the rest of the English curriculum.

In teaching reading, the teaching of phonics as the only approach to the early stages has been another of the features which is swamping the new English curriculum at Key Stage 1. Jonathan Solity evaluates carefully the kind of phonics which makes a difference and also that teaching phonics *within* the context of reading, rather than as a separate set of skills, is essential to support early reading development. His study suggests, in addition, that explicit teaching is essential to ensure that children make appropriate progress.

In a study which looks at young early readers, Rhona Stainthorp and Diana Hughes follow the reading development of children who read before they come to school and their matched pair who didn't. It is interesting to compare these findings with those of Jonathan Solity in the previous paper, as in this case of young early readers, explicit teaching was not available to the successful early readers. However, the high level of parental involvement in their reading, and the ways in which these regular behaviours supported their children's development, is a theme picked up in Section 4.

How a curriculum is implemented in practice is developed by Jacqueline Manuel in a very different context from that experienced in England and Wales. National Curriculum Statements in Australia are not yet mandatory although Curriculum Guidelines, State by State, offer general parameters within which schools are required to design their own curriculum. Here, Jacqueline Manuel outlines and describes an example of this in a College for older students. She underlines forcefully how teachers, using their professional autonomy and knowledge, contribute to and benefit from involvement with the process of curriculum development. Importantly, the students also gain a greater entitlement.

The three papers in Section 3 are all highly critical of National Curriculum assessment of English as practised in England and Wales, but using evidence from three very different perspectives to do so.

Julia Davies and Ivy Brember operate within the National Curriculum in England. They studied the Year 2 children in a group of schools in the north-west of England intensively over a period of four years, and gathered test evidence of reading attainment both on the 1991 and 1992 National Curriculum tests in reading at Key Stage 1, but also on the Primary Reading Test each year from 1989 to 1992. Their main finding is a contradiction in the trend of attainment between the *Primary Reading Test* and the Key Stage 1 tests in 1991 and 1992: up on the Key Stage 1 tests, but down on the PRT. They highlight this as a problem of concurrent validity, then go on to consider other evidence also, and conclude that the Key Stage 1 tests are unlikely to be reliable as evidence of attainment even taken one year at a time, still less over time.

Gerry Shiel and Patrick Forde present a review of the features which should characterise reliable and informative pupil profiles in reading for their own pupils in Ireland. They discuss interesting work in progress on such profiles in Hawaii and Australia. These developments seem to them to be proceeding positively. They then apply the same analysis to National Curriculum assessment of English in England and Wales, and find it seriously wanting. They conclude that this system cannot operate as a profiling system, at least in its current form. They consider the questions this raises for their own work in relation to assessment of reading in Ireland.

Roxana Mihail presents the most unusual perspective of the three, coming as she does from the Institute of Educational Sciences in Romania. She and her colleagues have also been grappling with the problems of producing valid and reliable assessments of language and literacy, and her paper is a timely reminder that such problems are by no means confined to the Anglophone world. After presenting in detail recent developments in the assessment of Romanian language and literature, complete with three translated test papers, she compares and contrasts that experience with what has been happening in the United Kingdom, not just in England and Wales, but also the monitoring surveys of performance in reading which took place in Northern Ireland in 1993. She suggests that the success of the Northern Irish system, and the relative failure of those in her own country and in England and Wales, is not unconnected with confusion over the purposes for which assessment is undertaken, and with the degree of interference from educational authorities in the mechanics of the assessments. It is worth quoting her overall judgement on the 1993 Key Stage 3 tests in English in England and Wales:

> From a Romanian perspective, the form of examination seemed to be of an eighteenth-century character in itself, and to be based on a curriculum which was more prescriptive than anything we had in Romania even in the "bad old days".

These three papers contribute further evidence to the growing and damning indictment of national curriculum assessment in English.

The seven papers in Section 4 focus on Family Literacy. Here we see a fresh and developing view of the roots of literacy in a society through its communities and the values which people themselves within their daily lives attribute to literacy. These papers fall into four main groups:

The first group focus on work within City Challenge-funded initiatives. The second focuses on family literacy in the early years and conditions for the early acquisition of literacy skills. The third is given over to a description of the UK government-funded Family Literacy programme, undertaken by The Adult Literacy and Basic Skills Unit (ALBSU), and the fourth revisits Hackney PACT and considers the impact of the National Literacy Association, the '99 x 99' campaign.

This set of 7 papers moves from a conceptual and definitional overview, to three examples of work in hand (2 UK, 1 Australian), thence to a major national government-funded initiative, and finally to a review of a long-standing London-based programme and consideration of the need for and the effects of a literacy campaign which is firmly within the broader public domain.

In this 1994 International Year of the Family, it was appropriate to gather together these seven linked papers on the theme of Family Literacy. They provide a forum which brings together a number of perspectives and contemporary developments on this ever-topical theme. 'Parental involvement in children's reading' as a key phrase of the 1980's has been superseded by broader connotations of Family Literacy, which embrace school and home dimensions to literacy acquisition.

It is hoped that these linked themes will continue to:

- bring together practitioners and researchers and others in dialogue and debate,
- facilitate exchange of information about current initiatives,
- encourage networking amongst interested professionals.

In appraising the progress of Family Literacy

i. there remains lively interest and involvement in Parental Involvement in Reading/Family Literacy

ii. there is a wave of current research and practice that builds upon earlier innovative work (Topping and Wolfendale, 1985; Branston and Provis, 1986; Bloom, 1987; Davis and Stubbs, 1988; Body, 1990; Beverton et al, 1993)

iii. this more recent research and practice encompasses a broader conception of home-school literacy ventures than did the earlier schemes (see Wolfendale, 1994 for a Time-Line of Developments, p.94)

iv. developments in the England and Wales are paralleled by considerable work in America, Canada, Australia, at least. Other sources confirm the fact that Family Literacy, whether predicated on deficit models or not, is perceived to be a potent societal-pedagogical vehicle to enhance levels of literacy competence in children as well as adults (Dickinson, 1994; Dombey and Meek Spencer, 1994; Walker, 1994; Wolfendale and Topping, in preparation).

As these papers attest, contemporary research and practice into Family Literacy is actively pursuing the most effective means of realising the goal of 'literacy for all'.

Bridie Raban-Bisby, Greg Books, Sheila Wolfendale
June 1995

Section 1

English in a National Curriculum

Chapter 1

Literacy and policy

Graham Frater
Educational Consultant and Inspector

Literacy, Illiteracy and Power

In Britain, we have long been ambiguous about literacy. Even King Alfred argued that learning to read might be confined to 'the youth in England *of men rich enough to devote themselves to it'*; he added that such learning might be accomplished *'while they are unfit for other occupation'*. When Florence Nightingale offered adult literacy classes to her recuperating soldiers at Scutari, the generals accused her of 'destroying discipline' and 'spoiling the brutes'.

> The authorities were afraid that the men would get above themselves if they read instead of drinking. (Woodham-Smith, 1950:239)

In his sermon for Queen Victoria's accession, 33 years before the 1870 Act, the Reverend Sydney Smith noted — and it still sounds uncomfortably familiar — that:

> There are, I am sorry to say, many countries in Europe which have taken the lead of England in the great business of education. (Smith, 1845a:232)

The advantages Sydney saw in literacy were all-embracing. He recognised, with a refreshing frankness, that learning to read is both to be empowered and to be subject to the shaping influence of print:

> When I see the village school and the tattered scholars and the aged master or mistress teaching the mechanical art of reading or writing and thinking that they are teaching that alone, I feel that the aged instructor is protecting life, insuring property, fencing the altar, guarding the throne, giving space and liberty to all the fine powers of man... (Smith, 1845a:232)

And lest you think that last phrase makes Sydney sexist, his essay of 1810 on 'Female Education' (Smith, 1845b) was among the first to argue for women's rights in education.

Deprivation, poor literacy and lack of power have always been closely associated. Writers have recognised this more readily than policy makers, as Dickens showed with Jo the crossing sweeper in *Bleak House,* closed off, in poverty and ignorance, from all:

> Those mysterious symbols, so abundant over the shops, and at the corners of the streets, and on the doors and in the windows!

More recently, ALBSU's evidence (ALBSU, 1987) has demonstrated that though Jo's 'absolute poverty' may have diminished, the underlying patterns are much the same. Those reporting difficulties with basic skills were more likely than others to:

- be the children of fathers in manual occupations — 3 out of 4;
- have been eligible for free school meals (at twice the rate of the rest of the cohort);
- come from families on low incomes (double the rate for the rest of the cohort);
- have been born 5th or later in a large family (double the rate of the rest of the cohort);

- (except for death of a parent) to have experienced all types of family difficulty, including housing problems, more than other children;
- have been in care at some point;
- have not lived with both parents throughout childhood.

The latest ALBSU study clearly shows an enduring association 'between poor literacy and [...] families in which the parents are unskilled and have not gained any qualifications' (ALBSU, 1994): 61% of those with parents in the bottom attainment group had low scores for literacy, while only 2% of those with parents in the highest group had low scores for reading.

Reporting in 1990, and drawing chiefly on the government's own statistics, Professor Bradshaw, of the University of York, was able to show that, for a period of about a decade:

> Children have borne the brunt of the changes that have occurred in economic conditions, demographic structure and social policies in the UK. More children have been living in low income families and financial poverty has doubled. (Bradshaw, 1990:66-67)

Department of Social Security figures published in July 1994 suggest that child poverty has now trebled[1]. The effects of the policies of one department of state may actually impede the delivery of the policies of another. Given ALBSU's clear evidence of links between parental circumstances and children's reading standards, universal literacy must be seen as a far more complex matter than books, method, content or curricula alone. Improved early literacy might be at least as well served by a direct address to such policy issues as poverty and nursery provision as to an energetic re-drafting of the reading provisions of the National Curriculum, as in the period 1992-4. In truth, none of these factors is sufficient on its own.

To be released from illiteracy, as many successful adult literacy students report, is to be released from a secret shame, to feel more human. Dickens was right — to be illiterate is to have severely diminished opportunities in a world infused by the technology of writing.

Perceptions of Declining Standards[2]

Falling standards have been perceived since the dawn of literacy — Professor Raban's inaugural lecture (Raban, 1992) records that one of the earliest cuneiform tablets contains a complaint about the declining standards of students' writing. King Alfred could at least blame the marauding Danes for slaughtering his scholars; ever since, those in power have blamed teachers and teaching methods.

Within 6 years of the passing of the 1870 Education Act, anxiety about reading standards was being expressed. By 1874, only 24% of children had reached the reading standards which qualified their schools for grants under the payments by results system. It was no better in 1880 and in 1886 the Cross Commission was set up — the first of a long line of enquiries into standards. HMI had been charged with carrying out the reading assessments under the payment by results system, by listening to children's reading. Rather as with the 'neck verse,' they soon found that meaningless learning emerged as a survival mechanism. The Rev. J. D. Stewart HMI, in evidence to the Commission, noted:

> I have seen children, reading apparently, with the book upside down.

The payment by results system, introduced in order to deliver a 'sound and cheap elementary education', had urged a concentration on the 'necessary drudgery' of instruction in basic skills. Exactly this focus had produced the upside-down reading which HMI Stewart had found. When asked about reading taught with due attention to sense and meaning, his proper respect for evidence prompted him to concede that:

> I have seen such an experiment as you seem to suggest tried, and I certainly think that the reading improved.

Since then, we have seen a steady flow of commissions and enquiries, each responding to disquiet about reading standards. Such bouts have followed the end of almost every war; and I estimate that a roughly fifteen year cycle obtains at other times. On this pattern, Turner's *Sponsored Reading Failure* (1990) was on cue, fifteen years after Bullock. Both events, it will be recalled, followed upon reports of falling standards, as measured by reading tests which were showing their age.

What emerges, from all those commissions, is that none used the same assumptions about literacy. Each had progressively *but tacitly* raised its criteria. The Newbolt report on *The Teaching of English in England* (1921) had expressed great concern about literacy on a definition far in advance of the 1870's. Employers, responding to market forces, were raising the threshold; thus, the Vickers engineering company claimed to have experienced:

> Great difficulty in obtaining junior clerks who can speak and write English clearly and correctly, especially those aged from 15 to 16 years.

Similarly, Lever Bros. expressed:

> A great surprise and disappointment ... to find that our young employees are so hopelessly deficient in their command of English.

And Boots the Chemists observed that :

> Teaching English in the present day schools produces a very limited command of the English language... Our candidates do not appreciate the value of shades of meaning, and while able to do imaginative composition, show weakness in work which requires accurate description, or careful arrangement of detail.

Without being declared, the field of focus was being extended. Newbolt's shift was from basic literacy, narrowly conceived, towards a notion of functional competence which now embraced:

- standard English;
- advanced writing skills ('shades of meaning');
- and spoken English.

'A taste for good reading and thoughtful study' had already been added by the Revised Code of 1904.

The pattern has continued unremittingly; indeed, in 1953, M.M. Lewis could say that:

> Common opinion is convinced that illiteracy is increasing [...] this conviction could have been recorded at any time during the last 80 years, if not earlier. [...] For about a century we have been concerned about the level of literacy, even though, in fact, our standards are rising as the actual level rises. In recent years the anxiety has become more insistent, more widespread, and sharper. (Lewis, 1953:48).

Loose Talk: The Synchronic Dimension

Literacy has a wide range of connotations, lacks a fixed definition and has no cut-off point. Functional literacy, which is about as far as we can go without greater confusion, relates to the match between an individual's abilities and the demands of his/her employment and lifestyle:

> A person is literate when he has acquired the essential knowledge and skills which enable him to engage in all those activities in which literacy is required for effective functioning in his group or community. (Gray, 1956:24)

It is *a relative not an absolute term;* its unavoidable relativism is inherently uncomfortable for policy makers; and it becomes inflexible and founders as soon as an attempt is made to pin it down by mass testing.

Many other views of literacy exist together at any one time:

> All my students are illiterate when they come to university — the best are literate when they leave. (DES, 1975:10)

> Please teach your radio announcers and script writers to be literate. I have heard several split infinitives and misplaced adverbs and prepositions this week. (Crystal, 1986)

> Complete illiteracy is extremely rare [...] Most respondents who said they had reading difficulties were talking about fluency rather than inability to read at all. (ALBSU, 1994:26)

> In truth most definitions of illiteracy amount to this — that he is illiterate who is not as literate as someone else thinks he ought to be. (Ministry of Education, 1950)

We Are Not Alone

Higher demands are being made upon more people for more and better literacy. Virtually all western societies with long-standing systems of compulsory education are expressing dissatisfaction about the literacy delivered by their school systems. And, just as the perception of decline has long been a persistent kind of folklore, so the statistics which are now brought to bear can begin to assume epic proportions.

Thus, France, which for several decades released only its 1946 illiteracy figures for the UNESCO tables (3.6% of 14 year olds), at last acknowledges a problem. But an estimate that 'between 50%-70% of the adult population is excluded from all forms of written communication' as claimed by the *Association Française pour la Lecture* is simply preposterous (Velis, 1988 in Hautecoeur, 1990).

And in Canada 'It is now estimated that one Canadian adult in four is functionally illiterate; the corresponding estimate for Quebec and the rest of Canada's francophone population is almost one in three' (Hautecoeur, 1990).

In the USA, literacy campaigners are ready to claim that 60 million people, representing more than a third of the entire adult population, are deficient in literacy (Kozol, in Hautecoeur, 1990).

As societies grow more complex, campaigners are sounding loud alarms, making extravagant claims and pressing simple solutions to complex problems. Indeed, the more we know about what is involved in the reading process, the more attractive the 'one club' solutions appear to pressure groups and policy makers. Marie Clay, among others, has made clear what a complex cognitive process reading behaviour is. HMI's antipodean visit (OFSTED, 1993) showed that the New Zealand education system, influenced by her research, provides its primary school teachers in training with twice the UK provision of instruction in literacy teaching. Her findings pose challenges to our system which, as the downgrading of formal teacher training and the half-hearted financing of the British version of Dame Marie's Reading Recovery scheme suggest, our policy makers, despite their public statements, are reluctant to meet.

The new generation of ethnographic researchers into literacy is revealing other kinds of complexity[3]. They are demonstrating something of the complex character of the social contexts and processes which support reading. Their understanding that reading is:

- not a set of processing skills alone;
- not an autonomous behaviour, but a social and interactive one;
- not value-free, but shot through with ideology;

poses a direct challenge to the validity of the skills-based agenda which underpins the revisions now confirmed for English in the National Curriculum in England and Wales.

Policy and the National Curriculum

At no time has literacy been more exposed to policy in England and Wales than during the last ten years. Indeed, the word 'national' has politicised the curriculum to an extent which nobody predicted. We may now see that the development of the National Curriculum has fallen into two phases.

The first phase was long and slow: it dates from Jim Callaghan's Ruskin speech. This was the first set-piece speech about education by a Prime Minister and it initiated the momentum of inspection, curriculum discussion, publication, evidence gathering and committee activity which, across political administrations, characterised the next 14 years. For English, the 1st of August 1989, the date when the Subject Order came into force, marked the end of the phase. We can now see that period to have been an innocent, pre-lapsarian era in which evidence, consensus and teachers' experience were accorded their due.

The second phase was much shorter; it was marked by two thrusts:

- the government's withdrawal from the consensus it had established through the Cox curriculum;
- and the rejection of the evidence and professional opinion with which the Cox curriculum had been infused.

This second phase is the premature revision of the English National Curriculum whose closing stages we are currently witnessing. It began, soon after the Order was published, with new appointments to direct the work of the government's education quangos — the National Curriculum Council and School Examinations and Assessment Council. Its first published signal was *The Case for Revising the Order* (NCC, 1992), from which everything else has followed. The *Case*, my focus from now on, shows us that revising the English curriculum is part of an ideological project to determine:

- the models of learning underpinning the English National Curriculum;
- the model of language development on which the curriculum shall be based;
- the body of content to be covered;
- and the teaching methods to be employed in its delivery.

Straighter Linearity

The linear pattern of progression in the National Curriculum has no basis in evidence either about children's development, or their progress in language. It is a fiction convenient only for some kinds of measurement.

One of the central arguments urged for revising the English National Curriculum lay in its repetitions of similar features at different levels. Those repetitions were rooted in evidence — not least that of the National Writing Project, which had reported that pupils do not develop their abilities in a linear fashion, but do so recursively. Omitting repetition has removed Cox's attempt to recognise that recursiveness in a curriculum modelled on a straight line graph. By assigning specific competencies to levels, *without repetition,* the attribution of attainment to level has become more arbitrary and remote from evidence about progression, than at present.

AT1. Speaking and Listening

The *Case* claims that 'The Current Order does not.....place sufficient emphasis on the requirement that all pupils [...] should become confident users of standard English'.

This is astonishing: Standard English (SE) is central to the current but outgoing Cox curriculum. No doubts about the importance of SE have been published by teachers in the lively debates which have followed the *Case.* Professional doubts concern the timing (the Key Stage and level) now proposed for the teaching of SE. By overruling evidence about language development, policy is plainly concerning itself with teaching method.

> To become competent users of standard English, pupils need to be taught to recognise its characteristics and the rules which govern its usage...[the present Order] will not necessarily encourage pupils to speak clearly, accurately and confidently. There is a case, therefore, for strengthening the references to the mastery of Standard English...and for requiring children to use Standard English before level 5.
>
> These requirements need to be based on a clear definition of Standard English.

These are no more than assertions. A model of teaching and learning is clearly in play: it is that of children as empty vessels, Mr Gradgrind's pot-filling. Against the trend of over thirty years of evidence about language development, the assertion is that early and explicit instruction in rules is going to be effective in the acquisition or development of SE.

As for legislating for a definition of SE, the hubris is amazing; let me remind you of the entry on SE in the *Oxford Companion to the English Language*:

> **STANDARD ENGLISH.** A widely used term that resists easy definition but is used as if most educated people nonetheless know precisely what it refers to. Some people consider its meaning self-evident; it is both the usage and the ideal of 'good' or 'educated' users of English. [...]It is also usually agreed that standard English is a minority form. (McArthur, 1992)

AT2. Reading

With regard to reading, the official proposition, which has indeed prevailed, is that:

> [The current Order] neither defines the skills involved in learning to read with sufficient precision nor provides teachers with a clear and balanced framework to support the teaching of initial reading. It should, in addition, pay greater attention to the development of more advanced reading skills.
>
> The programmes of study for literature are not sufficiently explicit about how pupils can best develop the habit of reading widely, and, as they mature, encounter texts which introduce them to the richness of great literature.

Rightly, the present curriculum does not describe skills in detail because, as required by his terms of reference, Cox was concerned with defining outcomes — what could be accomplished by pupils, not the processes by which accomplishment might be arrived at. Once again, and despite official denials, the new agenda is for the National Curriculum to engage with teaching method.

> The teaching of phonics and the use of reading schemes should ... be given greater prominence in the Order...

That the new Order was intended to engage directly with content is equally plain. It also looks like a settling of old scores between the curriculum council and the assessment council, both now amalgamated:

> The only statutory requirement in the Order is that pupils should read Shakespeare: no other texts, periods/movements or individual writers have to be taught. In the absence of such judgements, it is SEAC and the GCSE boards, who,... are defining the texts which pupils read. The issue ...is whether the Order needs to provide a more explicit definition of the literature pupils should read in order to further the objective of encouraging wide reading and developing an appreciation of great literature.

AT3. Writing

The argument for revision clearly proposes an alternative model of learning to the evidence-based one to be found in the present curriculum:

> [The present Order]... does not offer a clear definition of basic skills, the grammatical knowledge pupils must master if they are to become effective writers, and the variety of ways in which competence in spelling can be developed.

Again, this is an argument for teaching in a pre-determined sequence, with rules as pre-requisites to language use. No evidence is offered for the proposition, but unsupported assertion is readily found:

> This ability [to convey and construct meaning] depends upon the basic skill of handwriting and upon the ability to spell and to write grammatically. The issue ... is whether these basic skills are defined with sufficient clarity and emphasis...

If only this were true, life would indeed be simpler for all English teachers. If it had ever been effective the Spens Committee could not have reported:

> A common and grave criticism that many pupils pass through the Grammar school (and even through the University) without acquiring the capacity to express themselves in English. (Spens, 1938, p.174)

Spens was reporting when traditional grammar teaching, copperplate script and spelling lists were customary, when selective grammar schools were in the ascendant and when universities admitted a far smaller proportion of the population than they do now.

Scotched Myths

Myths people the world with villains and heroes, with problems and magical resolutions. Evidence is complex, messy and untidy: the solutions it suggests are long-term, costly and dependent on frail human agency. What I have classed as the second phase of the National Curriculum, the revision stage, has been characterised by a flight from uncomfortable evidence into comfortable myth.

It is a myth that primary school teachers in England neglect to teach phonic skills. It is a myth which provides convenient scapegoats and allows policy to stress these skills in the name of a balance that already obtains.

The facts are that phonic skills are 'taught almost universally and usually to beneficial effect', as HMI found in their major reading survey of 1990 and have continued to find ever since (DES, 1990:2). The Warwick University study on the Implementation of the National Curriculum for English (Raban et al, 1994) has given us the figures and shown that 98% of Key Stage One teachers employ phonics.

It is a myth that the 'real books' movement has had the effect of ousting the structured reading scheme from primary classrooms. It is a myth that permits policy makers to claim a role as saviours by emphasising the use of reading schemes — which have not only never been abandoned, but have seldom been less than dominant in most primary classrooms.

The facts are that 'Published schemes of graded reading books were used in more that 95% of classes' (DES, 1990:2).

It is a myth that most teachers have adopted single, partial or unbalanced methodologies for teaching infants to read and that 'balance' needs to be restored by means of a revised National Curriculum.

The fact is that 'there is no evidence of teachers and schools rushing into a single method of teaching reading. The great majority of teachers, almost 85%, used a blend of methods to teach initial reading

> skills. In less than 18% of classes was a single method — phonics, look-and-say, or 'real books' — used exclusively or even predominantly. There was clear evidence that adherence to a single approach, whatever the particular method, hindered the children's reading development' (DES, 1990:2)

And it is myth, prevailing in the face of such facts, that we find informing the latest official recommendations for the National Curriculum, where a single skill, that of phonic decoding, unaccompanied by any others, or by an appeal to meaning — remember 'the neck verse' — is isolated for the attainment of level one in reading at Key Stage 1.

Such myths have allowed policy makers and their acolytes to turn teachers, teacher trainers, advisers and researchers into villains whose inconvenient evidence and experience are now scorned. Policies rooted in myth are irrelevant to the raising of standards and may well depress them; the crude assessments those policies entail have already proved to carry a ludicrously high opportunity cost.

The simplifying drift of policies for literacy is nostalgic, an appeal to the mythical success of the way things were done in the past. And myths are confirmed by attributing to those ways the achievements which were accomplished *despite and not because of* them. Mis-attribution is one of the great persisting fallacies of educational debate; it was spotted as early as 1809 by Sydney Smith (alias Peter Plymley). In an essay on the curriculum of the English public school of his time (an exclusive diet of Latin and Greek), this reforming Wykehamist noted that:

> It is in vain to say that we have produced great men under this system. We have produced great men under all systems. [...] It is scarcely possible to prevent great men from rising under any system of education, however bad. Teach men demonology or astrology, and you will still have a certain proportion of genius, in spite of these or any other branch of ignorance or folly. (Smith, 1845c:197)

Puncturing the informing myths of policy is dangerous stuff: we should not wonder that, though they thought about it, nobody ever had quite the courage to make Sydney into a bishop. Nor should we wonder that, with scrupulously gathered evidence so contradictory to the thrust of policy, HMI has recently suffered a radical change of remit.

What is most vital is that we get the policies right. This means having policies which are firmly rooted in professional consensus and, above all, in evidence — however complex its nature, however challenging to popular assumptions, however demanding, or long-term, its implications for the system.

References

ALBSU (1987) *Literacy, Numeracy and Adults* London: The Adult Basic Skills Unit

ALBSU (1994) *The Basic Skills of Young Adults* London: The Adult Basic Skills Unit

Bradshaw, J (1990) *Child Poverty and Deprivation in the UK* London: National Children's Bureau

Crystal, D (1986) 'Literacy 2000' *English Today* 8

Department of Education and Science (1975) *A Language for Life* The Bullock Report, London: Her Majesty's Stationery Office

Department of Education and Science (1990) *The Teaching and Learning of Reading in Primary Schools* HMI Report, London: Her Majesty's Stationery Office

Gray, W.S. (1956) *The Teaching of Reading and Writing* Paris: UNESCO

Hautecoeur, J-P. (1990) 'Generous Supply, Flagging Demand' in *Alpha 90* Montreal: Ministère de l'Education du Québec

Kozol, J. (1985) *Illiterate America* New York: Anchor Press/Doubleday

Lewis, M. (1953) *The Importance of Illiteracy* London: Harrap

McArthur, T. (1992) *The Oxford Companion to the English Language* Oxford: Oxford University Press

Ministry of Education (1921) *The Teaching of English in England* The Newbolt Report, London: His Majesty's Stationery Office

Ministry of Education (1939) *Report ... on Secondary Education* Spens Report, London: His Majesty's Stationery Office

Ministry of Education (1950) *Reading Ability* London: His Majesty's Stationery Office

National Curriculum Council (1992) *English: The Case for Revising the Order* York: National Curriculum Council

OFSTED (1993) *Reading Recovery in New Zealand* London: Her Majesty's Stationery Office

Raban, B. (1992) *Literacy, Research and Debate* Inaugural Lecture, Coventry: University of Warwick

Raban, B., Clark, U. and McIntyre, J. (1994) *Evaluation of the Implementation of English in the National Curriculum at Key Stages1, 2, and 3 1991-3* London: School Curriculum and Assessment Authority

Smith, S. (1845a) 'Sermon on The Duties of the Queen' in *Works* Vol III, London: Longman, Green

Smith, S. (1845b) 'Female Education' in *Works* Vol I, London: Longman, Green

Smith, S. (1845c) 'Professional Education' in *Works* Vol I, London: Longman, Green

Spens Report (1938) *Secondary Education with special reference to Grammar and Technical High Schools* London: His Majesty's Stationery Office

Turner, M. (1990) *Sponsored Reading Failure* Warlingham: IPSET Education Unit

Velis, J-P. (1988) *La France Illettrée* Paris: Editions du Seuil

Woodham-Smith, C. (1950) *Florence Nightingale* London: Constable

Notes

1. I refer here to The Times 15/7/94, reporting the results of the 'Survey of Households with Below Average Incomes' which drew upon government statistics.
2. I derive much of the historical data for this section of the paper from M. M. Lewis (see citations), from Silver, P. and H. 'The Political Quest for Educational Standards' *New Society* 24/2/77 and from the Bullock Report (DES, 1975).
3. A ready source of research materials illustrating this line of evidence and thinking is to be found in the four readers associated with the Open University MA Unit E825, *Language and Literacy in Social Context* edited variously by Graddol, D., Maybin, J., Stierer, B. and Boyd-Barrett, O.

Chapter 2

Some current initiatives in language and literacy education in Australia

Paul Brock
Australian Language and Literacy Council
National Board of Employment, Education and Training

Australia's Language: The Australian Language and Literacy Policy

The single most important political impact upon literacy education in Australia in the past quarter of a century at least, was the 1990 decision of the Commonwealth government to implement a White Paper *Australia's Language: The Australian Language and Literacy Policy* which had its roots in and expanded upon (in politically and strategically important ways) the directions initiated in 1987 by the *National Policy on Languages* (Joseph Lo Bianco, 1987) I was fortunate enough to be involved in the construction and final drafting of the document which was endorsed by the Federal Cabinet in 1991.

The White Paper was finalised only after an extensive period of consultations with all States and Territories, professional bodies, and providers of language and literacy education prior to and, especially, after the release of an earlier — and in some ways deliberately provocative — 'Green (discussion) Paper'.

The four goals of the national policy are:

1. all Australians should develop and maintain effective literacy in English to enable them to participate in Australian society;
2. the learning of languages other than English must be substantially expanded and improved;
3. those Aboriginal and Torres Strait Islander languages which are still transmitted should be maintained and developed, and those which are not should be recorded where appropriate; and
4. language services provided by interpreters and translators, the print and electronic media, and libraries should be expanded and improved. (DEET, 1991:iii)

The Policy details 29 objectives which target the four goals. The Policy set out a most substantial agenda in the areas of school and adult literacy; school and adult ESL; Languages Other Than English (LOTE) in school and adult education contexts; Aboriginal literacy and languages; and advisory and other services.

During a period of substantial cutbacks in government spending, the White Paper represented a quite remarkable commitment of funds to language and literacy education in a way and scope unparalleled in Australia's history. The Policy indicated funding across all eight areas of over A$233 million in the 1990-1 financial year, over A$278 million in 1991-2, over A$320 million in 1992-3, and just over A$333 million in 1993-4.

The funding of the Policy is continuing and I believe that the government is likely to commit incremental amounts out to at least the end of the 1997-8 financial year.

Definition of Literacy

The White Paper's concept of 'Literacy', is a kind of 'objective correlative' for, or pointer to, the general spirit of the policy. The policy deliberately and explicitly rejects any narrow, functionalist or instrumentalist view of literacy. It aspires for all Australians to have 'effective literacy'. Rather than paraphrase the document, I would prefer to quote from it to give the substance and flavour of the policy.

> **Literacy**
>
> Literacy is the ability to read and use written information and to write appropriately, in a range of contexts. It is used to develop knowledge and understanding, to achieve personal growth and to function effectively in our society. Literacy also includes the recognition of numbers and basic mathematical signs and symbols within text.
>
> Literacy involves the integration of speaking, listening, and critical thinking with reading and writing. Effective literacy is intrinsically purposeful, flexible and dynamic and continues to develop throughout an individual's lifetime.
>
> All Australians need to have effective literacy in English, not only for their personal benefit and welfare but also for Australia to achieve its social and economic goals.
>
> One may acquire literacy in many languages. Some Australians are literate in languages other than English, including Aboriginal languages, as well as or instead of English. For many Australians of non-English speaking background, the development of initial literacy in the first language is desirable for personal development as well as for development of literacy in English. (DEET, 1991:9)

The Policy proceeds to articulate a supple, complex and comprehensive understanding of differing types of literacy

> Different types of literacy exist. Indeed, literacy can be said to be a continuum of skills. At one end of the spectrum, literacy could be limited to minimal reading ability without writing ability or the ability only to write one's own name. These capacities are often referred to as basic literacy.

The concept of functional literacy has gained recognition in recent years. It is commonly used by international organisations such as the Organisation for Economic Co-operation and Development (OECD) and the UNESCO. A distinction is made between basic literacy and functional literacy. UNESCO gives the following explanation:

> People are functionally literate who can engage in those activities in which literacy is required for effective functioning in their group and community and also for enabling them to continue to use reading, writing and calculation for their own and their community's development. (1978)

The notion of what it means to be literate will vary, therefore, from one society to another and within societies. Literacy is certainly not just a set of static, isolated skills through which people can decode and encode printed words. The concept of functional (or 'social') literacy highlights the uses which are made of literacy skills in a particular society. It has gained momentum because of awareness of the increasing everyday demands which modern society and the modern workforce place on the literacy capacities of individuals.

However, use of the term 'functional literacy' is not universally supported. Some argue that all literacy is functional and, therefore, that setting levels for functional literacy is not possible. Some maintain that the concept implies a tighter link between literacy skills and functional competence than actually exists. Others observe that the term suggests a high value placed on conformity to specific functional contexts when generalisable literacy and learning skills which contribute to problem-solving and adaptability are required. Nevertheless, the term is used internationally and is a useful way of explaining that literacy exists in context. It also distinguishes a higher level than basic literacy. However, functional literacy must be effective literacy, which, as stated [above], is intrinsically purposeful, flexible and dynamic, and which continues to develop throughout a person's lifetime. Effective literacy should become the commonly accepted term.

The Policy Directions Paper for the 1990 International Literacy Year Program in Australia referred not only to basic literacy and to functional literacy but also to the concept of active literacy. It stated, 'For an advanced technological society such as Australia, our goal must be an active literacy which allows people to use language to enhance their capacity to think, create and question, which helps them to participate more effectively in society.'

Along its continuum, literacy also includes the cultural enrichment which comes from immersion in and responsive reading of the body of Australian and world literature. It involves recognition of oral literatures, such as those of Aboriginal people. Literacy also includes the acquisition of strategies for writing, not only for pragmatic purposes, but also for personal development.

Literacy in Australia is both a means and a goal. Effective literacy in the broadest sense is the goal of all levels of education and training, and society more generally. As a means, the ability to read and write English effectively in Australia is an essential tool for education and training and for participation in all aspects of Australian life. Both aspects require national attention. (DEET, 1991:34-35)

2. The Australian Language and Literacy Council

Unlike the situation in Britain, the Australian Commonwealth government policy and program delivery areas of Education and Employment are within the one senior portfolio of 'Employment, Education and Training'. The bringing together of these three areas was one of the initiatives of the Australian Labor government which has been in power in Australia continuously since 1983.

In 1987 the Commonwealth Minister for Employment, Education and Training, John Dawkins, decided that he wanted independent comprehensive policy advice from experts acknowledged as such by their peers within the various academic, professional and industrial sectors of employment, education and training in addition to what he received from his Public Service Department. In order to do this, he established the National Board of Employment, Education and Training.

The Board has five Councils made up of nationally respected authorities in the respective fields. They are the Schools Council, the Employment and Skills Formation Council, the Australian Research Council, the Higher Education Council, and our Australian Language and Literacy

Council. The advice of the Board and its Councils in response to Ministerial References is formally tabled in the Australian Parliament, is subject to parliamentary debate, and can play a significant role in subsequent Australian government legislation.

Sometimes the Councils and the Board affirm public service advice to the Minister. On other occasions we modify or even vigorously oppose it. The Board strongly values its independence.

The role of the Australian Language and Literacy Council is to advise the Minister on the effectiveness of the Policy's implementation and possible modifications of the Policy and to provide him or her with formal Advice on any language and literacy References which she or he nominates.

Currently we are addressing a number of References for the Australian government.

They require the Council to

- critique teacher education, both in the preservice and the professional development arenas, in preparing teachers of literacy in the adult and school education sectors,
- assess the quality and quantity of teacher supply in the field of foreign languages,
- review the implementation of effective communication (sometimes termed, misleadingly, 'Plain English') policies in the public and private sectors, and assess the availability of accessible reading materials for people with intellectual or physical disabilities, and
- undertake a pilot study to evaluate ways in which English language and literacy competencies ought to be incorporated within national industry standards.

We pursue all References through extensive consultation within the associated fields to ensure that the Advice which we provide to the Minister for tabling in Parliament is as informed as much as possible by those working at the grass roots. The recent external review of the Board, undertaken by Professor Wiltshire, demonstrated that the Council, through the Board, provides a valuable, independent, and well informed source of policy advice for the Federal Minister and the Australian government.

The National Collaborative Curriculum

In Australia's system of federated government it is not easy to establish national goals upon which the Commonwealth and all State and Territory governments agree. Tensions between government bodies at the local, regional, State and Commonwealth levels are not uncommon. But the tyranny of unfettered partisan localism is surely to be resisted at least as forcefully as the tyranny of conformist centralism.

The historic and splendid *Hobart Declaration on Schooling* issued by the Australian Education Council (AEC) in 1989 marked the start of extremely significant national collaboration between Commonwealth, State and Territory governments in school education and formed the basis of the national collaboration on curriculum frameworks.

From 1987 until 1991, the collaboration between State/Territory and Federal governments of all political persuasions was a significant political factor in the development of language and literacy policy. For much of that period there was a majority of Labor governments represented around the table. Since 1992 the election of non-Labor conservative coalition State governments has complicated the process somewhat. But the Hobart Declaration of 1989 remains in place. It commences with five broad goals.

The Agreed National Goals for Schooling in Australia

1. To provide an excellent education for all young people, being one which develops their talents and capacities to full potential, and is relevant to the social, cultural and economic needs of the nation.
2. To enable all students to achieve high standards of learning and to develop self-confidence, optimism, high self-esteem, respect for others, and achievement of personal excellence.
3. To promote equality of educational opportunities, and to provide for groups with special learning requirements.
4. To respond to the current and emerging economic and social needs of the nation, and to provide those skills which will allow students maximum flexibility and adaptability in their future employment and other aspects of life.
5. To provide a foundation for further education and training, in terms of knowledge and skills, respect for learning and positive

> attitudes for life-long education. (Curriculum Corporation, 1994a:46)

Goal 6 focuses upon specifics. It is to develop in students:

- the skills of English literacy, including skills in listening, speaking, reading and writing;
- skills of numeracy, and other mathematical skills;
- skills of analysis and problem solving;
- skills of information processing and computing;
- an understanding of the role of science and technology in society, together with scientific and technological skills;
- a knowledge and appreciation of Australia's historical and geographic context;
- a knowledge of languages other than English;
- an appreciation and understanding of, and confidence to participate in, the creative arts;
- an understanding of, and concern for, balanced development and the global environment; and
- a capacity to exercise judgement in matters of morality, ethics and social justice.

It was upon this nationally agreed foundation that the Commonwealth, State and Territory governments erected the whole national collaborative curriculum edifice at the cost so far of somewhere around A$6 million.

All Ministers for Education agreed that there would be eight key learning areas: English; Mathematics; Science; The Arts; Health and Physical Education; Languages Other Than English; Studies of Society and the Environment; and Technology.

In some cases these Key Learning Areas (KLAs) are the direct equivalents of traditional school subjects; in others they represent amalgams —eg. 'The Arts' and, especially, 'Studies of Society and the Environment' which includes at least history, geography, consumer education, legal studies, environmental education and religious studies. 'Languages Other

Than English' (LOTE) covers many different languages. I am yet to be convinced, however, that 'Technology' ought to be a key learning area from Kindergarten to Year 10 equivalent in intellectual substance or content to, say, 'English' and 'Mathematics'. Interpenetrating all of these Key Learning Areas, schools are to incorporate the non-subject specific but generic key competencies.

Despite what some Australian academics have asserted or inferred, the national collaborative curriculum venture, even though it was initiated by John Dawkins, was not some Napoleonic grab by the Commonwealth government demanding conformist, reductionist, economic rationalist, so-called education. The process was *not* unilaterally controlled, manipulated or mandated by the Australian government.

Indeed, in its processes, as well as in its products, the Australian 'national curriculum' experience has been significantly different from what has happened in the United Kingdom. Collaboration among all governments and other bodies has been central to the Australian process.

Dr. Ken Boston, Director General of Education in New South Wales, who succeeded as Chair of Curriculum and Assessment Committee (CURASS), Garth Boomer (whose premature death last year saddened all of us who knew, loved and admired him not only in Australia but in Britain as well) has succinctly highlighted the principal differences between the Australian and the British experiences.

> Our so-called 'national curriculum' has not — as in the United Kingdom — been developed by a National Curriculum Council appointed by the Secretary of State and charged with the responsibility of preparing fully detailed curriculum material to be tabled in Parliament. Nor, as in the UK, has it been driven by a particular political agenda. The *Statements and Profiles* are the result of a voluntary and fragile alliance which has held together only because each of the States and systems judges it to be of benefit to them and the nation. (Boston, 1994:44)

The Australian Education Council of Ministers for Education in the Commonwealth, State and Territory governments established a comprehensive committee known as the Curriculum and Assessment Committee (CURASS) to construct the eight curriculum frameworks and profile frameworks to be deployed in assessment and reporting. The Commonwealth was only one of a number of bodies with a vote on CURASS. Membership also included representatives of each State and Territory curriculum authority and public education system; the National Catholic Education Commission; the Australian Teachers' Union; the Independent Teachers' Association of Australia; the Australian Parents' Council; the Australian Council of State School Organisations; the Australian Council of Educational Research and the Australian Curriculum Corporation. The New Zealand government was also represented on the committee. I was a Commonwealth government member of CURASS for twelve months up to the end of 1991.

Boston (1994) has also sketched the processes of consultation involved across the whole national project.

> The work took eighteen months. Some hundreds of people — selected competitively from across the nation and on the basis of their expertise — were involved in writing the briefs, the statements and the profiles for the (eight) key learning areas. More than 250 national organisations were consulted along with their State and Territory chapters. No fewer than 70,000 students, 2,400 teachers and 480 schools were involved in trialing the profiles. The validation process, carried out for us by the Australian Council for Educational Research, involved a further 1,600 teachers and 20,000 students. (*op.cit.*)

There are Australian critics of the national curriculum venture who would contend, with some justification, that this latter assessment paints too rosy a picture. Any implications that the quality of construction, consultation and trialing was consistently good within and across all eight key learning areas would be false. For example, the extent of teacher collaboration has varied quite significantly from curriculum area to curriculum area, as has the quality of the final products. Genuine and substantive criticisms have been made, for example, of the Science as well as the Languages Other Than English (LOTE) *Statements and Profiles.*

In my opinion English was probably the best as far as both the process and the product are concerned. Garth Boomer, while he was the Chair of CURASS, also chaired the sub-committee which took responsibility for the English curriculum project. Garth enjoyed an eminent international reputation in the field of English curriculum. I understand that the situation in England was different to this in that the equivalent figure was a medieval scholar with little, if any, academic or professional expertise in the English curriculum field.

I must also stress that unlike the British situation, the Australian national Statements are not formal classroom curricula. Rather, they are nationally agreed curriculum *frameworks* endorsed by all Australian Ministers for Education which each State and Territory is free to use and adapt — or even not use at all — in establishing their own specific curricula. In fact adaptation and implementation (and not rejection) of the national curriculum frameworks is now under way in all States and Territories. In this process there are specific directions or strategies being pursued in some States and Territories that are not being pursued in others.

The National Statement and Profile in English

The basic goals within which the English *Statement* is framed are as follows.

> Goals of the English Curriculum
>
> English is that area of the curriculum where students study and use English language and literature (including literature translated into English).
>
> The English curriculum encompasses studies which, in Australia, are called by a number of names, among them Language arts, English and English language. It also includes a significant part of English as a second language (ESL) programs.
>
> The English curriculum aims to develop the following:
>
> 1. The ability to speak, listen, read, view and write with purpose, effect and confidence in a wide range of contexts.
> 2. A knowledge of the ways in which language varies according to context, purpose, audience and content, and the ability to apply this knowledge.
> 3. A sound grasp of the linguistic structures and features of standard Australian English ... and the capacity to apply these, especially in writing.

4. A broad knowledge of a range of literature, including Australian literature, and a capacity to relate this literature to aspects of contemporary society and personal experience.
5. The capacity to discuss and analyse texts and language critically and with appreciation.
6. A knowledge of the ways in which textual interpretation and understanding may vary according to cultural, social and personal differences, and the capacity to develop reasoned arguments about interpretation and meaning.

> Students come from diverse socio-cultural and language backgrounds. The school curriculum must recognise this diversity and the important part language plays in students' educational achievements. (Curriculum Corporation, 1994a:3)

The English *Statement* is consistent with the *Australian Language and Literacy Policy.* It insists that literacy is more than a set of static, decontextualised skills. It endorses the concept of Australian English. It makes a strong endorsement of the view that

> at school, as in the early formative years, language is best learnt in use, with the aid of well-chosen teacher demonstrations, explanations, correction, advice and encouragement.
>
> Effective teaching is based on what children already know and can do. The teaching of English will achieve most where the considerable informal language knowledge and competence of students, whatever their cultural or language backgrounds, is acknowledged, used and extended. (*op.cit.*)

In some ways the national English *Profile* is the more strategically important document, since it sets out the principles upon which assessment of student achievement in English language and literacy should be based. It also incorporates an ESL component.

The *Profile* is to be used

> as a reporting framework by enabling teachers to make judgements about students' ability to use their English knowledge and skills to speak, listen, read, view and write with purpose and effect and are to

be used as part and parcel of classroom teaching and learning strategies. (Curriculum Corporation, 1994b:1)

The *Profile* booklet also provides teachers with:

- eight levels (from K-10)
- Strands (Speaking and Listening, Reading and Viewing, and Writing — even though there are only two Strands in the Statement — and Strands organisers
- Level Statements purporting to describe in general terms what student performance at each level should be
- Outcomes which describe in progressive order the essential skills and knowledge in English which students typically acquire as they become more proficient
- Pointers which are indicators or signals of a more generic achievement; and
- Annotated work samples.
  (Curriculum Corporation 1994b:1)

Unfortunately, the *Profile* was published separately from the *Statement*. The further that assessment instruments are removed from their relevant curriculum statement, the greater the risk that assessment and testing will drive the school curriculum.

I have some serious concerns about the Australian *Profile* as it stands. As is often the case in such global assessment and reporting frameworks, too many of the so-called levels of achievement seem to me to be more exercises in semantics rather than descriptors of real development that teachers observe in classrooms across the years. Some of the examples of progress from one 'level' to the next are, at best, problematic.

The ESL component is very problematic for a number of reasons — especially the fact that it makes too little recognition of the differences between oral and aural proficiencies. Other work, particularly the *ESL Bandscales* that have been developed within the National Languages and Literacy Institute of Australia, will have to be taken into consideration in the trialing of the national *Profile*.

It also seems to me that in constructing reporting and assessment templates like the Australian English *Profile*, those remote from classrooms too often make assumptions about student progression which fail to take account of some of those outside-of-school pressures which those of us who have spent years in the classroom are very familiar with. I refer, for example, to socio-economic and cultural inhibitors including the effects of poverty, the regression inevitably brought on by discontinuities as a student moves from being 'on top of the pile' in one schooling environment before hitting the 'bottom of the heap' in the next as they proceed from pre-school through to tertiary and other forms of post-school education.

I believe that the next few years of teachers trialing the *Profile* in classrooms around the nation will be critical to modifying and validating the individual descriptors as each State and Territory establishes its own set of assessment and reporting criteria.

Some Examples of Recent Federal Government initiatives in Language and Literacy

The Federal Government's National Professional Development Program

In a major professional development commitment which commenced during last financial year, the Australian government has committed A$60 million over three years for teacher development programs to support the national policy developments in Curriculum *Statements* and *Profiles*, incorporation of Key Competencies and developing accredited vocational education in schools. The grants are of two kinds and are generally submission-based on a competitive basis.

They seek to promote partnerships between teacher employers, universities and professional teacher organisations (such as the Australian Reading Association) in the provision of relevant, quality teacher professional development activities. Under the National Professional Development Program grants can be made direct to peak national bodies. For example the Australian Literacy Federation (which includes within its umbrella of five national associations the Primary English Teaching Association, the Australian Reading Association and the Australian Association for the Teaching of English) has just received a grant of

A$100,000 in addition to the A$150,000 it has received since 1991, to advance these national language and literacy agendas.

National Literacy Survey

Recent decisions announced in the Australian government's Budget demonstrated the government's commitment to literacy education. An additional A$10 million (over and above that already committed in the *Australian Language and Literacy Policy*) has been allocated for 1995 to assist education authorities in the States and Territories to promote and extend programs such as *Reading Recovery* and *First Steps* to improve the literacy and numeracy skills of students from Kindergarten to Grade 3, especially those from disadvantaged groups.

Three hundred long term unemployed people are to be trained as early literacy teacher support personnel.

Indicative of the Australian Commonwealth government's approach was its decision announced in the recent White Paper on Employment, *A Nation at Work,* to conduct a National Literacy Survey of students aged 7, 9 and 13 in order to obtain a snapshot of literacy levels amongst Australian students. This decision was in response to the ubiquitous claims and counterclaims consistently made about literacy levels and the need to have some reliable data on which to develop policies and to enable governments to assess the literacy problems that may be facing schools. As a result of this survey it is hoped that resources may be targeted more effectively. Furthermore, individual schools should be better able to assess their progress against national benchmark levels for Australia and set new goals if and where necessary. About A$3 million has been set aside for this national project which will, of course, require the co-operation of State and Territory governments for its success.

But the really notable feature is the approach which I understand is being advocated by the Commonwealth Department of Employment, Education and Training. Disavowing the standardised, simplistic and relatively a-contextual approaches characteristically displayed in 'pick-a-box' testing, I believe that the Federal Department favours the following parameters for any national assessment procedures:

- the process must be able to establish national benchmarks of student performance and to assist teachers in their diagnostic assessment of their students

- classroom teachers must be involved to ensure reliability and validity of the assessment instruments
- the assessment instruments must relate to the national English curriculum *Profile*
- the process will not be one merely of a norm referenced paper and pencil test but be a criteria referenced approach where open ended assessment tasks will be undertaken in classrooms and students' performance will be assessed or inferred against the levels and strands identified in the national *Profile*.

Indicative of the kind of approach that I believe the Federal Department is hoping to implement is the Australian Council for Educational Research's (ACER) Development Assessment Resource for Teachers (DART). The DART assessment package consists of sets of classroom activities which can be used by teachers as normal classroom activities. The assessment tasks are embedded in the activities carried out by students as part of the learning activities. Teachers are provided with guidelines for rating and judging students' performance. Importantly each DART activity is designed to assess a range of outcomes and teachers are able to interpret the results in terms of the *Profiles* strands for English

Of course, the success or failure of this venture will depend upon negotiations with the States and Territories and decisions taken by all Australian Ministers of Education.

Some Concluding Reflections

Having spent all the years of my adult life as a member of English teaching professional bodies and in championing their causes as well as researching their evolution, I wonder if I could offer a few words of reflection on a number of issues which I believe to be facing the English teaching profession today and in the immediate future.

The perennial 'Literacy Crisis'

There is no doubt in my mind that the most constantly recurring issue in our field since at least early Graeco-Roman history has been the lament of the aged and the conservative about the 'decline in literacy standards' in the young being perpetrated by dreadful, revolutionary 'soft, touchy, feely' cadres of contemporary teachers apparently lacking the intellectual rigour of their predecessors.

To say this is not to deny legitimate concerns about maintaining and increasing the literacy skills of our young people within a world of ever rapidly changing and demanding contexts for textual, oral/aural and visual literacies.

Invariably associated with the 'literacy crisis' syndrome are the cries of those who pursue their own exclusivist nostrums for literacy remediation and who fiercely oppose the claims of any other theoretical and pedagogical positions within language and literacy education. A British colleague of mine refers to those who fiercely adhere to their own narrow remedies and who refuse to consider the claims of other theoretical and pedagogical approaches — irrespective of the variegated nature of the learners and the diversity of learning contexts — as 'the intellectual terrorists'.

A statement from the Tasmanian Council of State School Parents and Friends Association Submission to a recent House of Representatives Inquiry into literacy education in the early years of schooling deserves to be 'up in lights' on noticeboards in every school and — perhaps more importantly — in the office of every newspaper editor and the studios of all talk-back radio pontificators.

> If anything has been learned from the research on teaching literacy skills, it should be that it would be arrogant to assume that all of the answers are known. It would also be misguided to assume that evidence points to a single model of learning or teaching, or that one model will be necessarily appropriate at all developmental levels or for all children. (House of Representatives Standing Committee on Employment, Education and Training, 1992:24)

Teachers need to be aware of a wide repertoire of theories and strategies from which to draw eclectically when teaching English language, literacy and literature within the particular educational contexts that they teach their students.

Incidentally, that famous dictum in the Newbolt Report (Ministry of Education, 1921) on the Teaching of English in England that 'every teacher is a teacher of English' has too often in practice been implemented as if it meant that 'anyone can teach English'. 'Anyone' cannot; and should not.

There is much ill-informed criticism about the literacy achievement of graduates of educational institutions — all the way from primary school graduates to university graduates. Now, I am not denying that there can be problems. But I believe that much of this is exaggerated because these criticisms often pay too little heed of the new linguistic contexts within which the educational graduate from the former 'institution' is usually expected to operate immediately, nor of the unfamiliarity of content with which the ex-student now has to deal. Transference of literacy skills from one set of contexts to another is not a simple process.

Such criticisms also often ignore the possibility that the new context in which the student finds herself or himself may be characterised by very poor English communication from 'above'. The need for effective communication (sometimes called, misleadingly, Plain English) reform in many public and private enterprises is witheringly obvious and our Council is currently addressing this very issue. How often, I wonder, is the 'illiteracy' not that of the reader or listener but, rather, that of the writer or speaker!

Practising what we preach

One of my favourite maxims comes from Chaucer's description of the 'poure persoun' — the humble and dutiful country priest whom we meet in Canterbury Tales: 'firste he wroghte, and afterward he taughte'. We must practise what we preach. All teachers of English need to be exemplary users of the language: to read widely and critically; to write with flair, imagination, accuracy and lucidity; to speak with clarity, verve and wit; to listen with acumen, accuracy and sensibility. To *teach* effective literacy we must be *'practitioners'* of effective literacy.

Retaining, cherishing and learning from the profession's history

From my own research and experience in related academic and professional fields I believe that it is absolutely vital for a professional body like the United Kingdom Reading Association not to lose a secure grasp of its own history. Your corporate memory, diverse and all as its content will be, will have been built up over 31 years not only through the accumulation and recording of documentation but also — perhaps pre-eminently — through the accumulation and recording of oral histories of your pioneers and their descendants.

Valuing the history of your development will not only help the profession to retain what is of value and let go what is not, but — perhaps even more importantly — will safeguard it against any later attempts to ignore or distort that history by any later whizz fad geniuses, gurus or whatever, who might seek to erect their 'new' empires by demolishing their own straw-person versions of earlier edifices.

Negotiating the battlegrounds

Professional bodies like the United Kingdom Reading Association need to be fully engaged in the 'politics' of the policy-making process. For there are those who are happy to cling together within their stockaded corrals and whinge bitterly about 'those up there' in their stockaded corrals who impose their world view upon the practitioners 'below'.

It is very difficult for anyone to build a road between entrenched corrals or camps. Too often those few who attempt to move between the teaching/academic camp into the policy/managerial camp end up being subjected to abuse from either or both. Inevitably, to enter into negotiations with those perceived to be 'the enemy' is to open oneself to allegations of compromise or even treachery by those perceived to have been one's former allies. Like the followers of the Oxford Movement such people too often are despised by their former colleagues and treated with distrust by their new colleagues.

But some of us have to do it. We have to wrestle with the issues of power and control. In the words of Lear's Fool

> He that has and a little tiny wit,
>   With a heigh-ho, the wind and the rain
>
> Must make content with his fortunes fit,
>   Though the rain it raineth every day

(William Shakespeare, *King Lear*, Act III, Scene ii, lines 74-77)

This may sometimes mean taking two steps forward while conceding one step back as the price for avoiding losing everything on a crash-through, 'all or nothing' approach against political masters whose intransigence and security of power constitute an immovable rock — at least until a subsequent election.

The educational community has been too prone to scorn those who attempt to cross sectoral boundaries. I believe it is true to say that some universities, for example, have demonstrated strong reluctance to reward interdisciplinary endeavour and have tended to look askance at academics who seek to communicate with 'the common throng' through the popular media.

It is so much easier to play to the immediate audience of one's colleagues within the stockaded corral. It is much harder, but essential, for English teachers individually and collectively as members of professional organisations, to become involved in the messy, often thankless and misunderstood task of attempting to reform policy through confronting and negotiating the political (in the broadest sense of that word) process with all the enthusiasm, tact, sensitivity and intelligence that this demands.

Rejecting ideological bigotry and respecting discriminating and informed eclecticism

As a profession matures and expands it is inevitable that theoretical disputation will occur. Sometimes this will be painful as old alliances and friendships creak, and even crack. That warm homogeneity which characterised the first flush of comrades-in-arms collegiality can break up. Ironically, this can occur soon after the fight to gain recognition from a formerly unresponsive world has been won. This process, I would argue, is a common experience for many, if not most, 'new' academic and professional disciplines. It is inevitable as disciplines 'grow up'.

But part of such maturity is the capacity to deal intelligently and constructively with diversity and not succumb to the 'us versus them' bitterness of ideological bigotry. I would suggest that the field of literacy education has already been hurt by this kind of immaturity.

In that inevitable process of maturation I would urge you to resist, as far as possible, empire building and destructive infighting within and between opposing 'camps'. You need to identify and resist those false either/or dichotomies and ideological entrenchments often predicated upon straw-person arguments and sometimes even 'the cult of personality'. You should be on your critical guard to identify and contest theory that becomes dogma; critical enquiry which becomes worship; leaders who become gurus; bridges that become barricades; concepts that become articles of faith; followers who become acolytes; approaches which become religions; and dissent which becomes heresy, irrespective of the various intellectual or professional cultures from which they may come.

Whether we are teachers, researchers, policy makers, bureaucrats or a mixture of any of these, we must always be, to quote from W.H. Auden's fine poem 'September 1, 1939', 'ironic points of light' — idealists but armed with a healthy and informed scepticism of all preachers of orthodoxies.

But, ultimately, irrespective of what governments proclaim, of what curriculum policy makers plan, or of what school principals and heads of departments decree, we must never forget this. That it will be the dedicated and informed parents or guardians in individual homes, and the talented and committed teachers in individual classrooms, who will continue to 'make the difference' to the quality of English language and literacy education experienced by the children, adolescents and young adults in our schools and colleges.

References

Australian Council for Educational Research (1994) *Development Assessment Resource for Teachers* Camberwell: Australian Council for Educational Research

Australian Education Council (1989) *Hobart Declaration on Schooling* Canberra: Commonwealth Department of Employment, Education and Training

Boston, K. (1994) 'A perspective on the so-called 'National Curriculum'' in G. Wilmot (ed) 'Points and Counterpoints: National Collaborative Curriculum Development — Enduring Achievement or Fading Dream?' *Curriculum Perspectives* 14,1

Commonwealth Government of Australia (1994) *Working Nation: The White Paper on Employment and Growth* Canberra: Australian Government Publishing Service

Curriculum Corporation (1994a) *A Statement on English for Australian Schools* Carlton: Curriculum Corporation

Curriculum Corporation (1994b) *English — A Curriculum Profile for Australian Schools* Carlton: Curriculum Corporation

Department of Employment, Education and Training (1991) *Australia's Language: The Australian Language and Literacy Policy* Canberra: Australian Government Publishing Service

Lo Bianco, J. (1987) *National Policy on Languages* Canberra: Australian Government Publishing Service

Ministry of Education (1921) *The Teaching of English in England* The Newbolt Report, London: His Majesty's Stationery Office

Chapter 3

National Curriculum English

Brian Cox
Chair of the English National Curriculum Working Group

Standards

In July 1994 I took part in a King's College, London, conference with teachers which began with three 20 minute speeches on English, Maths and Science. I spoke on English, Professor Paul Black on Science and Professor Margaret Brown of the Mathematics Working Party and the School Examinations and Assessment Council on Mathematics. We all agreed that the new draft proposals for a 'slimline' National Curriculum (SCAA, 1994) in fundamental ways are not in accord with research or good practice. The new curriculum would damage standards. Good teachers would be asked to implement a curriculum which they know to be flawed and this is a recipe for disaster. This applies only to State schools. Independent schools are allowed to make their own choices, and so good Independent school teachers will follow research and good practice. A gap between State and Independent schools will emerge, and State schools will acquire a major disadvantage. In the last year the media in this country has concentrated on testing and the boycott; just as important is the question of who should control the curriculum itself.

Political Interference

Why is this happening? The answer is political interference by John Patten, Baroness Blatch and various members of the Centre for Policy Studies and allied pressure groups. These people have in almost all cases no experience of teaching English in the classroom. They are highly prejudiced, dogmatic and narrow in their views of English, often ignorant of modern research in linguistics. Their views of education are based on nostalgia for a lost golden age.

Drafts of the new English Curriculum, 1992-1994

In September, 1992, NCC decided to revise the English curriculum set up by my Working Group in 1989 (NCC, 1992). Why? The research of Professor Bridie Raban and her team at Warwick University (Raban et al, 1994) on the class-room implementation of the English curriculum gave no warrant for radical change. The case for change was driven forward by a very small group of people, particularly David Pascall, then Chair of the National Curriculum Council, and various supporters of the Centre for Policy Studies and the Campaign for Real Education. The decision to rewrite the curriculum was carried through against the wishes of almost all teachers of English.

From 1992 to 1993 David Pascall, an oil executive with no experience of teaching English, took the lead in advocating that all children from the age of five should be made to speak what he called grammatically correct spoken Standard English, even in the playground. When a clever journalist asked him what 'grammatically correct' meant, he replied: they shouldn't split the infinitive. The *Times Educational Supplement* later said that in future children who wished to split the infinitive would have to go behind the bicycle shed. In academic and school circles this became the international joke of the year. But what is deeply disturbing is that a man so ignorant about the English language and teaching should have been given a major input into the National Curriculum, an input which still influences the new slimmed-down draft curriculum prepared under the rule of Sir Ron Dearing.

Since then a series of documents about National Curriculum English have been published, driven by three elements:

i. Attempts by professional officers of National Curriculum Council and more recently, the School Curriculum and Assessment Authority behind the scenes to save good practice from the wreckage imposed by David Pascall and his friends.

ii. Consultation exercises. Teachers have had some impact on the revisions of earlier drafts.

iii. Right-wing refusal to give way to the consultation process or the profession. The most recent example has been when the recommendations of the 1994 English Advisory Group, led by Alistair West and other teachers, were changed in important ways by right-wing members of SCAA.

The decision to base the draft slimline curriculum on the revised proposals of September, 1993, was undemocratic. In a letter of June 24, 1994 in the *Times Educational Supplement* Pat Baldry from Essex wrote:

> The subject working party for English took as the starting point the National Curriculum Council Consultation report (September, 1993) produced after last year's consultation process. In doing this, teachers' support for the current Order has been ignored. The new draft proposals are based, therefore, on a document that was neither circulated widely to schools, nor put before Parliament. The existing Order for English, which is the legal requirement for the content of teaching and learning of the curriculum for English, has been shuffled to one side. Why and by whom?

The result of this process, the draft slimline English curriculum is, not surprisingly, a confused document. It is better than the previous post-1992 drafts, but still contains major flaws.

The New Draft English Curriculum

The Cox curriculum is not perfect. The new slimline curriculum has introduced important improvements:

i. Teachers' responses to previous versions of the National Curriculum had made it clear that it was overloaded. It was thought necessary, therefore, to reduce the content. The slimline version should be more manageable, and so long as teachers work within this framework, they can still include things that they think are important that are not specified here; so some teachers will want to give more emphasis to media studies, some to Knowledge about Language, some to information technology, and so on.

ii. The new curriculum is the right way round. It starts with the programmes of study — what goes on in the class-room — and ends with the level descriptions — the hoped-for outcomes in teaching and learning (the Cox Committee advocated this, but were overruled).

iii. The atomised statements of attainment have been combined to produce a summary description of attainment for each level — synoptic description. (I have to say that many of these seem to me bland and cliché-ridden.) Graham Frater, previously Chief Inspector for English, has pointed out that the Cox curriculum was thought by right-wingers to be imprecise. The new atomised statements are often even less precise.

There are other major flaws. The most important are addressed below:

Spoken Standard English

It is in this area that the most important changes were made in the recommendations of the 1994 advisory group. In the *Times Educational Supplement,* May 20, 1994, Alistair West described the deletions. In the following sentences the section in brackets was deleted:

> Pupils (may be speakers of more than one variety of English and) should develop confidence in their ability to adapt what they say to their listeners and the circumstances.
>
> Pupils' understanding of English (both Standard and other varieties) should be enhanced through their reading.

Alistair West also said that in Key Stage 2 the requirement to 'consider some of the differences in vocabulary and grammar between standard and non-standard varieties of English' has been deleted. Who made these changes, and why?

Katharine Perera (1994) explains in what ways the sections on Spoken Standard English are harmful. She explains that the description of spoken Standard English is either unhelpful or downright wrong in a number of places:

> Core grammatical features of standard English are said to include: 'correct and consistent use of verb tenses'. It is easy to demonstrate that standard English does not require the consistent use of verb tenses: 'I am leaving now because I have been waiting since before the train arrived and there is no sign of the parcel that I thought John had promised to send.' Here, within one standard English sentence, there are five different tense/aspect verb forms.

In a number of places, the document uses the word 'correct' in relation to the forms of Standard English, but in fact this use depends upon an interpretation of the notion 'Standard English' which is completely circular, and therefore vacuous — ie Standard English is correct grammar, correct grammar is Standard English. In a *Times Educational Supplement* article of June 17, 1994 Michael Rosen enjoyed himself pointing out that whereas by level 5 commas are usually used accurately, Sir Ron and John Patten can't agree on it. Do you put a comma after Dear Ron or after Yours sincerely? Usage varies. Similarly with spoken Standard English, what is correct? If I say: 'Yesterday I motored to the aerodrome listening to the wireless' should a teacher tell me I'm wrong? The recommendations on 'correct' spoken standard English are impossible to apply in practice, and impossible to test. As professional linguists know, my use of grammar in speech — at my age of 65 — varies from that of highly intelligent educated young people under 30. Who will decide what is spoken Standard English?

Katharine Perera writes in her essay:

> As for the characterisation of the grammar of Standard English, the phrase 'conventions of grammar' which is used in the introduction is more helpful than the superficially appealing phrase 'grammatically correct expression' which features in the programmes of study. Both

> definitions skate over the issue of how and by whom the conventions will be agreed.

Spoken Standard English is introduced at an inappropriately early age. The programmes of study for AT1 introduce spoken Standard English in Key Stage 1:

> Pupils should be introduced with appropriate sensitivity to the importance of standard English. Pupils should consider their own speech and how they communicate with others, particularly in more formal situations or with unfamiliar adults. (Perera, 1994)

How will infant children in inner city schools cope with that? Spoken Standard English should not be introduced before Key Stage 2, and preferably not until Key Stage 3 in many schools.

Let me insist that in the Cox curriculum we strongly support the view that all children are entitled to be helped to speak Standard English by the age of 16. It is the language of power in our society. But our attitudes to language and identity are rapidly changing. Colin MacCabe (1990) wrote:

> In 30 years England has been transformed from a racially and linguistically homogenous society into a miscegenated and polyglot one. Of course one should not ignore the extent to which the earlier homogeneity was itself the product of a continuous process of repression in which the various races and languages of the British Isles were subordinated to English hegemony. But the reality of the change of the past 30 years cannot be underestimated either. If the initial response to this change was a multiculturalism, woolly or aggressive according to preference, the eighties saw the Conservatives attempting to impose an English identity on the country.

This aim lies behind the curriculum interferences of the last three years.

Phonics

In the 1989 English curriculum prepared by my Working Group the Attainment Targets say for Reading for Level 2 (5-7 year olds):

> 'Use picture and context cues, words recognised on sight and phonic cues in reading'.

In the Programmes of Study for Level 1 this is said:

> 'Through the programmes of study for reading pupils should be guided so as to:
>
> - appreciate the significance of print and the fact that pictures and other visual media can also convey meaning, eg road signs, logos;
> - build up, in the context of their reading, a vocabulary of words recognised on sight;
> - use the available cues, such as pictures, context, phonic cues, word shapes and meaning of a passage to decipher new words.'

In the new draft slimmed-down curriculum the Programmes of Study for Reading include a description of 'phonic knowledge' and the opportunities which should be made available for children aged 5 to 7:

> 'Phonic knowledge focuses on the relationships between print symbols and sound patterns'.
>
> 'They should be made aware of the sounds of spoken language and taught how symbols correspond to those sounds. Opportunities should be given for:
>
> - listening to sounds in oral language to develop phonological awareness;
> - recognising alliteration, sound patterns and rhyme and relating those to patterns in letters;
> - considering syllables in longer words;
> - identifying initial and final sounds in words, including sounds which rhyme;
> - identifying and using a comprehensive range of letters and sounds (including combinations of letters, blends and digraphs), and paying specific attention to their use in the formation of words;
> - recognising inconsistencies in phonic patterns;
> - recognising that some letters do not produce a sound themselves but influence the sound of others, *eg final 'e', soft 'c'*.'

These proposals have provoked considerable argument.

Graham Frater (1994) writes on the proposals for early reading:

> The programmes of study give prominence to phonic and graphical strategies, whilst context and meaning, as presented in this part of the document, are under-emphasised and ancillary.

What is less clear is how this phonic dogma is intended to be turned into practice. It does not fit with good practice.

Annabelle Dixon, who was a member of the 1994 English advisory group, writes in *The Times Educational Supplement,* June 17, 1994:

> Teachers want the children in their care to become fluent and competent writers and readers. What drives them to despair at present is the idea that in order to be able to prove such competence in public tests, children as young as five will have to undergo the drill of phonics such as 'the relationship between root words such as magic and magician', and also learn to 'recognise inconsistencies in phonic patterns.' Supposedly you first teach the children a rule and then confuse them by pointing out the exceptions. ..... The amount and nature of the phonic and spelling skills suggested as suitable for Key Stage 1 means that there will be no time for anything else. Most important of all, it will reduce the time children will have to read and be heard read. There are a minimum number of spelling and phonic skills that children need at this age to be useful, and better that they learn these well than be overloaded by work more suited to older children.

A reply to this was published in a later *Times Educational Supplement* by John Bald, July 1, 1994, with details of research that showed the value of more emphasis on phonics. The main point I wish to make is that the issue of the place of phonics in the teaching of reading ought to be left open to professional advice, and not enshrined in a statutory curriculum which often reflects the desire of politicians to return to the drills of the 1930s, rather than denying the importance of phonics in the teaching of reading. When professionals disagree we don't need a statutory curriculum which imposes only one side of the argument.

Prescribed Lists of Books

Beverley Anderson writes in *The Times Educational Supplement,* June 3, 1994:

> Nowhere is it suggested that English-speaking students be made aware of texts in other languages, nor that they appreciate bilingualism. There is no hint that the English we now read, write, hear and speak also belongs to the Welsh, Scots, Irish, Australians, Indians and Jamaicans, to name but a few.

In a brilliant essay in *The Independent* on November 2, 1990, Stephen Spender commented on the changes now going on both in the English language and in our reading of English texts. He explains that study of the London and East Anglia Group Examination Board Curriculum, with its inclusion of multicultural texts, had persuaded him to change his previous opinions. Before 1945, he says, it was taken for granted that children of every kind of social background (particularly from the working class) should ideally speak and write an English which conformed with the standards of the best speech and writing of the educated upper classes. The purpose of teaching them the traditional classics was that they should meet these standards. There really were no other standards; but in recent years we hear on the BBC new accents, new voices. Today our schools include thousands of children from various ethnic communities. The idea of 'correct' English as Received Pronunciation is no longer valid. The great tradition of Milton, Keats or Jane Austen, Spender says, is growing even further away from the present very fluid, Anglo-American language. Like many of the older generation, he finds this change unsettling. He writes:

> The idea of a future in which there is no single standard, but a multiplicity of standards, each with its separate variety of correctness, is indeed terrifying. (Spender, 1990)

However, he believes, as my Working Group did, that works by non-English modern writers must be a central element in the curriculum. For instance, the obvious political bias in the prescribed lists is shown by the omission of Tony Harrison.

Other arguments against prescribed lists are well-known. Teachers need freedom to choose texts which they and their children will enjoy.

The importance of media studies has been down-graded.

Conclusion

Annabelle Dixon (*op.cit.*) wrote that the new draft slimline curriculum is

> one of culpable ignorance, combined with a wilfulness based on prejudice — why else the bias against bilinguals? ... There is no evidence that the authors are familiar with the realities of teaching young children from other than literate middle-class families.

Teachers must take part in the consultation exercise; otherwise it will be claimed that the new draft proposals for the slimline curriculum is acceptable to them. But I have no faith that SCAA will listen to the major criticisms. We will be faced by a new slimline curriculum which will reduce the credibility of the National Curriculum and which will result in massive confrontations in 1995-6 when attempts are made to assess it. By that time, Sir Ron Dearing, if he has any sense, will have moved on.

In countries all over the world it is vital that the curriculum should not be controlled by politicians, but by the teaching profession. We have a great struggle ahead.

References

Frater, G. (1994) 'Third time lucky?' *The English and Media Magazine* 30, 4-5

MacCabe, C. (1990) ' Language, Literacy, Identity: reflections on the Cox Report' *Critical Quarterly* 32, 4, 7-13

National Curriculum Council (1992) *The Case for Revising the Order* York: National Curriculum Council

Perera, K. (1994) 'Language in the English National Curriculum' *The English and Media Magazine* 30, 5-7

Raban, B., Clark, U. and McIntyre, J. (1994) *Evaluation of the Implementation of English in the National Curriculum at Key Stages 1, 2 and 3* London: School Curriculum and Assessment Authority

School Curriculum and Assessment Authority (1994) *English in the National Curriculum: Draft Proposals* London: School Curriculum and Assessment Authority

Chapter 4

The state of English in the state of England

Bridie Raban-Bisby
University of Melbourne

In England and Wales at this time we have a statutory National Curriculum. Working parties were set up during the late 1980s and National Curriculum English, Mathematics and Science were introduced to our youngest children in 1989. Other subjects have followed. The English curriculum written at that time is still in place (December 1994), but only just. It has been re-drafted and revised and a new English curriculum (NCC, 1993) has been waiting in the wings to be implemented in September 1995. These proposals have now been overtaken by a 'slimmed-down' Dearing version (SCAA, 1994a) which was published for consultation. Responses to this round of consultations were due back during July 1994.

What is fascinating to notice are the differences and distinctions which can be drawn between these documents (DES/WO, 1990; NCC, 1993; SCAA, 1994a). They represent the polarities of teaching English which have been embedded in our work since the beginnings of mass public education. Teaching English; Speaking and Listening, Reading and Writing is a deeply political act and always has been. Because of this, the English curriculum at any moment in time will reflect dogma and ideology rather than reasoned and evidence-based decisions.

In contrasting the Cox curriculum (or Order, as it is called) with the 1993 revisions, the first thing to notice is that the first proposed revisions to the Programmes of Study, which outline the curriculum, take up twice the number of pages as those in the Cox curriculum Order. It is worth pointing out that the more text which makes up the statutory curriculum, the more opportunity there is for the writer to be directive. We have learned that it is advisable to keep statutory curriculum documents in broad brush strokes, leaving their interpretation to non-statutory guidance which may be kept under constant review and changed as appropriate. However, when I and my research team proposed this course of action in our evaluation report to the National Curriculum Council (Raban et al, 1994), NCC's response was to say that teachers would disregard anything they didn't have to do by law. This was a revealing statement. Clearly, the statutory Order is to be used as a vehicle to tell teachers what to do, although this has always been contested by the National Curriculum Council and by SCAA, the School Curriculum and Assessment Authority, who point out that all the subject Orders lay down what has to be legally covered, not how to teach the material.

In looking at Attainment Target 2 *Reading* for the Cox curriculum Order (DES/WO, 1990), an analysis of the discourse shows it to be couched in terms of these statements each mentioned once:

Activities should build on,
Teaching should cover,
Pupils should encounter,
Teachers should take account of,
Activities should ensure that,
Pupils should be guided to.

In contrast, the 1993 revisions (NCC, 1993) were couched in terms of the following statements, mentioned once unless indicated otherwise:

They should be taught, (4)
Pupils should learn, (2)
Pupils should be introduced to, (2)
They should apply knowledge, (2)

> It is essential that teachers should draw on,
> From the outset pupils should,
> At an early age pupils should,
> They should build up,
> They should be given extensive experience of,
> Pupils should read on their own, etc.

There is no overlap between these two sets of statements. They emanate from quite different belief systems concerning learning and teaching and this is more clearly seen when attention is focused on the content of required curricula. For instance in the Non-Statutory Guidance for the Cox curriculum Order, Reading is defined as:

> When we read we make sense of it for ourselves, not just by 'decoding' but by bringing our own experience and understanding to it. (NCC, 1989: C8)

In looking through the 'Detailed provisions' for the Programme of Study it can be seen how this view of reading has been translated into curricular terms and how teachers might be implementing these statutory requirements into classroom practice. For instance, the first requirement is that:

> Reading activities should build on the oral language and experiences which pupils bring from home.

This model of reading sees diverse literacies as a resource stemming from diversity of home experiences which children bring with them into the classroom, believing quite rightly that to ignore these experiences would be, at best, unhelpful to the children.

In contrast, the Programme of Study in the 1993 revisions addresses this issue as follows:

> Pupils who begin school with limited experience and understanding of literacy will need a planned and extensive introduction to the initial stages of reading. Pupils should learn the alphabet. Their awareness of sounds and patterns of sounds should be developed as a preparation for phonic work. (para 5)

Here we see a deficit model, repeated in the 1994 proposals, which is set to make up the shortfall which some children may be deemed to present as they begin compulsory schooling.

The 1993 revisions begin:

> Pupils should learn to read with fluency, accuracy and understanding. *Thus* they should be taught the alphabet, phonic skills, the basic conventions of books and print and effective techniques for decoding, understanding and responding. (para 1) (my emphasis)

The 1994 proposals repeat these two sentences, leaving out the entailing *thus*. Here we see phonic knowledge having a prominent section in para 7, listing activities such as 'considering syllables in longer words' and 'recognising that some letters do not produce a sound'. Graphic knowledge which children are required to have includes 'plurals — by adding s, es and ies' and 'prefixes and suffixes'. Again, these elements are repeated in the 1994 proposals.

Surprisingly, there are repeated references to phonics as the only valid way of achieving fluency in reading. Occasional references to other elements are made, but phonic skills are the only ones carefully described. It appears, therefore, that teachers could be constrained by decree to adopt a view of reading which evidence shows is inadequate.

For instance, the insertion at Key Stage 1 in Reading of a core sight vocabulary including, for instance, such common words as 'they', 'was' and 'had' seems more obviously the product of ignorance. Because of their lack of clear semantic content, these tend to be the very words that beginning readers find hardest. But to have tried to place the recitation of the alphabet as the very first test for reading in the 1993 revisions was to insist on engaging children in an activity which, until they learn how to use an index or a dictionary, would be no more than a mysterious ritual to them. Dombey (1993) goes on to suggest that perhaps this is intentional. After all the wayward classroom activities of the 60s (and 70s and 80s) classrooms should once more become the site where children are taught to submit to what they don't understand and what they have no use for.

This exclusive emphasis on phonic learning has caused disquiet among those concerned with early reading. Dombey (1993) notes that in our complex writing system the phonic rules are exceedingly complex and riddled with exceptions, among them most of the commonest words in the language. Many children find it exceedingly difficult to identify the final 'sound' in a word, and are usually unable to do so until well after they have learned to read (Johnston et al, 1990). And very often children appear to learn the complex sound-symbol relationships of English through perception of analogies, rather than following explicitly stated rules (Goswami, 1990).

The National Curriculum Council decreed, through their 1993 revisions for English, that all children should be able to 'identify two letter consonant blends and the most common digraphs'. Again, Dombey (1993) asks, is this stricture the product of ignorance of how children learn phonics, or does it spring from a deep-rooted anxiety about children working things out for themselves? Certainly the view of reading put forward in the 1993 revisions and the 1994 proposals is one that owes more to the prejudices of the ill-informed, rather than to reputable research findings like those mentioned above. Here we see nothing less than a tyranny of ignorance coupled with the folly of the prejudice.

Most marked, of course, are the differences in the Statements of Attainment between the 1989 and 1993 documents, and between those and the Level Descriptors (1994) particularly at Level 1.

1989

Pupils should be able to:

recognise that print is used to carry meaning in books and in other forms in the everyday world

begin to recognise individual words or letters in familiar contexts

show signs of a developing interest in reading

talk in simple terms about the content of stories, or information in non-fiction books

1993

Pupils should be able to:

say the alphabet

identify first and final sounds in spoken and written words

read aloud a minimum of 30 common usage words within simple short narratives

1994

> **Level 1** ...They use their knowledge of the alphabet and of sound-symbol relationships in order to read words and establish meaning...
>
> **Level 2** ...They use more than one strategy (phonic, graphic, syntactic and contextual) to establish meaning...

What we see happening here is a dramatic shift in the emphasis for describing and identifying early reading, a shift towards dogma as opposed to evidence and understanding based on successful practice. There is a widespread belief that teachers do not teach phonics to young children learning to read and this is the reason why reading standards have been falling in our schools. However, the evidence from the evaluation study (Raban *et al*, 1994) illustrates that teachers of young children spent most of their 'teaching reading time' teaching phonics and that phonic activities (eg. practising sounds, using phonic cues and sounding groups of letters) were those most frequently observed. These experiences were being provided for children while teachers were implementing the Cox curriculum.

In particular, it is evident that in the recent proposals, children at Key Stage 1 would be more likely to achieve Level 2 than Level 1 and these revisions would, therefore, be contributing towards falling standards as even more children failed to achieve appropriately.

This contrast between explicit ideologies of teaching and learning is also echoed in the statutory elements for *Writing*. As before, the first indicator is found through an analysis of the emphasis of statements surrounding the statutory requirements:

Cox Order:

> Pupils should have frequent opportunities to,
>
> Pupils should be enabled to,
> Pupils should undertake,
> Teachers should talk about,
> Pupils should write,
> Pupils should be introduced to,
> Pupils should be taught, (4)

1993 Revision:

> Pupils should write,
>
> Pupils should be introduced to, (2)
> Pupils should be taught, (10)
> Pupils should learn to, (5)
> Activities should help pupils, (3)
> Activities should encourage pupils, (2)
> Classroom activities should emphasise/extend/develop, (2)
> From the outset pupils should,
> At an early stage pupils should,
> Pupils should discuss,
> Close attention should be paid to,
> They should write word lists.

What we see here is a much wider set of demands of teachers in these revisions, with clear emphasis on explicit teaching and learning. It is proposed here that the transmission model should dominate the English classrooms of the future.

Close inspection of the content of the proposed Programme of Study for Writing indicates the view of writing which is to be fostered:

> Particular attention is paid to the acquisition of standard English: grammatically correct expression, accurate spelling and conventional punctuation and an extensive vocabulary. (NCC, 1993 para 1: 57)

Para 2 demands that 'From the outset, pupils should', for instance, 'hold a pencil correctly'. This paragraph continues: At an early stage, pupils should be taught to: start and finish letters correctly... use full stops... recognise the most obvious sound of each letter.' Later in paragraph 3 it is stated that pupils 'should be taught to apply their existing linguistic knowledge, drawn from oral language and their experience of reading, and understanding how word choice and word order is crucial to clarity of meaning' and 'pupils should learn to ensure that subject and verb agree'. These statements remain in the 1994 proposals.

Statements like these so clearly misrepresent what we know about children's linguistic sophistication on entry to school, that teachers are confused and confounded by revisions to the English curriculum which appear to ignore what children can already do and do well. How is it possible, teachers ask, for children to write with vitality if we first make them anxious about the mistakes they are going to make?

Again, if the Statements of Attainment for Level 1 are inspected across the three documents, the shift in emphasis can be judged more clearly:

1989

Pupils should be able to

> use pictures, symbols or isolated letters, words or phrases to communicate meaning.

1993

Pupils should be able to

> identify where a full stop should go in their own writing
>
> write each letter of the alphabet
>
> form letters controlling size, shape and left to right orientation

1994

> .....Pupils begin to show an awareness of full stops, identifying where they are needed in their own writing. Letters are usually clearly shaped and correctly orientated.

In the 1993 revisions and 1994 proposals, pupils are required to 'learn that a sentence is a unit of sense demarcated by an initial capital letter and final punctuation marks.' This statement is written in the face of, for instance, my own research (Raban, 1986) which attempted to reach children's understandings of features of print. For instance, when asked what they understood by the term 'a sentence', children aged 5 and 6 years pointed to the space between the full stop and the capital letter of the next sentence. This indicated the level of sophistication and experience of written language required before any formal teaching of the concept was possible. Children could internalise imposed teaching that a sentence needed a full stop and a capital letter, but their real understanding of this typographic device was neither accurate nor secure at these early stages.

With respect to writing, therefore, we see a similarly narrow aridity as we saw with reading. The secretarial aspects of writing have been brought firmly to the fore, in a way that indicates dogma at work, dogma which is uncurbed by familiarity with real children in real classrooms. Indeed, the over-concern with punctuation in children's earliest attempts at writing, accompanied by an insistence that children spell correctly from the earliest ages, would, if these revisions are implemented, lose for us all the exciting ground won by our National Writing Project, so successfully embraced by our primary teachers (Czerniewska, 1992). What we learned here were the rewards gained in terms of children's progress from an equal emphasis on process, as opposed to a single, central focus on outcomes for the development of writing.

When a desire to raise standards is couched in terms of external forms of assessment, then curriculum statements need to be formulated which can be readily and unequivocally tested. This is seen as the driving force wedging itself between the 1989 and 1993/94 documents. For instance, 'building on oral language and experiences which children bring from home' is going to be more difficult to assess than, for example, 'saying the alphabet' and essentially this is the difference between these documents. It is worth remembering what Ken Goodman has pointed out, that the easier a piece of language behaviour is to assess, the more likely it is to be trivial.

In addition, the recursive model of language development, found in the first statements of the Cox English curriculum, rooted in research and matched by the experience of teachers, is eliminated in both the revisions and the proposals. In short, the new assessment statements are even more arbitrary and remote from empirical evidence. As Britton and Martin (1992/93) have pointed out, the model of language and learning implicit in the revisions is that of developing language skills through conscious mastery of rules and much guided practice, rather than development through reflection on planned usage.

The long-term consequence if these revisions were to be implemented would be a narrowing of the curriculum with a heavy emphasis on 'correctness' as opposed to 'appropriateness'. The benefits which primary teachers have gained from a developmental approach which focuses on emergent literacy and values what children bring with them from home to school, will be lost as pressure is experienced to teach conventions and rules of speaking, listening, reading and writing to children who may not have enough experience to make them meaningful. As Dawes (1992/93) suggests, able pupils may leave our primary schools being accurate language users, less able pupils may have ceased to bother with their language resources altogether.

Our beliefs concerning teaching and learning will influence our practice whether these beliefs are explicitly held or implicit. They will influence how we behave towards the pupils we teach, how we organise our schools and our classrooms and the ways in which we choose resources and choose to organise our time. What is important to emphasise is that these government documents revising and proposing new English curricula also have value systems and beliefs concerning teaching and learning embedded in them. In the analysis of directive statements which has been illustrated earlier in this paper we can identify a definite trend. In the Table below those statements which begin *Pupils should be taught* have been isolated as a sub-group of all the directive statements mentioned in the two sections concerning Reading and Writing at Key Stages 1 and 2.

Table 1
Analysis of Directive Statements (1990-1993-1994)

Key Stages 1 and 2

'Pupils should be taught' as a percentage of the total number of directives

	1990	1993	1994
Reading	6	16	46
	0%	25%	49%
Writing	10	30	65
	40%	33%	54%

What we see happening here is a dramatic shift, especially with respect to teaching reading, concerning government dominance of the process. There is a clear will to direct what teachers do in their classrooms and for the teaching of reading to be dictated by politicians rather than professionals.

Stereotypically, in teaching English, the extremes of belief have embraced, on the one hand, the view that children will get better at it if they are exposed to written and spoken language and given opportunities to use them for their own purposes, language being seen as emerging as part of the child's development. On the other hand, there is the view that language has to be explicitly taught and imposed on the child by those who 'know best'.

Where are these extremes rooted and how can they be resolved?

The problems which the writers of the Cox English curriculum faced had been at the centre of passionate argument for decades. Their report was yet another concerning English which the government had commissioned in, for instance, 1921 Newbolt Report, 1975 Bullock Report, 1988 Kingman Report, and then the Cox Report which was published in 1989. *The Teaching of English in England* was the title of the Newbolt Report (Ministry of Education, 1921) which was produced out of widespread dissatisfaction, following the end of the First World War, about low educational standards that had been revealed by a conscript army.

What then, about the teaching of English in the 1990s? To a degree the same problems have to be addressed which were presented to the Newbolt Committee: low academic standards, lack of competitive edge in the world economy, failure of pupils to achieve their full potential, with the resultant social and political disaffection.

More than 70 years after the publication of the Newbolt Report, questions about national identity are what provide the ideological subtext of the Conservative party position on the National Curriculum. MacCabe (1990) points out that the political and personal desire to see the reintroduction of grammar, for instance, is directly related to questions of national identity rather than to questions of standards.

As one commentator put it in *The Sunday Times* (Nov. 1988):

> Grammar is the fastest rising topic in the Tory party firmament, now almost on a par with hanging and dole fraud....The nation's grammar stirs the juices.

Returning to the argument of alleged falling standards in our schools, the most sharply focused target for this debate has been levels of literacy and, more recently, teacher training. Indeed, an article in *The Spectator* (February, 1993) has illustrated the point succinctly;

> ...schools today turn out semi-literates whose principal talent seems to be for committing crime or collecting unemployment benefit. These people are not the victims of recession, but quite often the victims of their teachers. They are unemployed because they are

> unemployable. They are unemployable because those who taught them taught them nothing useful. In turn, the teachers are the victims of those who taught them at training colleges.

The article goes as far as to say that the recent disagreement between teachers and the Secretary of State over children sitting English tests in schools in 1993 and 1994 was because teachers knew that these test results would show that their pupils could not attain basic standards of literacy even by 14 years of age.

Questions concerning the teaching of English in our schools tend to relate to two very general areas:

Language — particularly issues related to Knowledge about Language and Standard English.

Literature — with its links to culture, heritage and national identity.

Over the past years, the parameters of the debate seem to have been set by people who have very little knowledge of real schools. Indeed, the 'educational establishment' has been deliberately excluded from much educational policy-making in England.

Hickman (in Bazalgette,1994) reminds us about what has been ignored:

- The nature of real schools and classrooms,
- The diversity of our school population,
- The issue of how learning takes place most effectively.

With respect to diversity, it appears to be the case that people who are in a position to affect the lives of teachers and their pupils believe that classrooms are made up of homogeneous groups of pupils who sit in rows, are at the same developmental stage of learning, have similar backgrounds, interests and expectations. However, the reality is very different and as teachers, we know we ignore the real differences between our pupils at our peril.

Clearly, in the context of any classroom, questions concerning the teaching of English become problematic. How is it best to approach, for instance, the issue of Standard English and of a cultural heritage? Here we come to the question of how learning takes place. The model of learning that many people in positions of political power seem to have of the learner is one of an empty vessel that the teacher fills with knowledge and understanding. This view of learning presumes that the learners are passive, compliant, of similar backgrounds, interests and abilities. To suggest that pupils come into classrooms as empty vessels is an insult to their experience of the world and to the different types of expertise they clearly possess.

If we attempt to funnel the richness and diversity of our classrooms into an inflexible mono-cultural curriculum framed in a rigid adherence to, for instance, Standard English for all purposes or phonics as the only or even the major initial teaching method for reading — then we deny everything we know about the way people learn and we shall, at best, marginalise and, at worst, destroy the voices of our pupils — and their voices demand and deserve our attention.

Cartmell (1993), during an investigation of English in institutions of higher education, asked how these departments saw the future of English studies. Their collective response was characterised by *diversity*. They saw new options coming on stream concerning cultural and media studies. They saw the widening of the canon of literary authors and texts to include more women and ethnic minority writers. They perceived the study of English literature becoming the study of literatures in English. They saw English as an increasingly inter-disciplinary study, with a fuller integration of language and literature studies within a view of 'literary' studies which would be sufficiently inclusive to embrace both canonical and non-canonical texts.

Staff in these University Departments of English agreed that recent government proposals to prescribe what happens in schools' English curricula is a thunderstorm on their horizon. They were vociferous in wanting to combat this whenever it appeared.

Forty professors and lecturers of English signed a letter which appeared in the national press strongly objecting to the proposed revisions to the school English curriculum. The revisions, they maintained,

> reject the consensus of professional opinion about the best practice in schools; they involve an unacceptable degree of political and statutory control over classroom teaching...a new curriculum which so misrepresents the subject of English is an inadequate preparation for its study at higher levels.

At University level there are exciting new developments and trends in the study of English leading to cultural and media studies, women's studies, creative writing and the study of other literature in English. What we see happening here through these revisions and proposals is that the study of English in schools is slowly but definitely being pushed out of earshot of the teaching of English at our Universities. Importantly, such a disjunction will fracture our intellectual heritage, destroy homogeneity within the profession and strangle the freshness of discourse which characterises the vitality and richness of English teaching throughout our schools.

How far do the new 'slimmed-down' proposals exacerbate or retrieve the already fractured English curriculum for pupils in our schools?

The first thing to notice again about the new curriculum for English (SCAA/COI, 1995) is that it takes up fewer pages than the 1993 revisions, the 1994 proposals and even the Cox curriculum itself, thereby offering less coverage for statutory mandate. The Professional Officers for English in introducing the new curriculum admit that the English team received the greatest number of responses overall with particular concerns for literacy about the place of phonic knowledge in teaching and assessment in early reading, and in writing, teaching and assessing the use of the full stop.

The outcome of the consultation sees little change in this kind of emphasis, regardless of what the SCAA conference presentations say concerning the fact that little has changed from the 1989 original Orders. They present a conciliatory front to the profession, arguing that teachers must now reclaim their role in curriculum development and that teachers should not think that they have to radically rewrite all their current curriculum plans. Such rhetoric is unjustified and even abusive after the way in which the English curriculum, in particular, has been wrested from the profession. None of us are foolish enough to believe that little has changed since the introduction of the Cox curriculum. Indeed, the new 'slimmed down' Dearing version, written in response to an over-loaded prescription, has offered the opportunity to reconstruct the teaching of English in England and Wales and enter it into schools subversively.

In the Programmes of Study for English the emphasis is still clear for the teaching of reading. While one sentence gives a broadly acceptable aim:

> Pupils should be taught to read with fluency, accuracy, understanding and enjoyment, building on what they already know.

We see later that the ordering of the text makes it quite unequivocal what the priorities for teaching reading must be by law:

> Within a balanced and coherent programme, pupils should be taught to use the following knowledge, understanding and skills:
>
> phonic knowledge
> graphic knowledge
> word recognition
> grammatical knowledge
> contextual understanding

However, the SCAA presentations of this document say that we are not to impute any significance to the ordering of these statements. Their lack of concern for media studies clearly places this plea within a context of ignorance and callous disregard for what we all know about the power of text, both explicit and implicit, in a nation state.

The English Professional Officers admit that they were allowed only two stems for the development of the Programmes of Study — *pupils should be taught* and *pupils should have opportunities to*. They never indicate who is 'directing' this and they have interestingly disregarded that directive. They use 12 different stems in Key Stages 1 and 2 Reading and 14 in Writing. While the overall use of *pupils should be taught* far exceeds the use of the other stems in both cases, the proportionate use is marginally less than the 1994 proposals:

> 44% Reading 51% Writing

How this increasing emphasis is reflected in other new subject Orders will need to be judged by those who have been monitoring the development of the curriculum for their particular subject. An analysis like this has been useful and SCAA (1994b) have been quick to react to this kind of discussion which has been taking place across the country;

> The use of *Pupils should be taught.....*does not suggest any methodology — it applies as much to investigative, individual or group work as to other teaching approaches. In the new Orders, what should be taught is defined, but it is for schools to decide how. (SCAA, 1994b)

It might have been more user-friendly to suggest that teachers might decide on teaching methodologies and approaches in discussion with their colleagues. However the discussion progresses, what English teachers know generally and teachers of early literacy know particularly is that the struggle to achieve a balance of approach for teaching literacy in our schools has been badly savaged by people who seemingly know little and wish to learn even less.

References

Bazelgette, C. (ed) (1994) *Report of the Commission of Inquiry into English: Balancing literature, language and media in the National Curriculum* London: British Film Institute

Britton, J. and Martin, N. (1992/93) 'The model of language and learning implicit in the new proposals' *Language Matters: Whose Orders?* 3, 3

Cartmell, D. (1993) 'Bright with occasional showers' *Times Educational Supplement* Dec 7, 17

Czerniewska, P. (1992) *Learning About Writing* Oxford: Blackwell

Dawes, L. (1992/93) 'Writing at Key Stage 1 and Key Stage 2' *Language Matters: Whose Orders?* 3, 19-21

Department of Education and Science/Welsh Office (1990) *English in the National Curriculum* London: Her Majesty's Stationery Office

Dombey, H. (1993) 'Social engineering or just plain ignorance?' *Primary Teaching Studies* 7, 2, 7-10

Goswami, U. (1990) 'Phonological priming and orthographic analogies in reading' *Journal of Experimental Child Psychology* 49, 323-340

Johnston, R.S., Anderson, M., Perrett, D.I. and Holligan, C. (1990) 'Perceptual Dysfunction in poor readers: evidence for visual and auditory segmentation problems in a sub-group of poor readers' *British Journal of Educational Psychology* 60, 2, 212-219

MacCabe, C. (1990) 'Language, literature, identity: reflections on the Cox Report' *Critical Quarterly* 32, 4, 7-13

Ministry for Education (1921) *The Teaching of English in England* London: His Majesty's Stationery Office

National Curriculum Council (1989) *English at Key Stage 1* Non-Statutory Guidance, York: National Curriculum Council

National Curriculum Council (1993) *English in the National Curriculum* NCC Consultation Report, York: National Curriculum Council

Raban, B., Clark, U. and McIntyre, J. (1994) *Evaluation of the Implementation of English in the National Curriculum at Key Stages 1, 2 and 3 1991-1993* London: School Curriculum and Assessment Authority

School Curriculum and Assessment Authority (1994a) *English in the National Curriculum* London: School Curriculum and Assessment Authority

School Curriculum and Assessment Authority (1994b) *Inform* London: School Curriculum and Assessment Authority

School Curriculum and Assessment Authority/Central Office of Information (1995) *The National Curriculum Orders* London: Her Majesty's Stationery Office

Section 2

Issues of Practice

Chapter 5

What's happening to knowledge about language (KAL) in the primary years?

Michael Lockwood
University of Reading

A Problem of Terminology

Many teachers in the primary years seem unsure about exactly what KAL is. My experience of providing in-service courses for primary teachers over the past few years has been that sessions entitled 'Knowledge About Language' are poorly subscribed and often cancelled. On the other hand, sessions advertised as featuring 'Grammar' are usually over-subscribed. Those teachers who do attend KAL sessions usually mention 'grammar' as the area they most expect to be covered and often deny any wider concern with language in their teaching. In discussion it usually emerges that they *do* regularly involve their pupils in activities which develop a broader awareness of language: sharing with a class the experience of learning Welsh, or looking at the language of RAP poetry, to mention two examples which came to light in recent in-service sessions.

I received 8 replies to questionnaires sent to 71 primary schools, a response rate of about 11%. Fortunately the replies I had were more detailed than expected, leaving me with an in-depth picture of practice in a small number of schools rather than the quantitative survey I had anticipated. Taking into account the deliberately open nature of the questionnaire, which invited teachers to decide for themselves what constituted KAL, and its distribution in the second half of the summer term, how is the 89% non-response rate to be interpreted? Not, I think, by assuming that nearly 9 out of 10 schools 'don't do' KAL, but that there has been a problem with terminology and its dissemination in this aspect of English.

The University of Warwick *Final Report* on the implementation of English in the National Curriculum confirms my experiences. The Warwick team found that, although 'teachers at KS1-3 explicitly taught the Knowledge about Language requirements of the Order', 'teachers found the Order unhelpful when they tried to establish terms of reference for the phrase Knowledge about Language' (Raban *et al*, 1994:9). The Report's recommendation was that 'Teachers need clear explanations of the term ... Knowledge about Language' (p.11).

The term has clearly not become familiar particularly to non-specialists in primary schools. It may be, as has been suggested, that it sets up unintended associations:

> Few if any teachers would have used this term to describe aspects of children's competence ... before the advent of the National Curriculum. Many still have difficulty with it, perhaps because of its association with 'knowledge' in the sense of rote-learned banks of fact. (Bain *et al*, 1992:8)

Where did KAL Come From?

The Bullock Report, *A Language for Life* (DES, 1975), still an important influence on professional debate about English, briefly discussed what it called 'Language Study' (11.15-11.40), coming to its well-known conclusion that 'children should learn about language by experiencing it and experimenting with its use' and rejecting the traditional prescriptive study of grammar as ineffective. This is an interpretation of research in this area recently challenged in a paper by Tomlinson (1994), seemingly influential in recent revisions to the English National Curriculum.

It was the HMI discussion document *Curriculum Matters I: English from 5-16* (DES, 1984) which introduced as an explicit aim teaching pupils '*about* language' and clearly foreshadowed the English National Curriculum by proposing age-related objectives for 'learning about language' at 11 and 16. The result of teachers' dissatisfaction with these objectives expressed in *Responses to Curriculum Matters 1* (DES, 1986) led to the enquiry into English Language teaching which produced the *Kingman Report* (DES, 1988). Here the term 'Knowledge about Language' was first actually used (but not the acronym) and a model of language constructed to 'inform professional discussion' of it. The model had four equal parts (p.17):

Part 1: The forms of the English language
Part 2: Communication and comprehension
Part 3: Acquisition and development
Part 4: Historical and geographical variation.

KAL was to cover experience and understanding of any of these aspects of English and of language, although the model was never intended for classroom use. The Report gave examples of practice in primary classrooms and commented:

> Knowledge about language is not a separate component of the primary or secondary curriculum. It should not be 'bolted on', but should inform children's talking, writing, reading and listening in the classroom. (p.48)

Kingman recommended Attainment Targets (ATs) for KAL at 7, 11 and 16, setting these out in two parallel columns: one set referring to pupil performance (implicit KAL), the other to understanding or reflection (explicit KAL).

The Cox Report (DES, 1989) National Curriculum incorporated these recommendations into the design of National Curriculum English and defined KAL as covering:

— language variation according to situation, purpose, language mode, regional or social group, etc.
— language in literature
— language variation across time. (6.16-6.21)

Following Kingman's advice, KAL is not 'bolted on' as a separate AT, as it is in *Curriculum Matters*, but is integrated throughout the five ATs for Speaking and Listening (AT1), Reading (AT2), Writing (AT3), Spelling (AT4) and Handwriting (AT5). It is recognised that: 'The form in which knowledge about language is communicated will vary with the age and ability of the pupil, from play activities in the pre-school to explicit systematic knowledge in upper secondary education.' Assessment begins only at level 5, the upper end of the Key Stage 2 attainment range.

The Language in the National Curriculum (LINC) Project (1989-92) was set up to support the implementation of English in the National Curriculum in the light of the views of language outlined in the Kingman and Cox Reports. The LINC project deliberately emphasised the third and fourth parts of the Kingman model over the first and second in its attempts to meet the classroom needs of teachers and pupils. Thus 'language variation' was the principal concern, with the 'forms of language' including grammar addressed within that context only. The LINC 'Materials for Professional Development' were never made available directly to schools because of the DES's disagreement with the outcomes of LINC's approach. This may have contributed to the failure of the terminology of KAL to catch on in primary schools, despite LINC's plan of 'cascading' training into every school in England and Wales via English co-ordinators.

Much of the most valuable development work by LINC was done at local level by various consortia. Materials generated from classroom work in these regions has only been made available nationally through commercial publication (Bain *et al*, 1992; Carter, 1990; Haynes, 1992; Harris and Wilkinson, 1990).

How are Primary Teachers Approaching KAL?

The eight schools which responded to my questionnaire followed the Cox National Curriculum Order in taking a broad view of what KAL is. 'It permeates everyday classroom activity' was a typical response. The requirements for KAL were being implemented through speaking and listening, reading and writing activities in the integrated fashion recommended by Cox and Kingman.

Speaking and listening activities were designed to develop KAL by giving 'opportunities to children to experience and consider different forms of spoken language', to quote one respondent. Examples of these were:

— storytelling
— drama and role-play
— discussion of dialects in books
— listening to tapes of dialect speakers.

Reading activities were designed to enable children to 'examine texts and discuss use of language'. These included:

— group reading
— poetry presentation
— book reviewing
— whole school book weeks.

Writing activities, similarly, were seen as providing opportunities for children to write in and reflect on different genres. Those mentioned, alongside stories, plays and poems, were:

— newspaper reports
— cartoons
— adverts
— invitations.

Some of the teachers surveyed also mentioned additional 'language skills lessons' which concentrated on specific features of punctuation, spelling or grammar. However, these were also often embedded in the context of pupils' own writing, one example given being work on speech marks designed to lead on to the writing of puppet plays.

The model of learning about language in these classrooms conforms to that suggested by Bain (1991), which might be set out diagrammatically as:

Use and Experience of Language — Description of and Reflection on Language — Analysis of Language

|

Teacher Intervention and Use of Metalanguage as appropriate at these points

Enabling pupils to describe and reflect on their experience of language, the middle stage in this progression, seems to be the crucial feature of KAL in the primary years, which these teachers are providing. Formal analysis, with appropriate metalanguage, may or may not follow at this stage. What is important here is the awareness of language use and the anchoring of both reflection and any analysis in the context of real experience.

Bain (1991) also suggests three levels at which teachers may approach KAL:

— reflection on language in use in the classroom
— planned contexts for more sharply focused reflection
— language investigations.

For the teachers I surveyed, incidental reflections on language in use and planned contexts occurred in specifically English activities. However, lengthier language investigations, as well as planned contexts, occurred most frequently in other curriculum areas. '*All* topics will include language-based work' and 'topic work often starts off an interest in the origins of words' were typical comments. The most popular areas mentioned were History-based topics arising from the National Curriculum Study Units, such as:

— Ancient Egypt
— Ancient Greece
— Romans, Anglo-Saxons and Vikings
— The History of Writing
— The History of Printing.

Here pupils were able, for example, to make a comparative investigation of languages and scripts; to investigate language change over time; or to investigate the derivations of English words.

Geography-based topics (Ghana, China) also provided opportunities for looking at other languages, as did RE (Arabic). Cross-curricular topics were less frequent, 'Communication' and 'Animals' were two cited, but they also presented scope for planned language investigation and study.

Teachers in the survey also frequently mentioned the vocabulary of different curriculum subjects (the language of Maths, Science and Art) and the written genres associated with them (Science reports) as fruitful areas in which pupils' KAL was developed outside of the English curriculum.

All the teachers concerned felt they had been influenced by the existing National Curriculum in their approach to KAL. The effects reported were:

— a greater awareness of KAL in the curriculum
— tighter planning
— broader and more specific teaching
— increased teacher knowledge
— more formal emphasis on language skills.

Of the eight English co-ordinators involved, however, only two had received specific support on KAL from their local LINC consortium. The others had relied on general in-service provision for English or had received none.

The snapshot provided by the replies of these eight schools where KAL *has* become a familiar terminology seems to resemble the more general picture assembled by the Warwick Report. The Cox English National Curriculum has positively influenced practice in these schools and the teachers concerned are explicitly developing pupils' KAL in the broad and integrated manner envisaged. They are doing so, however, often without specific in-service support and with few published resources, Chris Lutrario's *Exploring Language* (1994) being the only primary KAL series to have emerged yet, although both BBC and Channel 4 have produced relevant TV programmes in the series *English Express* and *Talk, Write and Read* respectively. These teachers are also finding the time and the contexts to develop KAL outside the English curriculum as well as through the English ATs, possibly as a result of an overloaded primary curriculum.

How is KAL Going to Change?

National Curriculum English: The Case for Revising the Order, published by NCC in July 1992, comments:

> The inclusion of this [KAL] strand has resulted in more attention being paid to knowledge about language. Nevertheless, early work by the Warwick University team emphasises the need for ... a review and is particularly critical of the fact that requirements ... do not begin

> until level 5. The Warwick study cites evidence that KS1 teachers believe 'that the KAL thread in the English Order needs to be signalled much more clearly than it is at present'. (p.7)

The document recommends that revision should both 'define the essential knowledge and understanding of grammar needed at Key Stages 1 and 2' and 'make the overall framework for KAL more consistent and precise throughout the Key Stage' (p.12).

The proposals which emerged the following April, *English for ages 5-16* (DES, 1993), addressed the first part of this recommendation but ignored the second. Reference to KAL, in fact, was omitted almost entirely, with the exception of the statements about grammar at Key Stage 1 and 2. The *Consultation Report* on English (NCC, 1993) made some modifications to these drastic proposals in the light of responses by those dismayed at the loss of KAL. 'Requirements for the investigation and discussion of language in AT1 have been expanded', claimed this document (p.9), but this did not amount to a great deal. In both these documents the use of Standard English, defined as 'the correct use of vocabulary and grammar', was made a much more important feature of the Speaking and Listening and the Writing ATs, as KAL was correspondingly reduced.

The proposals put forward in 1993 were never implemented, since the Dearing Review of the whole National Curriculum overtook them. This produced a new document *English in the National Curriculum: Draft Proposals* (SCAA, 1994) which was distributed for consultation. Here, encouragingly, KAL is reinstated as 'Language Study' (harking back to Bullock?) and is moreover a named strand or section of the Programmes of Study (PoS) for all three ATs at each Key Stage. Originally the English advisory group had proposed 'Language Study and Standard English' as the title of this section, but this was altered before publication to 'Standard English and Language Study' (*Times Educational Supplement,* 13 May 1994, p.12). This and other presentational changes and omissions have given Standard English a greater prominence in the new proposals.

The 'Standard English and Language Study' section is defined as 'including aspects of linguistic knowledge, such as grammar, vocabulary, Standard English and language in use' (p.iii). However, it is emphasised that this area is not intended to be taught separately, as the kind of 'bolt-on' component Kingman warned against. Looking at the details for the primary years, Language Study consists mostly of encouraging, developing and then extending 'an interest in words and meanings' (e.g. p.3). In terms of reading it also involves consideration of the features of different kinds of texts (p.10) and writing at Key Stage 2 includes reflecting on the use of language in spoken and written forms and developing an understanding of sentence grammar (p.24). No statements relating to Language Study appear in the Level Descriptions, the assessment apparatus of the new proposals, although statements relating to children's awareness and use of Standard English *are* included.

As NATE have commented in their response to the *Draft Proposals*:

> 'The overemphasis on Standard English ... has led to the omission of important aspects of language study ... language diversity, history of languages, language and power in society, acquisition and development of language, language as a system ... The concern for Standard English needs to be set within this broader context of Language Study.'

The debate is essentially between a cultural heritage view of English and language, which seeks to transmit values unchanged, and a cultural analysis view, which seeks to equip children to examine them critically, to use terms from the Cox Report.

Four of the eight English co-ordinators in my survey echoed the NATE view, complaining of 'an overconcern with Standard English too early' in the new proposals, of an approach which was 'too skills-based', and that there was 'no concern with what the child brings to the situation' in terms of language. By contrast, two respondents felt there was 'little change' in the proposals and two felt there was 'fairly good coverage' of KAL.

Conclusions

Although the term 'Knowledge about Language' has not become familiar to all primary years teachers, the evidence is that teaching and learning about language is taking place at present in ways envisaged and stimulated by the Cox English National Curriculum. Recent research on the benefits to literacy learning of awareness — awareness of what reading and writing are, for example — presented by Wray (1992) suggests a rationale for metacognition in general in the primary curriculum, of which metalinguistic awareness could be a part. As Wray notes, there are also many social benefits to an approach to KAL which values diversity. Documents produced in Scotland and Wales recently (SO, 1991; CCW, 1993) provide a marked contrast to recent English ones in this respect.

As far as their future training needs were concerned, the group of teachers I surveyed felt that guidance on KAL for *all* teachers was needed. Exchanges of ideas and resources with other teachers was seen as potentially valuable. There was a desire for support both in the area of grammar at pupil and at teacher level ('how to recognise an expanded noun phrase at 20 paces!') and in the broader field of KAL ('how to involve pupils in meaningful activities to develop appropriate language skills').

If the Language Study of the future is to build on the strengths and remedy the weaknesses of the existing Knowledge about Language, primary years teachers will need to be adequately supported in implementing a clearly-defined curriculum where an over-emphasis on Standard English does not produce a narrower view of what children need to know about language.

References

Bain, R. (1991) *Reflections: Talking about Language* London: Hodder and Stoughton

Bain, R. Fitzgerald, B. and Taylor, M. (1992) *Looking into Language* London: Hodder and Stoughton

Carter, R. (ed) (1990) *Knowledge about Language and the Curriculum* London: Hodder and Stoughton

Curriculum Council for Wales (1993) *Review of National Curriculum English* Cardiff: Curriculum Council for Wales

Department of Education and Science (1975) *A Language for Life* The Bullock Report London: Her Majesty's Stationery Office

Department of Education and Science (1984) *Curriculum Matters I: English from 5 to 16* London: Her Majesty's Stationery Office

Department of Education and Science (1986) *Responses to Curriculum Matters I* London: Her Majesty's Stationery Office

Department of Education and Science (1988) *Report of the Committee of Inquiry into the Teaching of English* The Kingman Report London: Her Majesty's Stationery Office

Department of Education and Science (1989) *English for Ages 5 to 16* The Cox Report London: Her Majesty's Stationery Office

Department for Education (1993) *English for Ages 5 to 16 (1993)* London: Her Majesty's Stationery Office

Harris, J. and Wilkinson, J. (1990) *A Guide to English Language in the National Curriculum* Cheltenham: Stanley Thornes

Haynes, J. (1992) *A Sense of Words: Knowledge about Language in the Primary School* London: Hodder and Stoughton

Lutrario, C. (1994) *Exploring Language* Aylesbury: Ginn

National Curriculum Council (1992) *National Curriculum English: The Case for Revising the Order* York: National Curriculum Council

National Curriculum Council (1993) *Consultation Report: English* York: National Curriculum Council

Raban, B., Clark, U. and McIntyre, J. (1994) *Evaluation of the Implementation of English in the National Curriculum at Key Stages 1, 2 and 3.* London: School Curriculum and Assessment Authority

School Curriculum and Assessment Authority (1994) *English in the National Curriculum: Draft Proposals* London: Her Majesty's Stationery Office

Scottish Office Education Department (1991) *English Language 5-14* Edinburgh: Scottish Office

Times Educational Supplement 13 May 1994

Tomlinson, D. (1994) 'Errors in the Research into the Effectiveness of Grammar Teaching' *English in Education* 28(1) 20-26

Wray, D (1994) *Literacy and Awareness* London: Hodder and Stoughton/UKRA

Chapter 6

Teaching phonological skills to reception age children

Jonathan Solity
University of Warwick

Introduction

Since the late 1970s there has been growing interest in the role of phonological awareness in the development of children's reading. A number of influential studies have set the agenda for research into the acquisition of early reading skills in young children which have had a sufficient impact on practice for these skills to be included in the revised English National Curriculum. However, the nature of the phonological training required to improve reading is not entirely clear and there has been a reliance on longitudinal studies without adequate recognition of the full range of explanations that these studies generate, which do not necessarily support the increasingly accepted view that phonological awareness is a critical determinant of future reading. The research reported in this paper attempts, in a small scale study, to address some of the unresolved issues in research into phonological awareness and children's reading development.

Background

The skill of being able to detect sound patterns in words has become known as phonological awareness (or phonemic or phoneme awareness) and has been defined in the following ways:

> 'phonemic awareness is the ability to explicitly manipulate speech segments at the phoneme level' (Cunningham, 1990:429)
>
> 'phoneme awareness is the ability to recognise that a spoken word consists of a sequence of individual sounds' (Ball and Blachman, 1991:51).

The essential characteristic of phonological awareness is that children have to manipulate sounds without associating those sounds with their written symbols. In contrast, 'phonics' is the term usually used to describe the process by which children decode and read words on the basis of sound-symbol associations.

Critical to the debate about phonological awareness and children's reading is the research methodology adopted to investigate the relationship between them. This has been achieved through one of two designs; longitudinal and training studies. In longitudinal studies the aim is to find out which early reading skills correlate highly with later reading. Thus various measures of children's reading and phonological skills are taken on school entry which are then related to future progress. However, finding a correlation (such as the one between children's phonological skills and future reading) does not demonstrate a causal effect. This can only be achieved through training studies (or experimental studies as they are also known) which involve instructional interventions with experimental groups. The question to be asked is whether such interventions have a significant effect on the learning of children in experimental groups when compared to the progress of those pupils in control groups. Much of the research into phonological awareness has used longitudinal rather than experimental studies, although there has been a shift in emphasis in recent years.

A number of standard tasks have conventionally been used by researchers to assess phonological awareness which include identifying rhyme and alliteration patterns in groups of words, phoneme deletion and phoneme segmentation. Brief descriptions of these tasks now follow.

Rhyme and Alliteration

Children have to listen to words and say which is the odd one out. The position of the crucial sound varies in the words:

eg Bun, *hut,* gun, sun (a rhyming task with the critical sound at the end); *hug,* pig, dig, wig (a rhyming task with critical sound in the middle); bud, bun, bus, *rug* (an alliteration task with the critical sound at the beginning).

(These tasks are known as 'oddity tasks' and were developed by Bradley and Bryant, 1978.)

Phoneme Deletion

Children have to say the new word when a sound is removed from the initial word:

e.g. what word do you have when you remove 's' from sat?
what word do you have when you remove 's' from slip?
what word do you have when you remove 't' from bent?

Phoneme Segmentation

Children on hearing a word such as 'ran' must:

- tap on the table for the correct number of phonemes or;
- place the correct number of counters in a row to correspond to the number of phonemes.

Currently the arguments being advanced about the role of phonological awareness in learning to read are similar, in a number of critical respects, to those articulated during the 1960s and 1970s by advocates of the learning disabilities movement. It was hypothesised that certain visual and auditory skills underpinned children's progress in reading and accounted for many of the difficulties they experienced (Frostig and Marlow, 1972;

Kirk and Kirk, 1971; Tansley, 1967; Walker, 1975). It was argued that problems could be overcome by teaching children the necessary visual or auditory skills which they were found to lack. However, research (Hammill and Larsen, 1978; Ysseldyke and Salvia, 1974) indicated that such underlying skills could be improved but did not necessarily lead to a commensurate improvement in reading performance, primarily because they were not skills deployed in reading. The same criticism can be levelled at the tasks used to demonstrate phonological awareness, since in many instances, children are required to display skills that are not used in reading. The reading process does not demand that children delete or segment phonemes or identify rhyming and alliteration patterns.

Thus one of the questions raised by the current research is the extent to which it is of value to facilitate children's phonological awareness through the activities described earlier, since they develop skills which are not used during reading. It will be suggested that it may well be of greater value to promote children's acquisition of phonological skills which are directly involved in the reading process.

Research into Children's Phonological Awareness

Attention to the role of phonological awareness was heightened through the influential work of Bradley and Bryant (1983). They conducted a longitudinal study over a four year period and demonstrated a link between phonological awareness and progress in learning to read. They tested 118 four year old and 285 five year old children and found high correlations between initial sound categorisation scores (using the oddity task described earlier) and children's reading and spelling three years later. They argued that pre-school children who were able to detect rhyming sequences in words (e.g. hat, cat, mat, bat) or alliteration patterns (e.g. pip, pin, pig, pit) would make better progress once formal reading instruction began.

Bradley and Bryant acknowledged that their results could reflect parental/adult input but have not pursued this line of enquiry in any depth. Nevertheless, it is quite possible that the development of phonological awareness merely demonstrates the impact of early parental involvement in their children's learning. This issue is developed at a later point in this paper.

Within the original longitudinal study, Bradley and Bryant included a training study involving 65 children drawn from those with lower scores in sound categorisation during the second year of the research. The children were then divided into four groups. Groups 1 & 2 received training (40 individual sessions over 2 years) in sound categorisation. Group 2 in addition, with the help of plastic letters, were taught how each common sound was represented by a letter of the alphabet. Children were thus being shown the link between sounds and their visual representation. Group 3 were taught to categorise at a conceptual level and Group 4 received no training at all. Group 1 were ahead of Group 3 on standardised tests of reading and spelling by 3-4 months. Group 2 made better progress than Group 1, suggesting that training in sound categorisation is more effective when it also makes explicit connections with the appropriate written symbols.

However, children's phonological awareness was assessed through a limited set of tasks (the oddity tasks) which require children to make judgements which are not used when reading. No phonological tasks directly involved in reading (such as blending sounds together) were involved. Lundberg, Frost and Petersen (1988) also noted that Bradley and Bryant's study took place as the children were learning to read. As a result it is difficult to interpret the effects of the training programme because it interacts in an unknown way with the teaching of reading. This point is also addressed in more detail in the final section of this paper.

Lundberg, Frost and Petersen therefore conducted a study in Denmark between September and the following May with 390 Danish pre-school children (aged 6-7). An experimental group received training in what were described as metalinguistic exercises which included listening and rhyming games, segmenting sentences into words and syllable counting. Children were assessed on a range of tasks including seven different phonological ones, two of which required children to use skills which would be helpful in reading (syllable and phoneme synthesis). They found that increasing phonological awareness can be developed before children learn to read and that the phonological skills assessed were not acquired spontaneously. They were learned through direct teaching.

Ball and Blachman (1991) found that increasing letter-sound knowledge is not sufficient to improve phoneme segmentation skills, nor does it appear to have an impact on early reading or spelling skills. Their study supports the notion that phonological training that closely resembles the task of early reading may have more immediate effects on reading than instruction which does not make this connection explicit. Furthermore Cunningham (1990), in another training study, found that explaining to children the purpose of their phonological activities was important in a number of critical respects. She also observed that, beyond a certain age, the quality of instruction is more important than developmental level since the kindergarten experimental group performed better than the Grade 1 control group.

Hatcher, Hulme and Ellis (1994) also hypothesised that training in phonological awareness, in isolation from reading and spelling skills, may be much less effective than training that forms explicit links between children's underlying phonological skills and their experience in learning to read. They conducted a study with 7 year old failing readers. Their sample of 128 children (finally reduced to 125) were divided and placed in one of four groups. Group 1 had phonological training only, group 2 had phonology training linked to reading, group 3 reading alone where no references whatsoever were made to the sounds associated with different words and finally the fourth group comprised the control group and received no extra time at all. Hatcher et al. found that interventions to boost phonological skills need to be integrated with the teaching of reading if they are to be maximally effective in improving literacy skills.

In summarising the research to date involving training studies, a number of factors can be seen to be important in facilitating children's reading. Phonological skills can be acquired before children begin formal reading instruction and it is quite likely, given the research of Lundberg, Frost and Petersen, that these skills are not acquired by children spontaneously. They require appropriate interventions by adults. This process is enhanced where the purpose of the activities is explained to children. However, learning letter sound-symbol associations are not sufficient to facilitate progress in reading, although the failing readers in Bradley and Bryant's (1983) training study, who received teaching in this area, made better progress than those children who did not receive training in these skills. Having learned letter sound-symbol associations, children appear to require direct teaching geared to developing their phonological skills. This appears to be most productive when actually linked to reading, rather than being practised in the absence of appropriate written material.

Aims of this study

The research reported here set out to investigate the following areas:

- whether four and five year old children can be taught to blend two and three letter phonically regular words;
- whether a good knowledge of letter sound-symbol associations façilitates children's blending skills;
- whether those with good blending skills are able to read previously unseen material more accurately than those who have not (i.e. are children being provided with a generalisable strategy?);
- the nature of the phonological activities which help children to apply blending skills to reading;
- in particular whether children who have phonological training linked to print make better progress than those who do not;
- the impact of phonological training on children's rhyming and alliteration detection and discrimination skills;
- whether phonological skills involved in reading (e.g. phoneme synthesis) are more useful skills for children to learn than those which are not (e.g. phoneme segmentation).

The distinctive features of the present study are that it was conducted with reception age children who had just started school and were not seen to be failing readers. Children were taught in groups of six. The study was experimental in design and took place over a six month period. The teaching was conducted by an experienced classroom assistant, rather than a teacher, who received training both before the intervention started, and during the project, on teaching young children in small groups.

36 children were involved in the research drawn from two reception classes within the same school. The children were divided into classes according to their ages with one class having children born between September and the beginning of the following January and the other with birthdays between the end of January and August.

All the children were assessed in the following areas on a range of measures in the two weeks before the autumn half term:

- reading 12 common sight words;

- reading test from the *British Ability Scales* (Elliott, Murray, and Pearson, 1983) (total number of words read correctly);
- *Neale Analysis of Reading Ability* (Neale, 1989) (number of words read correctly from Passage 1);
- letter sound recall;
- letter sound recognition (e.g. children asked to point to the letter which says 'a' from an array of three letters);
- reading 12 consonant vowel consonant (CVC) words (e.g. hat, men, run);
- reading a specially prepared phonically regular story;
- sound blending (an adult states the individual sounds in two, three and four letter words. Children then have to state what word is made from blending sounds together);
- initial sound segmentation (children have to identify the sound which given words begin with);
- rhyme detection (children are given three words and have to state whether or not they rhyme);
- alliteration detection (children are given three words and have to state whether or not they begin with the same sound);
- oddity tasks.

Within each class, 18 children were matched and placed in one of two experimental groups or a control group. Children were matched on the basis of their performance in naming letter sounds, letter sound recognition, identifying the first sound in a word and their gender. Thus in each class there were six children within each group making a total of 12 children overall in each of the three groups. Children in the first experimental group, the reading group (RG), received extra teaching in the area of phonics which was all related to print. They engaged in the following activities:

- saying sounds (i.e. practising sound-symbol associations);
- blending sounds to make whole words;
- whole word reading;
- rhyming but only changing the initial phoneme (e.g. rat, sat, hat);

- reading sentences and then short stories;
- discussion about stories.

Children in the second experimental group, the phonology group (PG), were engaged in the same activities and practised the same skills as children in RG but their work involved manipulating sounds only and was not related to print. So instead of reading sentences, they sounded out the words comprising those sentences but did not see the written symbols. They therefore had identical opportunities to children in RG to develop their phonological awareness, but not to relate any new knowledge to written symbols. Finally the control group listened to stories and had an equivalent amount of time as the two experimental groups. Teaching sessions took place for approximately 15 minutes a day, three times a week between November and May. Interruptions occurred from school holidays, trips, health checks from the school doctor, etc. Overall the children received 59 teaching sessions.

An area often omitted in reporting experimental data in reading research is the context and nature of everyday classroom teaching. In so doing, research is potentially decontextualised which may lead to exaggerated, premature or misleading claims being made for the impact and significance of the intervention strategies. The assumptions which are made in experimental research conducted under laboratory conditions are rarely maintained in classroom contexts. Experimental and control groups continue to be taught in ways which may have considerable implications for the way in which research findings are interpreted. Although it is more convenient to assume that children in experimental and control groups have comparable learning experiences so that differences in performance on the skills under investigation can be attributed to the intervention, this may not be the case. Teachers may alter what and how they teach if they believe some children are making better progress than others. So although longer periods for research interventions are usually desirable, this introduces the likelihood of classroom teaching having a confounding effect on research outcomes.

Thus, the effectiveness of phonological awareness training may be demonstrated for a number of reasons. If children are already receiving phonological training as part of their usual classroom activities, the experimental group may improve due to the practice opportunities provided by the research. Alternatively phonological training may be different to that taking place in the classroom and thus complement existing teaching. A third interpretation suggests that if children are not receiving any phonological training at all or receiving no appropriate instruction in reading, any kind of relevant intervention provided to the experimental groups may have an effect.

In the present study, the children were all learning letter sound-symbol associations through the *Letterland* materials (Wendon, 1985). Children were introduced to a new sound on a weekly basis and were engaged in follow-up activities during the week. The school used the *One, Two, Three and Away* reading scheme (McCullagh, 1977) and during the course of the research, children were gradually introduced to books and vocabulary from the scheme. Many children took home reading scheme books to read to parents, library books and individual words to be learned.

Results

The performance of the reading and phonology experimental groups was compared to that of the control group through carrying out an analysis of variance on the pre- and post-test assessments. No significant differences ($p<0.05$) were found between RG and the control group and PG and the control group on:

- Neale analysis;
- letter sound recall;
- initial sound segmentation;
- rhyme and alliteration detection;
- oddity tasks.

There was a significant difference between RG and the control group and PG and the control group in reading CVC words, the phonically regular story and sound blending. In each instance RG and PG performed better than the control group. There were also significant differences between RG and the control group on the BAS, reading the common sight vocabulary and in letter sound recognition. Again RG performed better than the control group. No significant differences were observed in these areas between PG and the control group. There was also a significant difference between RG and PG in reading the common sight vocabulary (RG read more words correctly than PG).

All three groups improved their recall of letter sounds and no significant differences existed between the experimental and control groups. It would appear that the teaching of letter sounds through the *Letterland* materials was highly effective. However, the respective performances of RG and the control group and PG and the control group on other phonological tasks suggests that learning letter sounds alone is not sufficient to enable children to use that skill in reading. This is reflected through the performance of RG and PG in reading CVC words, the phonically regular story, and sound blending. It appears that children require specific teaching to blend sounds together and that in young children this does not occur spontaneously. This result is similar to that obtained by Lundberg, Frost and Petersen (1988).

The only difference in learning experiences between the experimental groups were the opportunities given to RG to relate newly acquired phonological skills to print. Nevertheless, the performance of the experimental groups on phonic and phonological tasks was comparable and they displayed similar differences in relation to the control group. However, statistically significant differences existed between RG and the control group on the BAS and common sight words. Such differences did not exist between PG and the control group. This suggests that children need to be able to relate their phonological skills to print in order that they are generalised appropriately to reading words which are best decoded on the basis of their visual appearance.

The significant differences existing between RG, PG and the control groups did not extend to the tasks which are commonly associated with the assessment of phonological awareness (rhyme and alliteration detection and discrimination). Again all groups were significantly better at the post-test than they had been at the pre-test, but there were no statistically significant differences between the groups, even though RG and PG had opportunities to identify rhyming patterns in words (but only where the initial consonant changed). In this instance the teaching available within the classroom had a significant impact on children's rhyming and alliteration identification skills. Improvement in these areas appeared as a result of learning letter sounds and other work undertaken in the classroom and did not appear to require direct teaching. The additional teaching available to RG and PG, while improving sound blending, which is a phonological skill directly relevant in decoding unknown words when reading, did not facilitate children's acquisition of those phonological skills which are not directly applicable to the reading process.

Discussion

Reading Research with Young Children

The observed gains made by RG and PG in relation to the control group were achieved with only 59 teaching sessions. Inevitably with young children some time in the early teaching sessions was devoted to managing their behaviour and giving them clear expectations. Being taught systematically in small groups of six offered a different teaching approach to the one present in their classrooms which was based on giving children choice and encouraging their personal autonomy. Thus the children had contrasting teaching styles and this may well have caused difficulties for them so early in the school year.

More significantly it may well have presented the teaching assistant with problems as the children checked out the extent to which various aspects of their behaviour would be tolerated within the small group setting. Thus valuable instructional time was taken up in the early stages with managing behaviour rather than teaching. Had the research taken place over a longer period, the experimental intervention might have had a greater impact if all the available time had been devoted to teaching.

Phonological Awareness as a Predictor of Reading Progress

Longitudinal studies have suggested that phonological awareness is an effective predictor of future reading progress. Such a conclusion is based on a number of assumptions. First of all it assumed that the school-based learning experiences of all children are similar and that differences in reading can be attributed to different levels of phonological awareness when they begin school. However, it is highly unlikely that such an assumption can be substantiated. Children with different skills are likely to receive a different curriculum, especially in the area of early reading. Certainly Bennett *et al.* (1984) in their study looking at the match between children and the curriculum found pupils with different attainments had very different learning experiences.

Secondly, much of the literature fails to address the factors which account for differences in phonological awareness when children start school. Such differences can be attributed to the nature of their learning experiences and exposure to certain kinds of input provided from a variety of potential sources (for example parents, playgroups, nurseries, television, etc.). Bradley and Bryant (1983) comment that 'the awareness of rhyme and alliteration which children acquire before they go to school, possibly as a result of their experiences at home, has a powerful influence on their eventual success in learning to read and to spell' (p.421). It is, however, highly likely that those children with phonological awareness when they start school get differential forms of help outside school from parents when they start learning to read. Those parents that familiarise their children with nursery rhymes etc. are also likely to assist their children in reading in a variety of respects. Thus, phonological awareness merely parallels parental input and reflects the varying nature of parental support once children start school, rather than being in itself a critical feature of learning to read. This view is supported by the research of Lundberg, Frost and Petersen (1988) who pointed out that, in Denmark, children do not start school until they are seven and they are seldom subjected to the informal literacy socialisation by parents which characterises the experiences of many children in the U.K. As a result, the children in their study had not spontaneously acquired phonolgical skills before they started school.

The Nature of Phonological Awareness

The training studies reviewed earlier in this paper suggest that phonological skills need to be taught directly and that children are likely to make the greatest gains in reading when this training is related to print (i.e. they are receiving help with phonics). This study found tentative support for this position. RG and PG differed at a statistically significant level from the control group on a number of phonically regular tasks, particularly reading the phonically regular story. PG did not appear to be disadvantaged by not relating their phonological training to print.

However, RG and PG differed in reading the 12 common sight words and the BAS. It is perhaps here that RG's experience in relating their knowledge to print enabled them to utilise their skills more effectively and know when it is, or is not, appropriate to decode words phonically. In contrast PG may have attempted to read every word phonically and not yet appreciated that unknown words could be decoded through alternative strategies.

Although RG and PG made statistically better progress than the control group on a number of reading activities, these differences did not extend to the tasks usually used to assess phonological awareness such as the rhyming, alliteration and oddity tasks. All three groups showed significant improvements on those tasks at the post-test. However, RG and PG differed from the control group in sound blending, a phonological skill used in reading.

There is a need to urge caution about the role of phonological awareness due to the work of Hammill and Larsen (1978) and Ysseldyke and Salvia (1974) which indicated that the way to improve reading was not to concentrate on skills hypothesised to underpin the reading process, such as visual discrimination, but to teach directly to the tasks that you wish to improve. There is a parallel here since a number of tasks used to assess phonological awareness (e.g. rime and alliteration detection or phoneme deletion) require children to use skills which are not used in reading.

Classroom Teaching: Onset/rime or Letter Sound Correspondences?

The critical issue to be addressed, given the emphasis in this paper on teaching directly to the skill we wish children to learn, is the teaching implications of the research into phonological awareness. Within the training programme for RG, phonic skills were taught largely through letter sound correspondences and blending individual letters to comprise two and three letter words. However, Goswami and Bryant (1990) and more recently Goswami (1994) have argued that onsets and rimes are more suitable phonological units for reading whole words. Goswami (1994) states the onset in a syllable corresponds to the initial consonant(s) in the written word (e.g. *c* in cat; *pl* in plot) whereas the rime corresponds to the vowel plus any following consonants (e.g. *at* in cat; *ot* in plot).

From a developmental viewpoint, Goswami (1994) comments that 'young children find it difficult to detect phonemes in spoken words, especially if they have to segment the sound of a word into all of its constituent phonemes' (p.33). She continues 'in fact, the ability to detect and manipulate individual phonemes within words appears to be consequent upon learning to read, rather than a prerequisite for beginning to read' (p.33). However, the findings of Lundberg, Frost and Petersen (1988) lead to this assertion being questioned. They found that awareness of individual sounds could be taught to pre-readers without linking it to the teaching of reading.

Nevertheless, although Goswami's recommendations may be reasonable from a developmental perspective, it does not mean that the most effective instructional strategy is represented by a developmental sequence. Rather, once children start school and begin to learn to read, teaching letter sound correspondences rather than onsets and rimes may be the most constructive approach to facilitating their reading progress particularly given the demands each approach makes on children's memories. When learning sound-symbol associations children have to learn the 26 most fequent sounds of the alphabet letters, their symbols and how to blend them together with accuracy and fluency. In contrast, when learning onsets and rimes, children still have to learn all 26 sound-symbol associations as well as all the onsets in CCVC words and rimes when reading CVC and CVCC words. When learning to identify the onset and rime in a word such as 'set', it is worth asking the means by which children will memorise the rime 'et'. (as it will for any other rime). In effect, such rimes are being learned at a sight level before being combined with the appropriate onset. Where the onset has two letters, which are also learned at a sight level, the memory demand on the children is high. As a result the question to be asked is whether learning onsets and rimes is as efficient and as generalisable a skill as learning sound-symbol associations.

Goswami and Bryant's research into learning onset and rime has largely involved children learning through analogy and reading word lists rather than books. This has been acknowledged by Goswami (1994) who prepared a number of short stories so that children would have an opportunity to apply their knowledge of onsets and rimes to what she termed 'real reading'. While the result obtained on these stories demonstrated that children could use analogies when reading Goswami's passages, what has to be considered is the extent to which the skill would generalise to reading anything other than word lists or specially prepared passages where pre-taught onsets and rimes are guaranteed to appear. It is one thing for children to generalise a skill to a narrow area of reading activities, and quite another to enable them to utilise their full range of skills and knowledge when reading 'real books'. In addition, the view of 'real reading' conveyed by Goswami is very different to the one held by many other reading specialists who would argue that 'real reading' and 'real books' have very little to do with reading short specially designed passages.

Implications for the Concept of Learning Difficulty

The final issue raised by this research into phonological awareness relates to the concept of 'learning difficulties'. The research reported in this paper suggests that children learn what they are taught. Perhaps more significantly, unless certain skills are taught directly they do not appear to be acquired by children. The findings of this study support earlier research indicating that phonic skills can be taught to young children; that certain phonic skills are not acquired without systematic instruction and that children do not automatically learn how to use their knowledge of letter-sound associations. Their progress in this area is facilitated by systematic instruction. If this is the case, the question to be addressed is whether those children who are seen to be failing can also be seen to have a learning difficulty in the absence of evidence that they have received the appropriate instructional opportunities.

References

Ball, E. and Blachman, B. (1991) 'Does phoneme awareness training in kindergarten make a difference in early word recognition and developmental spelling?' *Reading Research Quarterly* 29, 49-66

Bennett, N., Desforges, C., Cockburn, A. and Wilkinson, B. (1984) *The Quality of Pupil Learning Experiences* London: Lawrence Erlbaum

Bradley, L. and Bryant, P. (1978) 'Difficulties in auditory organisation as a possible cause of reading awkwardness' *Nature* 271, 746-7

Bradley, L. and Bryant, P. (1983) 'Categorising sounds and learning to read: a causal connection, *Nature* 310, 419-421

Cunningham, A. (1990) 'Explicit versus implicit instruction in phonemic awareness' *Journal of Experimental Child Psychology* 50, 429-444

Elliott, C.D., Murray, D.J. and Pearson, L. (1983) *British Ability Scales* Windsor: NFER-Nelson

Frostig, M. and Marlow, P. (1973) *Learning Problems in the Classroom* New York: Grune and Stratton

Goswami, U. (1994) 'Phonological skills, analogies, and reading development' *Reading* 28, 2, 32-37

Goswami, U. and Bryant, P. (1990) *Phonological Skills and Learning to Read* London: Lawrence Erlbaum

Hammill, D. and Larsen, S. (1978) 'The effectiveness of psycholinguistic training: a reaffirmation of the position' *Exceptional Children* 44, 402-14

Hatcher, P., Hulme, C. and Ellis, A. (1994) 'Ameliorating early reading failure by integrating the teaching of reading and phonological skills: the phonological linkage hypothesis' *Child Development* 64, 1, 41-57

Kirk, S. and Kirk, W. (1971) *Psycholingistic Learning Dissabilities: Diagnosis and Remediation* Illinois: University of Illinois Press

Lundberg, I., Frost, J. and Petersen, O. (1988) 'Effects of an extensive programme for stimulating phonological awareness in pre-school children' *Reading Research Quarterly* 23, 263-284

McCullagh, S. (1977) *One, Two, Three and Away* St. Albans: Hart-Davis Educational

Neale, M.D. (1989) *Neale Analysis of Reading Ability: Revised British Edition* Windsor: NFER-Nelson

Tansley, A. (1967) *Reading and Remedial Reading* London: Routledge

Walker, C. (1975) *Teaching Prereading Skills* London: Ward Lock

Wendon, L. (1985) *Letterland ABC* Cambridge: Letterland

Ysseldyke, J.E. and Salvia, J. (1974) 'Diagnostic-prescriptive teaching: two models' *Exceptional Teaching* 41, 181-85.

Chapter 7

Young early readers:
a preliminary report of the development of a group of children who were able to read fluently before Key Stage 1

Rhona Stainthorp and Diana Hughes
University of Reading

Introduction

This paper presents the preliminary findings of a longitudinal project monitoring the reading development, meta-cognitive skills and school experience in Key Stage 1 (KS1) of a group of children who had been identified as being able to read fluently before they began their formal schooling. The data relate to a group of 17 children who were identified as being able to read fluently before they began school. Each child is being matched to a same age control child who was unable to read at the start of the study.

In 1976, Margaret Clark published her seminal work on *Young Fluent Readers*, detailing the cognitive, social and educational experiences of a group of Scottish children who had been able to read fluently on entry to school. At that time, research into the cognitive processes associated with reading development was in its infancy. Models of reading development such as Marsh, Friedman, Welch and Desberg (1981), Frith (1985) and Ehri (1992) were yet to be developed. However, Clark's work is frequently cited as a text which has had a major influence on subsequent research into reading development. She suggested that there was as much to be learned from studying success or 'supra-normal' development as there was from studying difficulties. With the evolution of models of reading development and our increased understanding of the cognitive processes that underpin reading performance (Bradley and Bryant, 1983; Treiman, 1992; Byrne and Fielding-Barnsley, 1991) it would seem an apposite time to re-address the issue of *Young Fluent Readers*.

The children in the original study, who had learned to read before formal schooling without any apparent teaching, were all of above average measured IQ, but that was not a sufficient characteristic to account for their 'precocious' skills. One of the major findings in 1976 was that the children seemed to have superior auditory discrimination and attention skills which, combined with their general cognitive ability and supportive home environment, may have provided the right combination of personal characteristics and environmental circumstances to enable them to achieve success without formal teaching.

This observation, about superior auditory discrimination, has been borne out by all the subsequent work on phonological awareness. There is increasing evidence from the experimental literature that phonological awareness is a meta-cognitive skill which is central to reading development, particularly in an alphabetic system (Adams, 1990; Ehri, 1992; Goswami and Bryant, 1990; Treiman, 1992; Tumner and Hoover, 1992; Yopp, 1988).

Our understanding of the nature of phonological awareness has become increasingly sophisticated in the past 20 years, with the suggestion that a degree of phonological awareness will facilitate subsequent reading development, whereas some aspects of phonological awareness may develop as a consequence of learning to read (Tumner and Rohl, 1991).

Besides identifying phonological awareness as an important precursor of reading development, Bradley and Bryant also pointed to knowledge of the alphabet as being essential. This was also recognised by Walsh, Price and Gillingham (1988) and Adams (1990).

This research project is aimed at monitoring the meta-cognitive skills as well as the literacy skills of the children who are identified as being able to read before schooling. We also aim to monitor their literacy experiences both in and out of school.

There is also a second focus to the research. We are now in an age of the National Curriculum where more formal assessment has become part of the ongoing processes of the Primary School. One of the benign aspects of assessment is that it does enable teachers to objectify the performance of children against the criteria laid down for the Attainment Targets. Children who are able to read fluently on entry to school may already be achieving levels 2/3/4 in some attainment targets. We are concerned to monitor the progress made by such children and to identify models of good practice where teachers are successfully differentiating and providing a suitable diet of experiences.

The research design is a longitudinal cohort study so that reading development and school experiences can be monitored throughout KS1. The data being collected cover a variety of measures including standardised assessments for language, cognitive functioning, reading and spelling, and non-standardised research tasks measuring phonological awareness and meta-cognitive skills. Parents are involved in providing detailed accounts of the children's early years as well as providing information about the progress the children are making through the keeping of diaries. The schools are involved by (a) allowing us to monitor the children throughout KS1 and by (b) agreeing that class teachers will take part in semi-structured interviews about their approaches to literacy and their strategies for making provision for the young early readers in their classes. We have added a dimension to this study which was not included in Clark's original work. For each of our early fluent reader children we have identified a control child who is matched for language development and socio-economic status and who is, or will be, going to the same class as the study child.

Identification of the Young Fluent Readers

Clark obtained her subjects by trawling through the schools in her local LEAs. We were wanting to begin studying the children before they had begun their formal schooling so we had to devise other procedures for identifying children. We began by putting up small posters in local libraries and sending the same poster to nurseries, nursery schools and play-groups in neighbouring LEAs with a covering letter asking the teachers or leaders to display the poster. The resulting response meant that this was the only advertising we needed to do.

Every parent who contacted the department was interviewed initially over the telephone to determine whether the child seemed a likely candidate for inclusion in the project. In some instances we were contacted directly by a teacher or play-group leader who had mentioned the project to the parents of potential children.

Following the telephone interviews, appointments were made to visit the homes of likely children. At this first meeting they were informally assessed using the procedures laid down for the KS1 SATs which were conducted in a non-threatening, friendly atmosphere. Parents were also interviewed and asked to fill in a questionnaire about their own educational experiences, the developmental milestones of the children and their recollections of the reading development of their children. They were asked to keep occasional diaries of literacy activities. Permission was sought to approach the Head Teacher of the child's intended school. All parents agreed to take part in the project. This gave a cohort of 17 children who formed the group of Young Early Readers (Study Group — Group S).

Once Group S had been identified and their future schools contacted the Control Group (Group C) had to be identified. The Nursery Teachers and Play Group leaders played a significant part in this. In each case they were informed that we were wanting control children who were going to the same primary school as the Young Early Reader. The control child should be the same age, same sex and same socio-economic background and, in their judgement, with roughly the same linguistic and cognitive ability but not a Young Early Reader. The schools then made the first contact with the parents of potential control children.

It is the intention of this paper (a) to report the results of some of the preliminary findings and (b) to present detailed biographies of two of the group with the biographies of their control pair.

Preliminary Findings

Assessment Procedures

All the children were given the *British Picture Vocabulary Scales* (BPVS) which is a reliable measure of receptive vocabulary and which correlates highly with verbal IQ; and the *Concepts about Print Test — Stones* (Clay, 1979). They were tested on their knowledge of letter names and letter sounds and asked to do a set of phonological awareness tasks which tapped both rhyme judgement and ability to manipulate phonemes. In addition, Group S were given the *British Ability Scales (BAS) Word Reading Test* and the *Neale Analysis of Reading Ability* (revised). In most cases these standardised reading tests were not given to the control children because it was inappropriate so to do.

Phonological Awareness — Rhyming Tasks

i Rhyme production

The children's knowledge of nursery rhymes was used to establish the idea of 'rhyme'. They were then given a word and asked to generate another word that rhymed to go with it. For example they would hear 'log' and be asked to give other words that rhymed. They were given five words for this task which led to a maximum possible score of 5.

ii Rhyme detection

There were two sets of rhyme detection tasks which were designed on the basis of the odd-one-out tasks developed by Bradley and Bryant. The first task required the children to listen to four words, three of which rhymed and one of which differed by the final phoneme. The task was to detect the odd-one-out. An example is *fin, sit, win, pin* with *sit* being the odd-one-out. There were two practice items and five test items. The second task was similar but the odd-one-out differed by the medial vowel. An example is *red, fed, lid, bed* with *lid* being the odd-one-out. There were again two practice items and five test items.

Phonological Awareness — Phoneme Manipulation

i Phoneme Deletion

For this task the children heard words and were then asked to say the word without either the first sound or the last sound. For example they would be asked to take the 'l' from *leg* and to say the word that was left (*egg*) or to take the 'k' from *bike* which left *by*. There were practice items for both the initial and final phoneme task and then 5 test items in each case.

ii Phoneme Addition

This task was similar to phoneme deletion but the children were asked to add sounds to the words they heard. Again there were practice items before both initial and final phoneme test items and there were five of each test item.

Results

Standardised Measures

The mean BPVS score for Group S was 80.5 (sd 14.4) and for Group C was 75.8 (sd 13.6). A t test comparing the performance of the two groups showed no significant difference ($t(16)=1.16$, $p=0.26$). The mean score for Group S on the *Concepts about Print* (CAP) test was 19.3. The mean score for Group C was 11.9. A t test showed that Group S were able to score significantly higher than Group C ($t(31)=8.71$, $p<0.0001$).

The mean Reading Age from the BAS *Word Reading Test* for Group S was 8 years 7 months with a range of 7 years 10 months to 10 years 10 months. Eleven of the children were between 4 years 6 months and 4 year 11 months when they were tested. Four of them had Reading Age scores between 7 years 6 months and 7 years 11 months; six had Reading Age scores between 8 years and 8 years 11 months; and one had a Reading Age of 10 years 10 months. Six of the children were between 5 years and 5 years 5 months when they were tested. Of these, three had Reading Age scores between 8 years and 8 years 11 months; two had Reading Age scores between 9 years and 9 years 11 months; one had a Reading Age of 10 years 10 months.

Group S had a mean chronological age of 5 years when they were tested. A t test showed that their reading ages were significantly above their chronological ages ($t(16)=17.46$, $p<0.0001$).

Eight of Group C were able to score on the test. They had a mean Reading Age of 5 years 6 months with a range of 5 years to 6 years 5 months. These children had a mean chronological age of 5 years 2 months when they were assessed.

The mean Reading Ages for Group S on the *Neale Analysis of Reading Ability* were 8 years 4 months (range 6:7 — 13+ years) for accuracy; 7 years (range 5:10 — 7:9 years) for comprehension; and 8 years 7 months (range 5:6 — 10:11 years) for speed.

In each case the reading ages were significantly greater than the chronological age (Accuracy — $t(16)=9.069$, $p<0.0001$; Comprehension — $t(16)=14.3$, $p<0.0001$; Speed — $t(16)=9.53$, $p<0.0001$).

Five of the control children were asked to read the Neale passages. It is problematic to give a mean score for accuracy because three of them were scored with a reading age of 'less than 5 years'. One child had an accuracy score of 5 years 3 months and one had an accuracy score of 5 years. The mean score for comprehension was 5 years 4 months with a range of 5 years 3 months to 5 years 5 months. The same problem of calculating a mean score for reading speed arose: two children had a reading speed of 'less than 5 years 1 month', two children had a reading speed of 5 years 1 month and one had a reading speed of 5 years 9 months.

Letter Knowledge

Eleven Group S Children knew the names of all the letters; 4 made a mistake on one letter and two knew 22 letters. Their knowledge of letter sounds was not as accurate although the lowest score was 17. They were significantly better at naming the letters than giving their associated sounds (Wilcoxon $N=12$, $p<0.01$).

None of Group C children knew the names of all the letters. There was a great deal of variability in this group from one child who could name 22 letters to one child who could not name any. There was the same degree of variability with knowledge of letter sounds ranging from zero to 24. There was no difference in their performance on letter names and letter sounds (Wilcoxon $N=15$, $p=0.6$).

Mann-Witney tests showed that Group S had significantly greater knowledge of letter names ($U=1/U'=271$, $p< 0.0001$) and letter sounds ($U=29.5/U'=242.5$, $p<0.0001$) than Group C.

Phonological awareness — rhyming tasks

i Rhyme production

The mean score for Group S was 4.2. Two children were unable to score. The mean score for Group C was 2.8. Group S were significantly better at rhyme production than Group C ($t(31)=2.19$, $p.<0.05$).

ii Rhyme detection — Odd-one-out, end sound

The mean score for Group S was 3.1 and for Group C was 2.3. Because of unequal variances a t test was not appropriate. A median test using Fisher's exact probability test gave an associated probability of $p=0.057$. Tocher's modification applied and the null hypothesis was rejected. Group S were significantly better than Group C at this task.

iii Rhyme detection — Odd-one-out, medial sound

The mean score for Group S was 3.5 and for Group C was 2.3. Group S were significantly better than Group C ($t(31)=2.39$, $p<0.025$).

Phonological Awareness — Phoneme addition and deletion

Table 1 shows the means scores for these tasks.

Table 1: Mean Scores obtained by each group on the phoneme addition and deletion tasks

	Phoneme	Addition	Phoneme	Deletion
	Initial sound	Final sound	Initial sound	Final sound
Group S	4.1	3.8	4.7	3.8
Group C	0.8	0.2	0.4	0.3

Of the 17 Group S children, only one was unable to do the tasks at all and one was weak on all but the initial phoneme deletion task. Of the 15 Group C children who tried these tasks, only one was able to score on them all; 9 failed to achieve any score; 3 got a score of 1 on the initial addition task; 2 got a score of 2 on the initial addition task and of these one was able to score 1 on the initial deletion task.

Because of the number of zero scores in the Group C data set, statistical analysis comparing the two groups was not appropriate. An analysis of variance (2 within subject factors) was carried out on the data set for Group S. This showed that there was a significant difference between the addition and deletion tasks ($f(1,16)=4.77$, $p<0.05$). The deletion task was easier than the addition task. There was also a significant effect due to the position of the sound to be manipulated ($f(1,16)=10.11$, $p<0.01$); the initial sound being easier to manipulate than the final sound.

Discussion

The BPVS scores showed that both groups of children had the same high level of vocabulary development. This means that any differences in reading performance could not be accounted for by the Young Early Readers having superior language skills.

Performance on the BAS word reading test showed that the parents and teachers who reported these children to us were accurate in their assessment of their reading skills. The use of the SAT tasks to confirm their assessment had also been useful in enabling us to pick out a group of children who were clearly functioning at above what would be expected for children of their age. The BAS word reading test results compare favourably with the Reading Ages on the Schonell test that Clark reported for her group of Young Fluent Readers. This suggests that we are studying a similar population of children.

The results of the Neale Analysis showed that the children were, on the whole, less advanced in their comprehension skills than in their accuracy and speed. Whilst recognising that comprehension is a vital part of reading, this discrepancy should not worry us unduly, since the later passages in the Neale Analysis are well outside the range of experience of such young children. The Neale Accuracy scores combined with the BAS word reading scores indicated that they had achieved a level of word reading accuracy which enabled them to tackle complex texts with confidence. It should of course be remembered that, though accuracy was ahead of comprehension, their comprehension scores were significantly ahead of their chronological ages.

Letter knowledge in Group S was very high and they were better at naming the letters than giving their associated sounds. This knowledge was much better than in Group C. It is not possible to say how this knowledge affected the development of their reading performance; however, in monitoring the development of letter knowledge in Group C, it will be possible at the end of the project to study the relationship between letter knowledge and reading performance.

The phonological awareness of Group S was always significantly better than Group C. Their rhyming skills were approaching ceiling. This result confirms the work of Bradley and Bryant and Treiman. However, it will be interesting to monitor the performance of the two children who could not rhyme. One of these had a reading accuracy of 7 years 5 months when she was assessed at age 4 years 9 months and the other had a reading accuracy score of 9 years 5 months when assessed at 5 years 4 months.

Though the rhyming skills of Group C were not as good as those of Group S, they were able to show some rhyme awareness. However, Group C's performance on the phoneme addition and deletion tasks would suggest that these data provide evidence to support Tumner and Rohl in their assertion that some aspects of phonological awareness may develop as a result of learning to read.

The data from Group S on the phoneme addition and deletion tasks provide useful support for the view that children find the onset and rhyme segmentation to be the most natural (cf. Treiman, 1992).

These preliminary data provide support for the view that children who are phonologically aware are able to develop their reading skills with greater ease and efficiency than those children who are not phonologically aware.

Biographies

As well as collecting quantitative data on the performance of these children, it was felt important to collect qualitative data. In this section we will present biographies of two children from Group S with their matched controls. Information was obtained through questionnaires and informal interviews with parents or teachers. All comments in quotation marks were made by the parents or teachers of the children. SA and CA are girls due to start full-time school in September 1994. SA is the young early reader and CA is her paired control child. SB and CB are boys who started full-time school as 'rising fives' in September 1993. SB is the young early reader and CB is his paired control.

Table 2 shows a comparison of their family background, developmental milestones and pre-school educational experience. It can be seen from table 2 that it was possible to obtain a close match for both pairs of children in terms of family background.

Table 2: Comparison of the family background, developmental milestones and pre-school experiences of SA, CA, SB and CB.

	SA	CA	SB	CB
Maternal age - years	25	26	25	
Paternal age - years	25	26	32	24
Maternal education	no qualifications	8 'O' levels	BA Hons	B.Comm
Paternal education	HND	HND	BSc	BSc
Paternal occupation	Analyst Programmer	Project Manager	Management Consultant	Marketing Consultant
Siblings	sister +2yrs brother -4yrs	sister +2yrs brother -2yrs	sister - 2yrs	brother -2yrs
Sitting	6 mths	5 mths	6 mths	unsure
Crawling	7 mths	8 mths	9 mths	unsure
Standing	8 mths	11 mths	12 mths	unsure
Walking	9 mths	12 mths	15 mths	9 mths
First words	'Held back - shy'	'Not much until 2'	unsure comp	'Not vocal, good
Later Language	'5 mths later than average'	'Said every-thing from 2'	'Not as adv. as friends	'Vocab good once speech appeared'
Nursery/ Playgroup	Nursery class 3 terms, mngs	Nursery class 4 terms, mngs	Nursery 6 terms 2 days + 1 am	Playgroup/ Nursery 6 terms 5 sessions

It is interesting that none of the children showed early linguistic facility. SB's mother reported that '......his hands showed his intelligence more (than his speech)'. CA is said to have communicated 'through her older sister' (c.f. Crain-Thoreson and Dale, 1992).

Family reading habits

Three families — CA, SB and CB — made regular visits to the library, usually for children's books; SA's father made occasional library visits. All families read local or national newspapers either on a daily basis or at weekends. Both SA's parents read fiction, her mother described herself as being '.........*more patient with less interesting works*'. SA's father purchased reference material on computer science. CA's parents reported that they did not have a great deal of time to read. SB's mother was more likely to read non-fiction than fiction, but she reported that SB's father '.......*rarely reads a book*', however he regularly read newspapers and P.C. magazines. Both CB's parents read a wide variety of fiction and non-fiction: '.....*all family members read something most days*'. His mother reported reading '......*more children's than adults' books*'. The older sisters of SA and CA were both described as having above average reading ability for their age.

Current Assessment

Table 3 gives details of individual scores. At the time of assessment SB and CB were in their second term in a reception class. This may account for CB's ability to give letter names and sounds; he had also used 'Letterland' material at home. SA was unable to give the sounds for three vowels — u, i and e; she gave 'w' as the sound for 'y' (see Treiman, Weatherson and Berch (1994) for a discussion of letter names).

Neither SA nor SB were able to say what a comma or speech marks were, nor could they point to a capital letter — items 17, 18 and 24 in 'Concepts about Print' assessment.

These two pairs of children do not appear to demonstrate the significant difference in rhyme production and detection that was shown by the group as a whole. However, the ability of SA and SB to manipulate phonemes is clearly superior, as shown by their performance on phoneme addition and deletion tasks. CA and CB have not yet reached a level of phonological awareness which enable them to do these.

Development of reading

Parents reported that they believed SA's reading ability was '....achieved through participation in reading sessions with her older sister', (cf. Norris and Stainthorp, 1991). SA was said to have started to learn to read at three years of age and to have always been motivated to read. She has been observed in her nursery class reading in the book corner.

SB's parents reported that he '...*loved books from about a year*'. His mother described frequently reading an ABC of cats with him and she

Table 3: Comparison of Individual Scores on the BPVS, CAP, Letter Knowledge and Phonological Awareness tasks and Standardised Reading Tests

	Young Early Reader — SA	Matched Control — CA	Young Early Reader — SB	Matched Control — CB
C A yrs mths	5.0	5.0	5.4	5.1
BPVS — centile	52	70	68	72
CAP	19	12	21	15
Letter name	26	7	26	15
Letter sound	19	2	26	15
Rhyming	11	10	14	12
Phoneme addition	7	0	9	2
Phoneme deletion	9	0	8	0
Neale Reading Age				
— accuracy	7.11		8.6	<5.0
— comprehension	6.1		7.6	5.4
— speed	8.6		10.0	5.1
BAS word R Age	8.6		9.5	6.0
— centile	>99		>99	75

speculated that he learned his alphabet from this. SB initially acquired letter names but he '....*absorbed*' the sounds and was using them interchangeably by two years of age. By this time he was also playing hangman, word lotto and word games on the computer. By three years of age he was able to blend CVC sequences — d-o-g. No formal reading scheme was used: SB's mother tried one widely available scheme but described it as '.....*so deadly boring*' that she abandoned it. SB was said currently to read as '...*a means to an end*' such as reading the rules of a game, and to '....*rarely spontaneously read a book unless it had a purpose*'.

Both CA and CB showed an early interest in books. CB is reported to have spent up to an hour in his cot looking at books when only a year old. Both children enjoyed listening to and making up their own stories. CA was unable to score on any of the standardised reading tests but CB was able to score on the Neale Analysis with an accuracy score of less than 5 years, a comprehension score of 5 years 4 months and a reading rate of 5 years 1 month. On the BAS word reading test he scored 6 years which was at the 75th centile.

The group data showed that there were clear significant differences between the Young Early Readers and their control pairs in all the meta-cognitive tasks even though they were matched on all their other attributes including vocabulary scores. The individual comparisons presented here show that the mean data does not mask individual differences. Indeed, it can be seen from table 3 that, though SA scored considerably less than CA on the BPVS, her meta-cognitive skills were high and she was reading at an advanced level whereas CA was unable to score on the standardised tests.

As was stated initially, these are very preliminary findings. We look forward to reporting on the progress that all these children make over the next two years.

Acknowledgement

This research is funded by the Research Endowment Fund of the University of Reading.

References

Adams, M. J. (1990) *Beginning to Read: Thinking and learning about print* Camb. Mass.: MIT Press

Bradley, L. and Bryant, P. E. (1983) 'Categorising sounds and learning to read: A causal connection' *Nature* 30, 419-321

Byrne, B. and Fielding-Barnsley, R. (1991) 'Evaluation of a program to teach phonemic awareness to young children' *Journal of Educational Psychology* 83, 451-455

Clark, M. (1976) *Young Fluent Readers* London: Heinemann

Clay, M. M. (1979) *Stones: the Concepts about Print Test* Auckland: Heinemann

Crain-Thoreson, C. and Dale, P. S. (1992) 'Do early talkers become early readers?: Linguistic precocity, pre-school language and emergent literacy' *Developmental Psychology* 28(3), 421- 429

Ehri, L.C. (1992) 'Reconceptualising the development of sight word reading and its relationship to recoding' in P. B. Gough, L.C. Ehri and R. Treiman (eds) *Reading Acquisition* Hillsdale: Lawrence Erlbaum

Elliot, C.D., Murray, D. J. and Pearson, L. S. (1983) *The British Ability Scales* Windsor: National Foundation for Educational Research

Frith, U. (1985) 'Beneath the surface of developmental dyslexia' in K. E. Patterson, J. C. Marshall and M. Coltheart (eds) *Surface Dyslexia: Neuropsychological and cognitive studies of phonological reading* Hillsdale: Lawrence Erlbaum

Goswami, U and Bryant, P. E. (1990) *Phonological Skills and Learning to Read* Hillsdale: Lawrence Erlbaum

Marsh, G., Friedman, M., Welch, V. and Desberg, P. (1981) 'A cognitive-developmental theory of reading acquisition' in G. E. MacKinnon and T. G. Waller (eds) *Reading Research: Advances in Theory and Practice* Vol 3 San Diego CA: Academic Press

Neale, M. D. (1958) *Neale Analysis of Reading Ability* Southampton: Macmillan Educational

Norris, E. and Stainthorp, R. (1991) 'Reading tuition by elder siblings' *Reading* 25, 13-18

Treiman, R. (1992) 'The role of intrasyllabic units in learning to read and spell' in P.B. Gough, L.C. Ehri and R. Treiman (eds) *Reading Acquisition* Hillsdale: Lawrence Erlbaum

Treiman, R. , Weatherston, S. and Berch, D. (1994) 'The role of letter names in children's learning of phoneme-grapheme relations' *Applied Psycholinguistics* 15 97-122

Tumner, W. E. and Hoover, W. A. (1992) 'The role of cognitive and linguistic factors in learning to read' in P. B. Gough, L.C. Ehri and R. Treiman (eds) *Reading Acquisition* Hillsdale: Lawrence Erlbaum

Tumner, W. E. and Rohl, M. (1991) 'Phonological awareness and reading acquisition' in D. J. Sawyer and B.J. Fox (eds) *Phonological Awareness in Reading: The evolution of current perspectives* New York: Springer-Verlag

Walsh, D. J., Price, G. G. and Gillingham, M. G. (1988) 'The critical but transitory importance of letter naming' *Reading Research Quarterly* 23, 108-122

Yopp, H. K. (1988) 'The validity and reliability of phonemic awareness tests' *Reading Research Quarterly* 23, 159-177

Chapter 8

Strategies for curriculum diversity and decentralisation, professional autonomy and quality outcomes:

the experience of post-compulsory English education in the Australian Capital Territory

Jacqueline Manuel
University of New England, Australia

The substance of my paper is to share with you my personal and professional perspectives on the construction of the English curriculum and the teaching of English in schools in the Australian Capital Territory. In many ways, the ACT education system is striking and indeed unique in its process of curriculum design and implementation and in the very high level of professional responsibility entrusted to the staff by the educational bureaucracy or government.

For those of you who are perhaps unfamiliar with the internal geography of our country, the Australian Capital Territory is one of eight Australian states and territories. The ACT, with its capital city Canberra, is the seat of the Australian Federal government.

In the ACT, the subject of English and its curriculum continues to occupy a pivotal place in the entire compulsory and post-compulsory sectors. I'd like to examine with you the processes of the creation and delivery of the English curriculum in this particular system. I would also like to elucidate the ways in which the ACT's model stands as a means of responding to both the instrumentalist or vocational demands driven by industry and employees, and also the wholistic requirements of the subject English. I would then like to spend some time talking about practical examples of the what and how of teaching English in the ACT — about what goes on inside and outside the classroom on a typical day in this part of Australia.

In our country, each of the eight states and territories determines the nature and delivery of its own curriculum. Through national collaboration between all states and territories — and that has meant representatives from public, Catholic and independent school sectors, parents, students, and teachers working in consultation with government bodies — Curriculum Statements and Profiles have been produced in each of the eight areas of knowledge and experience offered to students in Australian schools.

These eight areas are English, Mathematics, Science, Technology, Languages Other Than English (LOTE), Health and Physical Education, Studies of Society and Environment, and the Arts.

While neither prescriptive nor mandatory, the National Statements in each of these key learning areas offer curriculum developers a coherent framework for approaching their task and are based upon the agreed national goals for schooling. The Statements encourage innovation and experimentation in each learning area and embody and articulate the philosophical tenets upon which our teaching and learning is predicated.

At the national level there are the agreed upon Statements and Profiles for each learning area. While each state or territory can select or reject aspects of these shared educational goals, at the state level in the ACT, the Department of Education adheres very closely to the national principles and goals.

The ACT Department's 'Curriculum Guidelines' establish general parameters within which schools are required to design the curriculum — in the broadest sense of the word. Courses within that curriculum may be proposed by any individual or group within the community through the agency of the local school board. What is to be stressed here, is that it is the school community itself, and this includes parents, students, community representatives, and finally teachers, that shapes and formulates the what and the how of its specific English programme.

All courses are submitted to the Accreditation Authority which is a panel appointed by the Department to administer the whole process of course accreditation. Each course submitted is reviewed according to a comprehensive and educationally rigorous set of criteria.

Utilising the broad ACT Curriculum Guidelines with National Statements and Profiles, English teachers in the ACT design courses which reflect both the national goals and also, importantly, the particular needs and requirements of their own clientele — the students who attend the school at which they teach. It is axiomatic that schools can differ remarkably in their make-up and ethos and as a consequence, any student-centred curriculum must validate notions of difference whilst at the same time ensuring an overall coherence in its objectives.

If a student is bilingual or has originated from a culture apart from Australia, they will generally encounter a curriculum which is sensitive and responsive to their particular needs. What this means in practice is a recognition and valuing of the language experience, cultural mores and academic skills with which they are already equipped. There are, for example, specific ESL programmes at the College to cater for students who may require assistance with literacy skills. When I turn to aspects of the curriculum in closer detail you will see how the needs of bilingual students are written into each course.

In the ACT there is no such thing as a central syllabus — each school proceeds to write its own syllabus which seeks to enflesh in practice the educational philosophies inscribed in the Guidelines and the Statements.

Let us look more closely at an English curriculum — the English curriculum created and implemented by the English staff at Lake Tuggeranong College, one of a number of senior secondary colleges in the territory which caters for students completing the final 2 years of post-compulsory education. The majority of students in the ACT attend government public schools, which are roughly the Australian equivalent of your comprehensive schools.

A student can attend the government school of his or her choice and pay no more than a nominal levy and a contribution for the use of equipment and facilities in specialist subjects like photography or art. This is an ongoing manifestation of the egalitarian values espoused by many politicians, bureaucrats and educationalists alike in contemporary Australian society, despite the ways in which it has often been caricatured by foreign media. The maxim of a 'fair-go' for all is clearly evident in our country's commitment to quality comprehensive education for every individual in our society, regardless of income, ethnicity or linguistic heritage. This has a great deal to do with the political fact that the Labour Party has been in power at a Federal level for over 10 years.

It also has a great deal to do with committed, progressive educationalists becoming involved in the political system in order that change for the good be enacted.

The system in which we operate in the ACT has not happened by accident — we continue to carefully guard what we have and to work for change where we believe it is necessary.

The colleges themselves are well appointed centres of learning. At Lake Tuggeranong College the entire school, internally and externally, is very welcoming and attractive. The college is sited in an enviable position. To the west it is flanked by the Brindabella mountains and to the east it rests on the shores of the lake. The physical environment both inside and outside the school is, at the very least, a pleasure to teach in.

All staff-rooms have current model computers linked to laser printers. Each faculty has for its use video recorders, televisions and sound equipment, and we have generous access to an extensive range of stationery requirements for ourselves and our students. We have literature resources which are constantly being added to and updated. The students themselves have access to many personal computers and we encourage their use in English.

As a consequence, the students engaged in post-compulsory education in the ACT do so within well equipped institutions where staffing levels and choice of courses are in many cases at an optimum level. There are over 100 members of staff at the college, catering for a student body of between 800-900.

By far the majority of the 800 or so students undertaking an English programme at College enrol in what is called a 'Tertiary' programme. The equivalent of a Tertiary programme in Britain would be an A-level. This course is fully accredited for entrance into tertiary or further education. Only a small percentage of the student population undertakes a more vocationally-oriented English programme, called an 'Accredited' programme. This accredited programme has links with local businesses, other education providers and industry, affording the students a wide range of training opportunities during their two years of post- compulsory education.

In constructing an English curriculum for the group of tertiary-bound (or A-level) students, we assume that their previous learning experiences have provided them with a demonstrated competence in the use of language and an ability to understand, and respond to, a wide range of adult literature. We expect that they come to us with capable reading and writing strategies together with some sense of English and Australian literary history. While all 14 year olds in Britain are required to read a Shakespearian text, we would not insist upon such a pre-requisite until we considered that the students had the linguistic skills and sheer life experience to enable them to engage meaningfully with one or more of Shakespeare's plays.

And the point needs to be made that content, no matter what it is, is irrelevant if a student doesn't know how to read or write. What is vitally important is the focus on the quality of the reading and writing processes at junior secondary level — on developing in our students the kinds of reading and writing strategies or practices that will *then* lead to personally enriching experiences with challenging literature such as that by Shakespeare.

In designing the curriculum in the ACT to serve the needs of our particular student body, we as English teachers are provided with a set of guidelines called the *English Course Framework.* I will now explore this in some detail and then go on to provide examples of how particular Literature units at the college embody its inherent philosophical principles and adhere to its explicit parameters for content selection, and teaching and learning practices.

The *English Course Framework* consists of firstly a 'Rationale' which states the guiding principles for English and its place in a student's education. This is as follows:

> 'English is an area of learning through which students develop their language skills for a variety of purposes and audiences. As students gain control of a wide range of oral and written skills, they develop their potential as human beings and are capable of assuming an active role in society.
>
> English equips students with the communications skills to meet a broad range of needs — their own need for self-definition and expression, and the need of society for literate people.
>
> Through the study of English, students develop an understanding of our community's and culture's diverse linguistic and literary heritage. By studying classic and contemporary literature, students hone their ability to empathise and demonstrate tolerance and understanding, including cross-cultural understanding. As they engage with literature, students acquire critical-thinking and problem-solving skills which are applicable in a wide range of contexts.
>
> As students develop a command and appreciation of a range of written and spoken texts, including non-literary and media texts, they are better able to consider, analyse, interpret, make decisions and communicate. These skills empower students in their own lives and enable them to contribute to society in a time of rapid social change. Through the study of English, students develop their skills for the appreciation of literature and life-long learning, enabling them to live in a satisfying way, deriving both pleasure and enlightenment from the rich encounter with language.' (*English Course Framework* ACT BSSS 1993:1)

Secondly, there is a statement of goals, in the form of objectives for students to achieve. The goals are in line with those set out in the National Statement on English for Australian Schools and the National English Profile and should enable students to:

- become analytical, critical and creative thinkers
- become independent users of language with strategies for effective reading, writing, viewing, speaking and listening
- develop skills in effective interaction and communication in groups
- understand the range and diversity of spoken and written literature and language
- appreciate cultural and social contexts in spoken, written and visual texts
- respond creatively and imaginatively to texts
- critically appraise texts.

(*English Course Framework* ACT BSSS 1993:2)

A third and important area of the Framework are the 'Across Curriculum Perspectives.' These are those educational and societal issues which are of such significance that they should permeate the curriculum. All courses should embody a clear awareness of these perspectives in the selection of content and teaching and learning strategies. These perspectives have been identified as follows:

- Aboriginal and Torres Strait Islander Education
- Australian Perspectives
- Environmental Education
- Gender Equity
- Information Technology
- Language for Understanding Across the Curriculum (LUAC)
- Multicultural Education
- Special Needs Education
- Work Education.

Most of these are self-explanatory so I will not go into detail here about each one. It is sufficient to say that in designing the curriculum, we must be mindful of these perspectives, although, obviously all perspectives are not applicable to all units in an English Programme. It is, for instance, inappropriate to incorporate an Aboriginal perspective when studying the poetry of Wordsworth or Shelley. It is, on the other hand, entirely possible and indeed necessary to incorporate such a perspective in the selection and teaching of material in an Australian Literature course.

The fourth element of the Framework is 'A discussion of learning and teaching in English':

> 'Students will be encouraged to become active and reflective learners with a wide range of strategies at their disposal for reading, viewing, speaking, listening and writing. Students will use strategies to develop their appreciation of the importance of cultural, social and individual perspectives in determining the interpretation and understanding of texts. Other strategies will focus on increasing students' understanding of how language is shaped and manipulated according to context, audience, purpose and content.
>
> Teachers will foster independent learning habits, heightened understandings about texts and language, and skill and confidence in the use of language through supportive strategies which include:
>
> - small-group and whole class discussions
> - workshops
> - role-play
> - negotiated and student initiated written analytical and creative responses to texts
> - research and reporting
> - debating
> - recasting of texts in a variety of forms
> - dramatic presentation of material
> - seminar presentation
> - teacher exposition, demonstration and modelling
> - guest speakers

- journal writing in response to texts, for personal reflection and self-monitoring of learning
- critical and expository essays and creative responses
- excursions.

(*English Course Document* Lake Tuggeranong College 1994/7)

We come to the fifth and particularly relevant guideline in the Framework: 'An outline of criteria for the selection of content.' In this area, reference to *A Statement of English for Australian Schools* (*SEAS* Curriculum Corporation 1994) is crucial for a rounded understanding of the nature of the content of the English programme. The English Curriculum includes two Strands — Texts and Language.

Both Strands are comprehensive and encompass the language modes of speaking, listening, viewing, reading and writing. They provide very inclusive and extensive definitions of literature and language and embody what enlightened teachers of English have long perceived to be the breadth of these two terms.

The Texts strand defines texts as 'any communication written, spoken or visual, involving language' (*SEAS* Curriculum Corporation 1994:6). For instance, texts would include novels, plays, poems, letters, articles, feature films, conversations, advertisements, and journals. Now in order to ensure the quality of an English programme in terms of the texts that are explored, the guidelines call for three categories of text: literature, everyday texts and the mass media.

In the study of literature as part of a wider reading and writing programme, the curriculum seeks to develop students' knowledge and appreciation of :

- Literature's potential to provide a source of enjoyment
- Literature's potential to inform and educate through its imaginative representation of human experience
- The opportunity literature presents to discover a diverse range of socio-cultural values, attitudes and beliefs
- The opportunities literature provides to reflect on the ways writers use language, including linguistic structures and features

- The ways in which literature can shape the reader's or listener's perceptions, and the ways these can be discussed and challenged
- The different ways people respond to texts, depending on their context.

(*SEAS* Curriculum Corporation 1994:7)

The literature category suggests that, in our teaching, we select from classic, contemporary and popular material. Classic literature refers to texts that have been recognised as part of an inherited literary canon. What must be stressed in the approach to classic texts is that critical reading and analysis are necessary if students are to understand how cultural beliefs and values have shifted or indeed continue to be woven into the fabric of our present lives. Of course, in the study of classic literature notions of literary value and the reasons why some texts are included in the canon and others are not make for fruitful and challenging explorations. The range of classic literature could include:

- myths, legends, fables, fairy tales, traditional tales, ballads
- extracts from the Bible, Aboriginal Dreaming stories, legends of the Torres Strait
- essays
- expository texts in disciplines such as history and science
- novels and short stories
- films
- autobiography and biography
- drama
- narrative, dramatic and lyric poetry.

(*SEAS* Curriculum Corporation 1994:8)

Contemporary literature indicates those works which are deemed to be significant texts dealing with complex ideas in contemporary language. Students derive a great deal from the study of contemporary literature because it enables them to 'experiment with similar techniques' (*SEAS* Curriculum Corporation 1994:8) in their own writing. In the critical contrast and comparison of classic, contemporary and popular literature students explore the ways in which contemporary works reflect or subvert current thinking and values.

In the contemporary literature component, students could examine:

- picture books, storytelling, wordless books
- novels and short stories
- films and television drama and comedy
- autobiography, biography and documentary
- performances of classic and contemporary poetry
- students' own writing
- poetry
- scripted and improvised drama and modern plays.

(*SEAS* Curriculum Corporation 1994:8)

The third component of the literature category is popular texts. It really refers to works whose primary purpose is to entertain rather than educate. Typically, these works lack an exploration of complex issues and ideas in a complex way.

The literature of popular culture is an important ingredient in the English Curriculum, however, because it exerts such a strong and continuing influence over the lives of our students, and indeed ourselves. Hence, it is vital that our students learn to approach and appraise such recreational reading and viewing with the same sort of discriminating and critical eye that we would expect them to use in the encounter with classic or contemporary texts. We should have the opportunity in our classrooms to explore with our students the more subtle and covert powers and values of the material which they are choosing to read, view, play on a video game or listen to on the radio.

Almost each year that I have taught, at least one student for his or her seminar presentation in English has examined an aspect of popular culture — e.g. the ways in which visual material, such as advertising and gender-targeted magazines, shape and manipulate young consumers. Such seminars are examples of the ways in which students can engage in sophisticated and challenging studies of the power of language in our lives. It is here that the intersection of literature and life can occur in dramatic and productive ways and can lead students into critiques of more complex contemporary or classic literary texts.

In the category of popular literature we could include:

- popular romance and thrillers
- television soap operas, serials and video clips
- cartoons and comics
- song lyrics
- jokes, riddles, humorous verse.

(*SEAS* Curriculum Corporation 1994:8-9)

The second category in the Text strand is Everyday Texts. These are texts associated with daily life such as

- classified ads
- invitations, apologies, complaints
- personal letters and telephone conversations
- messages, questionnaires and forms
- instructions, labels, captions, notices, pamphlets, brochures, catalogues
- diaries and journals.

In addition there are those texts associated with the specialised demands of schooling such as:

- recounts and descriptions
- informational texts
- notes, summaries
- arguments, written and spoken, speeches
- discussions and debates.

There are also texts associated with the world of work, including unpaid work such as

- formal letters, reports, job applications, C.V.s and resumes
- interviews and questions
- formal meeting procedures

- small group work
- public speaking.

(*SEAS* Curriculum Corporation 1994:10)

Obviously, as the student proceeds through school the curriculum would shift in emphasis from these everyday texts used in the home and at school to those occurring in the wider community.

The third category of the Texts strand is the Mass Media — including 'all print, non-print and electronic forms that communicate with a mass audience.' (*SEAS* Curriculum Corporation). These products are shaped by technology and occupy a central role in the shaping and defining of cultural values and issues. An understanding of the process of news-gathering and selection and the power of advertising would all be pursued in this Text category.

In summary, the breadth and range of texts available for selection as part of the content of an English curriculum is impressive:

> ... • news reports • documentaries • reviews • editorials • classified ads • invitations, apologies, complaints • personal letters and telephone conversations • messages, questionnaires and forms • instructions, labels, captions, notices, pamphlets, brochures, catalogues • diaries and journals • recounts and descriptions • informational texts • notes, summaries • arguments, written and spoken, speeches • discussions and debates • formal letters, reports, job applications, C.V.s and résumé • interviews and questions • meeting procedures • small group work • public speaking • popular romance and thrillers • television soap operas, serials and video clips • cartoons and comics • song lyrics • jokes, riddles and humorous verse • picture books, storytelling • wordless books • novels and short stories • films and television drama and comedy • autobiography, biography and documentary • performances of classic and contemporary poetry • students' own writing • poetry • scripted and improvised drama and modern plays • myths, legends, fables, fairy tales, traditional tales, ballads • extracts from the Bible, Aboriginal Dreaming stories, legends of the Torres Strait • essays • expository texts in disciplines such as history and science • novels and short stories • films • autobiography and biography • drama • narrative, dramatic and lyric poetry ...

That is just the Text Strand of the Curriculum. There is also the Language Strand. Again, within this strand there are three categories and several components. Within the 'Contextual Understanding' category, students study the socio-cultural context and the situational context of language use. Within the 'Linguistic Structures and Features' category, students learn the linguistic structures and features of Standard Australian English. Then, the final component of the Language Strand is 'Strategies', which includes strategies for speaking and listening, reading and viewing and writing.

The final area of the *English Course Framework* is 'Assessment and evaluation procedures.' Students are assessed on their performance and achievement levels in three 'umbrella' areas:

- Thought, Interpretation and Appraisal
- Oral Communication
- Written Communication.

Typically, a student undertaking a one semester unit in English (approximately 4 hours of tuition per week), would complete two major essays — 1000 words each, a formal seminar presentation, ongoing class tasks and minor pieces and an examination. The assessable items are marked according to sets of criteria and major pieces are moderated with other members of the faculty.

Post-Compulsory students do not sit for any external English examination as such. All final year students in the ACT sit for a common writing task which is a 600 word paper on a current issue or topic, and a multiple choice paper on Social Sciences and Mathematics. These papers are used to moderate school-based assessment. The results of these two external examinations do have an impact on students' final Tertiary Entrance Score. It is important to note that the Tertiary Entrance Score, based on the student's school-based assessment during 2 years at college, is recognised by all Tertiary institutions in Australia and indeed many overseas.

So these are the guidelines, the goals and the framework for constructing the English curriculum. What does it look like in practice?

A student undertaking an English programme at Lake Tuggeranong College must complete 4 one semester units of English over a period of two academic years. They can study up to 8 one semester units if they wish to major in English. We define a unit as 66 hours of face-to-face tuition during a semester. Each unit is taught for four periods per week (which is approximately equal to three and a half hours per week).

Each English teacher in our college teaches four classes in their discipline, one 'R' unit for two hours per week, and an 'Advisory Group' for two hours per week. The total face-to-face teaching time is 18 hours per week. Lake Tuggeranong is a relatively young college so our choice of units is moderate in comparison to the older colleges whose English curricula offer 60-80 individual units. Of course, these could not all be taught simultaneously: they are rotated so that a core of about 30 is offered each semester.

No unit can be repeated and several units have pre-requisites. There are two types of units, once again reflecting the Text and Language Strands of the National Statement. Each student must complete at least one unit from a Literature strand and at least one unit from a Language strand. This counters the potential for a student to complete college English without ever having engaged with literary texts nor having developed the skills of literary analysis, argument and exposition.

A student could, for example, undertake Communication Skills, Creative and Expressive Writing I and II and Travel Writing and complete an English programme without ever having had to study classic literature. When constructing this English curriculum, we as a staff had to decide whether or not we believed that a student need necessarily study classic literature in an English programme. After much debate the consensus was a firm 'yes' despite the fact that many of our students are initially resistant to literature which is outside their immediate, personal and sometimes limited experience.

In stipulating this course pattern we affirmed our belief that it is through literature and language, and the critical, creative and engaged response to its many forms, that individuals extend their understanding of the world and of themselves. But once again, this was a decision made by the members of the English faculty at Lake Tuggeranong College, rather than a unilateral decision anonymously imposed by a political or bureaucratic body.

The compelling feature of our school-based curriculum model is the integral place occupied by classroom teachers in the design and accreditation of the courses we deliver. The Accreditation Authority, the body which credentials all curricula in the ACT, is itself constituted by many

At our college, we offer students a choice of around 30 units in English.

Literature Units
Aboriginal Literature
Australian Literature
Black American Literature
Comedy and Satire
Conflict and Resolution
Crime and Detection
Drama as Literature
Fantasy Literature
Gothic Literature
Literature of Other Cultures
North American Literature
Myths and Legends
Science Fiction
Shakespeare and His Contemporaries
Short Forms of Literature
The Novel
Women in Literature

Specialised Literature and Language Units
Children's Literature
Communications Skills
Creative and Expressive Writing 1
Creative and Expressive Writing 2
Issues of Our Time
Language and Literature A
Language and Literature B
Life Stories
Looking at Language
Poetry: Past and Present
Research Studies in English
Travel Writing

former teachers and others who have a strong and recognised expertise in the subject area over which they have jurisdiction.

The most compelling feature of the curriculum in its design and implementation is that we as teachers own what we are teaching: we are accorded rightful autonomy and professional status in determining the nature of the content and delivery of the subject English. There is no prescriptive content to which we must over and over adhere. The professional experience and judgement of the teacher is valued as the ultimate source of authority for deciding what is appropriate and necessary for the achievement of the English goals within a particular unit, with a new group of students, during each new Semester. The pedagogical and broader educational implications of this are far-reaching to say the least. The results and achievements of our students in the ACT relative to those of students studying within other state or territory systems provide on-going evidence of the success of our devolved model of curriculum design and delivery.

One Head of English in the ACT, who had taught in another system years before, declared that he could not imagine going back to a system of teaching courses posted to him from above in brown envelopes and of having them examined by people who had never taught, nor even seen, the students (Brock, 1987:90).

From my own experience in this system, I can only concur with this perspective.

References

Board of Secondary School Studies, Australian Capital Territory Department of Education (1993) *English Course Framework* Canberra: ACT Department of Education

Brock, P. (1987) *Who's Doing What?: The senior English curriculum in Australian schools* Adelaide: Australian Association for Teachers of English

Curriculum Corporation (1994) *A Statement on English for Australian Schools* Carlton: Curriculum Corporation

Section 3

Assessing English

Chapter 9

Reading standards: a Key Stage 1 study

Julie Davies and Ivy Brember
University of Manchester

Introduction

The most significant changes since 1944 occurred in the primary phase of education when the Education Reform Bill became law and imposed a National Curriculum on all state funded primary schools. One of the reasons given for the introduction of a National Curriculum was the desire to raise standards in primary schools. Whether this occurs, and to what degree, in English Attainment Target 2 (Reading) is the main focus of this investigation.

Learning to read is one of the most critically important and empowering skills that children will acquire at school. Society expects children to become literate as a result of the education they receive. If it is believed that their standards of literacy are falling, considerable public concern is expressed and action demanded to ensure that children learn to read fluently. However, evidence for changes in primary school children's standard of literacy has often been fragmentary in Britain in the past because of the lack of a systematic and comprehensive means of assessment. The absence of such information encourages speculation and conjecture.

A dictionary definition of 'standard' is:

> 'a basis of measurement, a criterion, an established or accepted model... in schools and grade of classification; a definite level of excellence or adequacy required, aimed at or possible.'
> (Chambers, 1980)

The word 'standard' to denote an actual level of performance, which is acceptable, is being used by politicians and the public so that when they talk of falling standards they are referring to actual performance levels dropping as a result of some factor such as poor teaching. Though the concern over standards in reading has always been with us, during the last four years it has reached fever pitch. This has been due, in part to the publication by Turner of his analysis of some Local Education Authorities' (LEAs) data concerning their children's reading attainments on a variety of standardised tests, which indicated a drop in literacy standards since 1985 (Turner, 1990; 1992). It is pertinent and necessary at this point to briefly review what evidence there is concerning children's literacy standards. The Secretary of State acted with alacrity after the Turner investigation. Two HMI reports were quickly produced (DES, 1990a; 1991a). The lack of representativeness of the schools sampled is acknowledged in the first report as is the subjectivity of the methodology involved. However the first report was based on 3,000 inspection visits involving 120 primary schools where HMI observed the teaching and learning of reading in 470 classes and listened to over 2,000 pupils read aloud.

Their conclusion was that :

> 'In 80% of the schools the standards of reading were satisfactory or better and in about 30% of those the reading standards were high...'

The survey points to about 20% of the schools where for one reason or another the work in reading was judged to be poor and required urgent attention. But serious as that level of poor teaching and learning is, the broad picture has changed little since the findings of the 1978 HMI

National Primary Survey (DES, 1978). That does not suggest that there has been a fall in the overall standards of reading in primary schools. Nor does it suggest all is well, rather

> 'that we have the long standing task of raising standards of achievement beyond their current levels' (ibid: 1).

A follow up HMI survey a year later noted there had been little change in the broad picture of standards of work in reading in primary schools from that described in the previous report (DES, 1991a).

At the same time as HMI were investigating reading standards, the Secretary of State asked SEAC to carry out a survey of arrangements made by the LEAs for monitoring standards. The National Foundation for Educational Research (NFER) undertook this work and reviewed evidence made available by LEAs about the reading performance of 7-year-old pupils in the previous decade (DES, 1990b). It was found that 59% of LEAs in England and Wales used norm referenced tests. Twenty-six LEAs provided evidence of 2,000 children aged between 7 and 8 from which trends in performance over time could reasonably be assessed. Some decline in reading performance was found in 19 of the 26 LEAs : a six month decline in average reading levels was noted between 1987 and 1991. A major survey of 17,000 children's reading performance over ten years was also published at this time indicating a small but measurable decline in reading standards. It involved the administration of the Chiltern Reading Test to 1,500 7 to 8-year-olds from 1979 to 1991 in schools with low turnover of teaching staff and relatively little movement of children (Lake, 1992).

The Secretary of State was appraised of the nature, extent, purpose and generalisability of the results of LEA testing of reading for national monitoring purposes by the NFER report which concluded:

> 'The attempt to discern a national picture of pupils' performance from disparate methods of assessment highlights the need to have national assessment procedures with agreement as to the forms in which test results will be analysed and reported, together with the statutory obligation to make data publicly available.' (DES, 1990b)

The assessment procedures attached to the National Curriculum were welcomed by the Secretary of State for Education as filling this need. The

Standard Assessment Tasks (SATs) undertaken by all Year 2 children were expected to become the common currency that could be used to highlight the effective school, the effective teacher and the achieving child:

> This will give us the chance to measure children's progress against standards that are set nationally and held in common across England and Wales. In this way, we can have confidence in the results. We can have confidence that our children are being assessed against objective standards rather than being judged against the relative performance of their classmates.' (Patten, 1993)

The 'confidence' referred to depends crucially on the validities, and thus on the reliabilities, of SATs. The Secretary of State for Education recently pronounced that the national testing was here to stay as a means of checking at intervals on levels of educational attainment and progress. In practice, education is as much concerned about the latter as the former. However, it should be noted that the majority of such procedures, of which SATs are an example, rely upon data derived from cross-sectional studies. Such procedures cannot be as authoritative as direct study of progress through longitudinal monitoring of the same, or equivalent, groups of learners. Strictly speaking, then, true norms of progress are not available.

The SATs' intended use both as a measure of school effectiveness on which parents may base their choice of schools and also as a measure of teacher effectiveness is of central professional concern and warrants careful analysis of their validity and utility. The assertion that SATs will provide valid measures of the progress of pupils individually and collectively, and enable comparisons to be made over a period of years, has been challenged recently (Pumfrey and Elliot, 1991; Pumfrey, 1992; Pumfrey, Elliot and Tyler, 1992; Black, 1993; Kirkham, 1993; James and Conner, 1993; Davies and Brember, 1994). The criticisms centre on the SATs' validity based as they are on the over-dependence of subjective judgements of vague criteria. SATs' use both as formative and summative indicators of attainment has also received criticism, as has the ten point scale.

This study has a two-fold purpose. Firstly it reports the findings of a four year cross sectional study of Year 2 children's reading attainments as measured on a standardised reading test (France, 1981). At the same time, a report of head teachers' perception of the National Curriculum's effect on reading is given . Two main surveys have recently been published which include data on this aspect. The Campbell and Neill survey of teachers' perceptions indicated the majority of their sample thought that reading standards had been adversely affected by the introduction of the National Curriculum (Campbell and Neill, 1994). Pollard et al's survey (1994) of headteachers' views found that, while most welcomed some aspects of the curriculum content associated with the National Curriculum, half of the sample also saw a threat to depth because of the breadth of the new curriculum. Headteachers in this investigation also said that the inappropriateness of the SATs and the time consuming and disruptive aspects of standardised assessment were particularly problematic to them and their staffs (Pollard, Broadfoot, Croll, Osborn and Abbot, 1994).

Secondly, this investigation focuses on whether the reading SAT (En2) is a reliable, accurate and consistent measure of pupils' reading standards and progress by which parents can rank their child within the class, or the school within the LEA or the LEA in the national league tables. In other words, when a parent is told that their child is at Level 1, 2 or 3, does this correlate with the child's attainment on another, more common measure of reading attainment such as a standardised reading test?

Sample

For the four year cross-sectional study six schools were selected at random from the 85 within one LEA. Simple random sampling was employed to identify the six schools for research on the premise that such a sample would provide a basis for generalisation within the LEA. Within the schools, Year 2 children were chosen for specific study because they were the cohorts to be assessed by the first and second Standard Assessment Tasks (SEAC, 1991a; 1991b; 1991c; 1991d; 1991e; 1992a; 1992b; 1992c).

Within cohorts 3 and 4, one school did not make available their children's SAT scores, giving a sample size of 171 children in both 1991 and 1992 for the comparison of reading attainments.

Procedure

At the start of the research the headteachers were interviewed about their attitude to the National Curriculum and the effect they thought it would have on standards generally and reading standards in particular. In each of the four years the Primary Reading Test (PRT) was administered according to the instruction manual in the second half of the summer term (France, 1981). The test was standardised in 1981. More than 20,000 children were involved in the validation and standardisation stages. The test is an untimed multiple-choice group reading test which takes on average 30 minutes to complete. In 1991 and 1992, the SATs in English, Mathematics and Science were administered to all Year 2 children in the sample as instructed by SEAC (1991a; 1991b; 1991c; 1991d; 1991e; 1992a; 1992b; 1992c).

The null hypothesis that there would be no change over the four years in the raw reading and standardised comprehension scores on the PRT was tested by two one way analyses of variance with cohort as the independent variable and test scores as the dependent variable.

In order to test the null hypothesis that there would be no significant difference between the raw reading scores and the standardised comprehension scores for children at the same SAT level in years 1991 and 1992, two way analyses of variance (using harmonic means to compensate for unequal numbers in cells) were performed on the PRT raw reading scores and the PRT standardised comprehension scores, the independent variables being Year Group and SAT level. It was decided to use the PRT raw reading scores rather than the standardised reading ages because children scoring twenty or less are not given a reading age (6 being the lowest reading age on this test). In our sample 25% of the children in 1991 and 26% of the children in 1992 had reading ages of less than 6.

Results

Firstly we will deal with the four year cross-sectional study of the four cohorts. Our sample's reading scores increased consistently over the four years but none of these differences were statistically significant. The comprehension scores increased over the first three years and then fell slightly but again none of the differences were statistically significant.

Table 1: Sample Size and Means for Raw PRT and Standardised Comprehension Scores.

Year	Status	Mean R	Mean C	N
1989	Pre-National Curriculum	23.17	92.96	213
1990	National Curriculum	23.41	93.64	207
1991	National Curriculum+SAT	24.39	95.91	218
1992	National Curriculum+SAT	24.43	95.76	216
	Overall	23.86	94.59	854

R = Raw PRT Score. C = Standardised Comprehension Score.

We will now concentrate on the comparison of the last two cohorts for which we have the SAT scores. The national figures show an improvement in the attainment level of children between 91 and 92: a smaller percentage of children were at Level 1 and a higher percentage at Level 3 in 92. Table 2 shows the percentage of children at each level for the national results and for our sample.

Table 2: Children Attaining Each SAT Level (%)

	Level 1	Level 2	Level 3	Level 4
England and Wales 91	28	50	21	
England and Wales 92	24	50	24	2
Sample 91	22	56	22	
Sample 92	16	51	31	2

In both years the percentages at each level in our sample follow a similar pattern to the national figures and show an improvement in 1992. In 1992 only it was possible for Year 2 children to be given a SAT Level of 4. Only 3 children attained this level and for the purpose of our analysis these were combined with the children at Level 3 as this was the highest level achievable in 1991. Examination of the mean PRT raw reading and standardised comprehension scores for each year group shows that overall, the group means are lower in 1992 than in 1991. Only for the raw reading score at SAT Level 1 is the 1992 mean slightly higher.

Table 3: Means of Raw Reading Scores and Standardised Comprehension Scores at each SAT Level.

	Level 1	Level 2	Level 3	Total
1991	17.27	25.29	31.62	24.92
	82.24	97.67	109.84	96.96
	37	97	37	171
1992	17.74	23.27	29.86	24.55
	82.11	93.12	106.16	95.65
	27	88	56	171
Total	17.47	24.33	30.56	24.74
	82.18	95.51	107.62	96.20
	64	185	93	342

Line 1 = Raw Reading Scores. Line 2 = Standardised Comprehension Scores.
Line 3 = Number at SAT level.

The analysis of variance table shows that the differences between the year groups are significant at the 1% level for the raw scores and at the 0.1% level for the comprehension scores, thus allowing us to reject the null hypothesis that there is no difference between the year groups on the PRT scores.

Table 4: Analysis of Variance of the Primary Reading Test Raw Reading Score.

Source	F Reading	F Comprehension
Year groups	9.56**	10.35***
SAT Levels	171.17***	129.36***
Year v SAT Level	1.93	1.15

** Significant at 1% level. *** Significant at 0.1% level.

Conclusion

In answer to our research question: Is there evidence that reading standards have gone up in Year 2 children as a consequence of the National Curriculum and assessment procedures? The answer must be it all depends on which measure you use. The SATs say yes: the PRT says no. Two important points need discussing. Firstly it is true to say that the two tests (SATs and PRT) are both designed to measure the reading ability of children but do so in different ways. The SATs are determining whether or not the children can complete a certain task, so the result is dichotomous, while the PRT score is indicating the child's position on a continuous scale with a mean of 100 and a standard deviation of 15 in which scores were summed on a pass-fail basis. Our results clearly show that, for our sample, children who were tested in 1992 were achieving higher SAT levels with the same PRT score. Indeed from our results it appears that attainment in reading had fallen in the second cohort. This conflict of results should engender great caution in the interpretation of SAT scores.

Secondly, it could be argued that the disparity between SAT levels and PTR scores in 1991 and 1992 was a reflection on the validity of the PRT test rather than on the SATs' levels. However, the PRT was constructed using the generally accepted well-tried authenticated procedures for test construction. The same can hardly be said of the SATs. They were trialled for a year before their introduction but it is not clear on what basis the changes were made (and are constantly being made) to them. From this we may conclude that it is not possible for a school to make a meaningful comparison between two years' SATs results. Our results tend to confirm they are useless both for this purpose and as data for indicating where children stand in relation to other children locally and nationally.

Overall the evidence raises severe doubts about the validity of SAT levels. It echoes the significant reservations among the teachers about the validity and usefulness of the outcomes of the SAT process (Shorrocks et al, 1992). This small study suggests that the SAT results in reading should be viewed with a degree of caution as summative indicators of children's reading attainments. It reinforces Paul Black's view that programmes to evaluate the reliability of SATs must be undertaken and their results must be published (Black, 1993).

The SATs are criteria-referenced and attempt to provide summative as well as formative data. The Reading Standard Assessment Task requires the child to read a book (from a choice of modern children's books) to the teacher who makes an informal observational assessment of the child's fluency amongst other skills. This aspect makes the Task a more valid assessment of reading than traditional standardised tests in that the task the child is required to do matches more closely actual reading activity. However this factor limits the reliability of the assessment because given the choice of books it cannot be assumed that the task is comparable or of comparable difficulty for all the children, and given the reliance on judgemental factors in the assessment teachers may not be assessing children at the same level in the same way. Thus the Task in reading gives an assessment which is more valid but less reliable. In addition there is the problem of the 10 point scale covering achievement across the entire school age range . In effect assessments of pupils' reading attainment have been reduced to a four point scale. With such a crude scale, adequate precision, reliability and validity are not achievable. It is a fact that a restriction in the range of test scores reduces the reliability of the test. The SATs, it would appear, are useful for formative purposes but do not provide detailed data on standards over time and cannot contribute to year-on-year comparison (especially as they have been changed each year since their introduction).

The PRT on the other hand is a standardised test which is easy to administer and is therefore cost effective in terms of the teachers' time. Provided one does not want detailed information for individual diagnostic purposes the test serves well its purpose of giving an overall measure of the child's reading ability.

The fact that the PRT and SATs measure a child's reading in different ways is not a cause for concern; it is important to have several instruments available and to use the one that is most appropriate for a specified purpose. However what does give cause for concern is when these instruments move in opposite directions as they did in our sample.

The headteachers we interviewed were strongly in favour of the National Curriculum but were concerned at the speed at which it had been introduced, the constant changes in the assessment and some of the content. They were asked how they thought the content of the National Curriculum would affect reading standards and Headteachers thought that these would inevitably drop because of the pressure on time engendered by the new subject areas they had to cover. Our data shows that these fears have not been realised and this must reflect great credit on the teachers who have managed to maintain reading standards despite all the other pressures on their time.

References

Black, P. (1993) 'Pressing Priorities' *Times Educational Supplement* (23.4.93)

Campbell R.J. and Neill S.R.St.J. (1994) *Curriculum Reform at Key Stage 1: Teacher Commitment and Policy Failure* Harlow: Longmans

Chambers (1980) *Twentieth Century Dictionary* Revised Edition, Edinburgh: Clarke Constable

Davies, J. and Brember, I. (1994) 'The First Mathematics Standard Assessment Tasks at Key Stage 1: Issues raised by a five school study' *British Educational Research Journal* 20, 1, 35-40

Department of Education and Science (1990a) *The Teaching and Learning of Reading in Primary Schools* A Report by HMI London: Her Majesty's Stationery Office

Department of Education and Science (1990b) *An Enquiry into LEA Evidence on Standards of Reading of Seven Year Old Children: A Report by the National Foundation for Educational Research,* London: Her Majesty's Stationery Office

Department of Education and Science (1991a) *The Teaching and Learning of Reading in Primary Schools 1991* London: Her Majesty's Stationery Office

Department of Education and Science (1991b) *The Parents' Charter: You and Your Child's Education* London: Her Majesty's Stationery Office

Department of Education and Science (1991c) *Testing of 7 Year Olds in 1991: Results of the National Curriculum Assessment in England* London: Her Majesty's Stationery Office

Department for Education (1992) *Testing of 7 Year Olds in 1992: Results of the National Curriculum Assessment in England* London: Her Majesty's Stationery Office

France, N. (1981) *The Primary Reading Test* Windsor: NFER-Nelson

James, M. and Conner, C. (1993) 'Are reliability and validity achievable in National Curriculum assessment? Some observations on moderation at Key Stage 1 in 1992' *The Curriculum Journal* 4, 1, 5-19

Lake, M. (1992) 'Social Background and Academic Performance: Evidence from Buckinghamshire' in Pumfrey P.D. (ed) *Reading Standards: Issues and Evidence* Leicester: The British Psychological Society

Kirkham, S. (1993) 'Outlook variable' *Times Educational Supplement* (19.3.93)

Patten, J. (1993) 'School tests are here to stay' *The Observer* (18.4.93)

Pollard, A., Broadfoot, P., Croll, P., Osborn, M. and Abbot, D. (1994) *Changing English Primary Schools* London: Cassell

Pumfrey, P.D. and Elliott, C.D. (1991) 'National Reading Standards and Standard Assessment Tasks: An educational house of cards'. *Educational Psychology in Practice* 7, 2, 74-80

Pumfrey, P.D. (1992) 'Conclusion: Après Le Déluge' in Pumfrey P.D. (ed) *Reading Standards: Issues and Evidence* Leicester: The British Psychological Society

Pumfrey, P.D., Elliott, C.D. and Tyler, S. (1992) 'Objective Testing: Insights or Illusions?' in Pumfrey, P.D. (ed.) *Reading Standards: Issues and Evidence* Leicester: The British Psychological Society

School Examinations and Assessment Council (1991a) *SATs for 7 Year Olds in 1992: Information* London: School Examinations and Assessment Council

School Examinations and Assessment Council (1991b) *School Assessment Folder: Key Stage 1* London: School Examinations and Assessment Council

School Examinations and Assessment Council (1991c) *Handbook of Guidance for the SAT: Key Stage 1* London: Her Majesty's Stationery Office

School Examinations and Assessment Council (1991d) *Teacher's Book: Key Stage 1* London: Her Majesty's Stationery Office

School Examinations and Assessment Council (1991e) *Assessment Record Booklet: Key Stage 1* London: Her Majesty's Stationery Office

School Examinations and Assessment Council (1992a) *Teacher's Book: Key Stage 1* London: Her Majesty's Stationery Office

School Examinations and Assessment Council (1992b) *Assessment Record Booklet: Key Stage 1* London: Her Majesty's Stationery Office

School Examinations and Assessment Council (1992c) *National Curriculum Assessment: Core subjects Standard Assessment Tasks for 1992 Reference Notes*, Windsor: NFER-Nelson

Shorrocks, D., Daniels, S., Frobisher, L., Nelson, N., Waterson, A. and Bell, J. (1992) *Testing and Assessing 6 and 7 year olds. The Evaluation of the 1992 Key Stage 1 National Curriculum Assessment: Final Report* London: National Union of Teachers

Turner, M. (1990) *Sponsored Reading Failure* Walsingham: IPSET

Turner, M. (1992) 'Organised Inferiority? Reading and the National Curriculum', *British Psychological Society Education Section Review* 16, 1, 1-8

Chapter 10

Profiling pupil achievement in language and literacy: current issues and trends

Gerry Sheil and Patrick Forde
St. Patrick's College, Dublin, Ireland

Introduction

Pupil profiling is an approach to assessing and recording achievement that is primarily based on teachers' judgements about pupil performance in a variety of instructional and assessment contexts. In this paper, the main characteristics of pupil profiling systems in language and literacy are enumerated, and five dimensions along which pupil profiling systems may be evaluated are put forward. Then two profiling systems — the *KEEP Early Literacy Assessment System* (Paris, Calfee, Filby, Hiebert, Pearson, Valencia, Wolf and Hansen, 1992) which was developed in the United States, and the *Victoria Reading Profile* (Victoria Department of School Education, 1991) which was developed in Australia — are examined with reference to the five dimensions. Following this, there is a discussion on National Curriculum Assessment in England and Wales as a pupil profiling system. The paper concludes with a look at future directions in the development of profiling systems in language and literacy.

What are Language and Literacy Profiles?

Educators have profiled students' achievement in language and literacy for many years. Traditional profiles such as the *Neale Analysis of Reading Ability* (Neale, 1989) provide valuable information about the strengths and weaknesses of individuals who may be experiencing reading difficulties. Now, as the use of performance-based assessment procedures becomes more widespread, pupil profiling systems which address such dimensions of language and literacy as oral language, reading strategies, visual language, writing and attitude have been developed, and are used to assess pupils of all ability levels. Indeed, such systems are appearing at national, state and local levels in most English-speaking countries.

The basic elements of a profiling system are its indicators, its levels (or bands), and its assessment tasks and contexts. Indicators are statements which describe pupil achievement and are generally linked to the objectives of a curriculum. An example of an indicator of reading comprehension is 'describes what has happened in a story and predicts what may happen next' (Schools Examination and Assessment Council, 1993). Such indicators are generally difficult to interpret when they stand alone. When grouped with other indicators that describe related behaviours and attitudes, they become more meaningful. Groups of related indicators are referred to as levels, which are associated with discrete points of development, or bands, which suggest continuity and development. In most profiling systems, pupil achievement is rated holistically across the indicators within a level or band. Raters may be guided by the results of assessment tasks linked to the profiling system, by pupils' portfolios of their work, and/or by documented evidence of pupils' achievements during instruction.

Evaluating Profiling Systems

Profiling systems in language and literacy may be evaluated along several dimensions. In this section, five such dimensions are considered: function, structure, curriculum relatedness, technical adequacy and manageability.

Function

The function(s) of a profiling system may be classified with reference to the type of assessment information it is primarily designed to provide. The scheme outlined in the *Report of the Task Group on Assessment and Testing* (TGAT) (Department of Education and Science, 1988), which iterates that assessment information may be formative, diagnostic, summative and/or evaluative, is useful for describing a system's functions. It is often claimed that a particular profiling system (and its related assessment measures) meets the needs of all relevant stakeholders, including politicians, policy makers, teachers and parents. However, problems of interpretation and status may arise if a system designed to provide formative information is used to generate summative/evaluative information, or if summative/evaluative information is used for formative purposes (Gipps and Stobart, 1993).

Structure

The structure of a profiling system can be determined by examining the range of areas covered by the system and the depth and complexity of the assessments and allied reporting schemes within and across each area. Some profiling systems are comprehensive to the extent that they cover many aspects of language and literacy and their interrelatedness. Other systems may focus on a specific aspect of literacy, but in considerable depth.

An important aspect of a profile's structure is its cumulativeness. Cumulative profiling systems typically span several grades. Each profile level consists of different (though connected) sets of indicators describing progressively more complex literacy behaviours and attitudes. In continuous cumulative systems such as the *Victoria English Profiles,* the levels represent progressions or stages through which pupils pass (see Griffin, 1993), while, in non-continuous cumulative systems such as National Curriculum Assessment in England and Wales, they represent anchor points or benchmarks. In non-cumulative profiling systems such as the *KEEP Early Literacy Assessment System,* pupils are assessed on a series of indicators at a specific point in time. Inferences can be made about achievement but not progress.

Curriculum Relatedness

An important benefit of profiling systems over other assessment systems is that they are criterion-referenced (Griffin and Nix, 1991), and hence, are related to a particular curriculum. Profiling systems whose indicators clearly reflect the content and processes underlying a language and literacy curriculum, and which are informed by performance-based classroom-level assessments, are often evaluated more positively in terms of curriculum relatedness than systems which are underpinned by externally-developed indicators and/or tasks. A useful insight into a system's curriculum relatedness is the manner in which it was developed. Top-down profiling systems which are developed by experts with only token levels of consultation are generally perceived as being less relevant and less useful than systems characterised by high levels of teacher involvement at relevant stages in their development (Griffin and Nix, 1993).

Technical Adequacy

Among the factors to consider in evaluating the technical adequacy of pupil profiling systems and the performance-based assessments that typically underlie them are reliability and validity. According to Haertel (1992),

> 'the same issues of reliability and validity arise for the interpretation of performance assessments as for other kinds of assessments. However, the relative emphasis on different aspects of reliability and validity may differ, and evidence of reliability and validity may take somewhat different forms.' (p.986)

Profiling systems linked to classroom-level performance-based assessment are reliable and valid to the extent that multiple sources of evidence converge to support particular conclusions (Calfee and Hiebert, 1991). Therefore, such systems are appropriate for generating formative assessment information. Where profiling systems incorporating large-scale performance-based assessments are concerned, traditional indices of reliability may be subsumed by considerations of transfer and generalizability (Linn, Baker and Dunbar, 1991). Using generalizability theory (Cronbach, Gleser, Nanda and Rajaratnam, 1972), the variance or error due to raters and to the sampling of assessment tasks can be estimated, and these estimates can be used to establish an estimate of reliability.

Evidence for the validity of large-scale performance-based assessments should encompass curriculum relatedness, but should also include a consideration of such issues as the quality and comprehensiveness of the content covered, the fairness of assessments, the meaningfulness of the tasks for teachers and pupils, and the intended and unintended consequences of the assessments (Linn et al., 1991).

Manageability

The manageability of a profiling system appears to be critical to its success. The preparation and administration of assessment tasks, the documentation of performance, the development and evaluation of portfolios, moderation procedures, and the communication of results to parents and others all take time and effort. When demands on teachers are excessive, either due to the sheer volume of assessment and recording, or to a lack of adequate training and support, a profiling system which might otherwise be expected to have a positive influence on instruction and learning may be regarded as unmanageable.

From Theory to Practice: Two Case Studies

In this section, two recently developed profiling systems are discussed in terms of the five dimensions set out above. These systems were selected for review because they focus on the assessment of language and literacy, and because they represent contrasting approaches to pupil profiling.

The *KEEP Literacy Assessment System*

The *KEEP Literacy Assessment System* (Paris et al., 1992) was developed by a team of researchers to evaluate literacy achievement in the *Kamehameha Elementary Education Programme (KEEP),* a special 'whole literacy' programme for native Hawaiian pupils in grades K (kindergarten) to 3.

The primary function of the *KEEP System* is to gather summative data in order to evaluate programme effectiveness. However, the system appears to be adaptable to a range of different settings and purposes, and might be useful for generating formative information. Indeed, its authors suggest that users might

> 'record pupils' achievements with narrative comments rather than numerical scores, noting particular talent or weakness.' (p.97)

The *KEEP System* covers seven aspects of literacy including reading comprehension, strategy knowledge, motivation and attitude, and social participation in literacy. For each aspect, two attributes are rated. The attributes pertaining to reading comprehension are 'reading is constructive' and 'reading is evaluative'. Each attribute is accompanied by several performance indicators that define high and low engagement on the attribute. The evaluator's task is assemble a portfolio of a pupil's work in language and literacy (i.e. reading logs, journal entries, essays, etc.), to interview the pupil regarding the content of the portfolio, and to rate the pupil holistically on each attribute using a four-point scale, where 4 represents high engagement and 1 low engagement. Pupils' total scores across the 14 attributes range from 14 to 56 points. Although *KEEP*'s authors claim that the system can be used to evaluate both 'whole literacy' and 'skills-based' programmes, the indicators and attributes appear to reflect a 'whole literacy' perspective.

KEEP evaluates and records achievement in English reading and writing in considerable depth. However, the system is neither cumulative nor continuous. Instead, pupil performance is rated at a particular point in time. This may be sufficient for programme evaluation, but does not provide data on progress or development.

The assessment framework underpinning *KEEP* was developed in a top-down manner (see Au, 1994). While there was much discussion among the team of literacy experts who developed *KEEP* in order to reach agreement on the different elements (Paris et al., 1992), the non-participation of practising teachers in the project is unfortunate in that an opportunity to establish a stronger curriculum relatedness may have been lost.

The authors of *KEEP* admit that they are unable to provide numerical indices of validity and reliability for the system, but argue that performance-based assessments should not be examined against traditional psychometric standards. Reference is made to such aspects of validity as the fairness of tasks and the consequences of assessment, and it is claimed that acceptable standards have been reached in relation to these aspects of validity, but no specific evidence is provided. Hence, the practice of aggregating profile results across classes and schools must be questioned.

Administration of *KEEP* is manageable to the extent that it is carried out by external evaluators who conduct extensive interviews with pupils in order to arrive at their ratings. It might be useful to examine whether teachers could be trained to conduct the interviews, apply the rating scale, and generate the data required for an external evaluation.

As it stands, *KEEP* raises as many questions as it answers. The failure to address reliability in a systematic manner is a major problem. Nevertheless, the assessment framework is a comprehensive description of reading and writing behaviour that is worth referring to in the development of any new system, and the use of pupil portfolios as a basis of assessment is an important emerging trend.

The *Victoria Reading Profile*

In the late 1980s, the Victoria (Australia) State Department of Education developed pupil profiles in English and in mathematics. The *Victoria English Profiles* provide a system of assessment and recording based on the teachers' holistic judgements of their students in three areas: spoken language, reading and writing. In this section, the *Reading Profile* is discussed in detail. The *Spoken Language Profile* and the *Writing Profile* were developed and are used in the same way as the *Reading Profile* (Roe, 1992).

The function of the *Reading Profile* is somewhat ambiguous. The *Profile* is primarily designed to provide teachers with formative information that can be shared with parents and with pupils themselves (Griffin and Nix, 1991). However, the *Reading Profile* has also been used in state-level evaluations of literacy achievement and appears suited to that purpose (see Victoria Department of School Education, 1993).

The *Reading Profile* consists of a sequential series of 9 bands ranging from Band A, which describes behaviours and attitudes associated with emergent literacy, to Band I, which consists of indicators of advanced (high-school) reading skills. The *Profile* is cumulative in that the bands represent a continuum of achievement in reading, and continuous in that they represent stages through which pupils pass rather than benchmarks or standards. Pupils are rated according to whether the indicators within each band have been developed (3 points), are developing (2 points), are emerging (1 point), or have not yet appeared (0 points). While various assessment contexts, including standardised tests, are suggested in the materials accompanying the *Reading Profile,* no specific guidelines are given on linking test results to teachers' ratings, although it would be possible to establish such links.

An important feature of the development of the *Reading Profile* was the manner in which indicators were distributed across bands. The application of an item response theory (IRT) partial credit scoring model (see Masters, 1988) enabled the *Profile* developers to map a large number of indicators onto an underlying scale of achievement. Adjacent indicators were subsequently grouped into bands. Indicators which did not possess the mathematical properties of the IRT partial-credit scoring model were not included in the bands.

Griffin (1990; 1993) has described the *Reading Profile* as criterion-referenced because teachers rate pupils' achievement according to developmental indicators rather than expected grade- or age-level performance. The term 'instructional level' is used to describe the band or bands at which a pupil is developing specified behaviours and attitudes. While this suggests that the bands provide general directions for subsequent instruction (see Griffin, 1990), it should be noted that any set of indicators is only a sample of the total possible pool of indicators. Hence, instruction related only to those indicators specified in the *Profile* would be inadequate.

Considerable care appears to have been taken to ensure the active participation of teachers at all stages in the development of the *English Profiles* (see Griffin, 1990), including the development of indicators and the selection of assessment contexts. The involvement of teachers in the development process may explain why both standardised tests and performance-based assessments are included among the assessment contexts.

Evidence for the reliability and validity of the *Reading Profile* is along traditional lines. Data from the *Victorian 100 Schools Study* (Griffin and Rowe, 1988), in which the *Profile* was completed for over 5,000 pupils, provides evidence of internal consistency and test-retest reliability. The concurrent validity of the *Profile* was established by correlating ratings on the *Profile* with pupils' overall scores on a standardised test. The expanded view of validity put forward by Linn et al. (1991) and others does not appear to have been considered.

The *Reading Profile* appears to be easy to use. This conclusion does not, however, address the issue of how useful administrators, principals, teachers or parents find the information yielded by the *Profile*. Some research on how teachers use the *Profile* and the effects of the *Profile* on schools and on teachers would be helpful in addressing the issue of manageability and in generating additional evidence of validity.

The *Reading Profile* appears to be a useful tool for documenting pupil achievement. From a technical perspective, it provides a bridge between traditional standardised tests, on the one hand, and profiling systems based exclusively on performance-based measures, on the other hand.

National Curriculum Assessment as a Pupil Profiling System

The evolving system of National Curriculum Assessment in England and Wales yields two profiles of pupil achievement at the end of each Key Stage — one based on the administration of standard tasks to pupils in the core subjects, the other based on teachers' judgements of pupils' ongoing work across all aspects of the curriculum. In this section, strengths and shortcomings of National Curriculum Assessment as a pupil profiling system in language and literacy are examined with reference to the five dimensions discussed above.

It is unfortunate that standard tasks and teacher assessments have emerged as competing approaches to pupil assessment when the two could coexist as complementary approaches, each informing the other, as is the case with formal and informal assessments in the *Victoria English Profiles*. The higher status accorded to standard tasks by researchers, the media and the general public may be explained by their summative/evaluative function. In contrast, teacher assessments, which primarily generate formative information, are not perceived as being useful outside the context of the classroom. One outcome of this situation is that the systematic assessment of speaking and listening, which is a relatively new focus of classroom-based assessment, has not received the attention it deserves.

The current structure of National Curriculum Assessment in English can be criticised on the grounds that the number of attainment targets and statements of attainment may contribute to a fragmentation of the curriculum, and that educators and policy makers may focus only on those discrete elements of the curriculum that are assessed in the standard tasks. Perhaps recent proposals to reduce the number of attainment targets and to replace statements of attainment with level descriptions (School Curriculum and Assessment Authority, 1994) will, if implemented, lead to a more integrated assessment system that is easier to use and provides more relevant information on pupil achievement. However, level descriptions cannot, in and of themselves, ensure improved assessments. The assessment tasks themselves should be carefully looked at, and some consideration should be given combining performance on standard tasks with teacher judgements in arriving at indices of pupil achievement — a practice that is widespread elsewhere.

National Curriculum Assessment appears to be criterion-referenced in that there is a direct link between the content of the curriculum and the content of the assessments. However, many of the statements of attainment are imprecise in terms of how outcomes are specified and are open to varied interpretations (see William, 1993). Furthermore, the criteria for success or failure on standard tasks such as oral reading appear to reflect a norm-referenced perspective on assessment. The specification of the precise number of oral reading errors that a pupil may make on a passage (e.g. School Examinations and Assessment Council, 1993) may be seen as an attempt to set a standard or to ensure that there is an appropriate distribution of pupils across performance levels. Its relation to the evaluation of language processes is less clear.

Much has been written about the validity and reliability of National Curriculum Assessment. The following points, which are particularly relevant for assessment of language and literacy, have been made:

1. There is a lack of standardisation in the administration of SATs and in making judgements about students' performances (Madaus and Kellaghan, 1993; James and Conner, 1993).

2. Different statements of attainment have been interpreted in different ways by different teachers (Shorrrocks, Daniels, Frobisher, Nelson, Waterson and Bell, 1991; James and Conner, 1993).
3. Moderators in English are inconsistent in terms of the advice they offer, and the documentation provided to moderators is often insufficient to allow them to appraise the validity of assessments (James and Conner, 1993).
4. There are significant reservations among teachers about the validity of standard assessment process (Shorrocks, Daniels, Stainton, and Ring, 1993) and many teachers believe that the outcomes of teacher assessment are fairer reflections of student ability than scores on standard tasks (Shorrocks et al., 1993).
5. Levels within the National Curriculum may not be cumulative or scaled (Wiliam, 1993) so a student might achieve a Level 3 in English but fail to achieve a Level 2. Moreover, a Level 2 at Key Stage 2 may be different from a Level 2 at Key Stage 1 (Pollitt, 1994).

Taken together, these problems strongly undermine the fairness and quality of National Curriculum Assessment. Further, comparisons across different attainment targets in English are generally untenable since the scales for the different attainment targets are not linked conceptually (for example, in terms of interactions between reading and writing) or statistically, raising questions about National Curriculum Assessment as a pupil profiling system.

On the credit side, however, some improvement in consistency between standard task scores and teacher assessments for specific Statements of Attainment in English has been found (Shorrocks and Nelson, 1994). Furthermore, researchers have begun to look at different approaches to establishing reliability for the different purposes associated with National Curriculum Assessment (see Hutchison and Schagen, 1994). For example, it has been suggested that an index of dependability, defined as the percentage of students who are assigned the 'correct level' at a particular Key Stage for a given year, might be an appropriate index of reliability for the summative aspects of National Curriculum Assessment (Wiliam, 1993).

While numerous reports attest to the unmanageability of National Curriculum Assessment (e.g. Shorrocks et al., 1991; Madaus and Kellaghan, 1993), some improvement can be expected as a result of the current curriculum changes. However, there is, as yet, no comprehensive evidence that the investment of considerable time and energy in administering and scoring assessments, in maintaining extensive records of pupil achievement for auditing purposes, or in reporting results to relevant parties has had positive effects on teaching or on pupil learning.

Conclusions

In the past decade, there have been many changes in the ways in which pupils are assessed, and in how achievement is reported. Some of these have been brought about because of dissatisfaction with traditional assessment paradigms. Others are the result of concerns about the quality of instruction and standards of performance. Profiling systems in language and literacy appear to be particularly appropriate for documenting the achievement of pupils in classrooms or systems where newer instructional approaches are being implemented. However, the development of profiling systems and their related assessments is an ongoing process. Most of the projects described in a recent book on authentic assessment (Valencia, Hiebert and Afflerbach, 1994) were incomplete at the time of going to press. The current re-evaluation of National Curriculum Assessment in England and Wales is further evidence of unfinished work.

In this paper, some serious threats to pupil profiling and the performance-based assessments that underlie them have been identified. These include problems with function, structure, curriculum relatedness, technical adequacy and manageability. Quite clearly, all of these must be considered in the development of new systems or in the improvement of existing systems. However, the issues of reliability and manageability must be given the closest attention if pupil profiling is to have a viable future. The reliability of teachers' evaluations and ratings can be enhanced by providing adequate inservice education, by providing effective moderation, and by effectively developing assessment tasks in the first instance. Manageability must take into account the realities of classroom environment and the resources available for assessment.

As in other English-speaking countries, proposals for a pupil profiling system for Irish schools have been put forward (Irish National Council for Curriculum and Assessment, 1993), and these include the development of language and literacy profiles. Although it is not anticipated that the new system will generate data for evaluative purposes, the development of the system and its effects on schools, teachers, and pupils should be of considerable interest, and will, it is hoped, contribute to the broader development of more effective assessment systems.

References

Au, K. (1994) 'Portfolio assessment: Experiences at the Kamehamea Elementary Education Program' in S.W. Valencia, E.H. Hiebert, and P.P. Afflerbach (eds) *Authentic Reading Assessment* Newark, DE: International Reading Association

Blackburne, L. (1994) 'English: All present, but not quite so correct' *Times Educational Supplement* May 13

Calfee, R. and Hiebert, E. (1991) 'Classroom assessment of reading' in R. Barr, M.L. Kamil, P. Mosenthal and P.D. Pearson (eds) *Handbook of Research on Reading* (Vol. 2 81-309) New York: Longman

Cronbach, L.J., Gleser, G.C., Nanda, H., and Rajaratnam, N. (1972) *The Dependability of Behavioural Measurements* New York: Wiley

Dearing, R. (1994) *The National Curriculum and its Assessment: Final Report* London: School Curriculum and Assessment Authority

Department of Education and Science (1988) *Report of the Task Group on Assessment and Testing* London: Her Majesty's Stationery Office

Gipps, C. and Stobart, G. (1993) *Assessment: A teacher's guide to the issues* (2nd edition) London: Hodder and Stoughton

Griffin, P.E. (1990) *Developing Literacy Profiles* Paper presented at the Thirty-fifth Annual Convention of the International Reading Association, Atlanta, GA.

Griffin, P.E. (1993) *Profiles: Issues, assumptions and standards* Paper presented to the Faculty of Education Conference, University of Southern Queensland, Toowoomba, 7-8 June

Griffin, P.E. and Nix, P. (1991) *Educational Assessment and Reporting: A new approach* Sydney: Harcourt Brace Jovanovich

Griffin, P. and Rowe, K. (1988) *The Victoria 100 Schools Study* Melbourne: Ministry of Education, Victoria Australia

Haertel, E. (1992) 'Performance measurement' in M. Alkin (ed) *Encyclopedia of Educational Research* (6th edition) New York: Macmillan

Hutchison, D. and Schagen, I. (1994) (eds) *How Reliable is National Curriculum Assessment?* Slough: NFER.

Irish National Council for Curriculum and Assessment (1993) *A Programme for Reform: Curriculum and assessment policy towards the new century* Dublin: Government Publications

James, M. and Conner, C. (1993) 'Are reliability and validity achievable in national curriculum assessment? Some observations on moderation at Key Stage 1 in 1992' *The Curriculum Journal* 4, 5-19

Linn, R. L., Baker, E.L. and Dunbar, S.B. (1991) 'Complex performance-based assessment: Expectations and validation criteria' *Educational Researcher* 20, 15-21

Madaus, G. and Kellaghan, T. (1993) 'The British experience with authentic testing' *Phi Delta Kappan* 74, 458-469

Masters, G.N. (1988) 'The analysis of partial-credit scoring' *Applied Measurement in Education* 1, 279-297

Neale, M. (1989) *Neale Analysis of Reading Ability - Revised British Edition* Windsor: NFER-Nelson

Paris, S.G., Calfee, R.C., Filby, N., Hiebert, E.H., Pearson, P.D., Valencia, S.W., Wolf, K.P. and Hansen, J. (1992) 'A framework for authentic literacy assessment' *The Reading Teacher* 46 (2), 88-99

Rowe, K.J. (1992) *Subject profiles: What, how and why?* Paper prepared for the '150 Schools Project' Steering Committee: Victoria, Australia, Department of School Education,

School Curriculum and Assessment Authority (1994) *English in the National Curriculum: Draft proposals* London: School Curriculum and Assessment Authority

Schools Examinations and Assessment Council (1993) *Assessment Handbook: English (Key Stage 1)* London: School Examinations and Assessment Council

Shorrocks, D. and Nelson, N. (1994) 'The reliability of national curriculum assessment at Key Stages 1 and 2' in D. Hutchison and I. Schagen (eds) *How Reliable is National Curriculum Assessment?* Slough: NFER

Shorrocks, D., Daniels, S., Frobisher, L., Nelson, N., Waterson, A. and Bell, J. (1991) *The Evaluation of National Curriculum Assessment at Key Stage 1 1990/1991* (ENCA 1 Project) London: School Examinations and Assessment Council

Shorrocks, D., Daniels, Stainton, R. and Ring, K. (1993) *Assessing Six- and Seven-year-year-olds at Key Stage 1: A report on the 1992 Key Stage 1 assessment* Leeds: National Union of Teachers

Pollitt, A. (1994) 'Measuring and evaluating reliability in national curriculum assessment' in D. Hutchison and I. Schagen (eds) *How Reliable is National Curriculum Assessment?* Slough: NFER

Valencia, S.W., Hiebert, E.H. and Afflerbach, P.P. (eds) (1994) *Authentic Assessment: Practices and possibilities* Newark, DE: International Reading Association

Victoria Department of School Education (1991) *English Profiles Handbook: Assessing and reporting students' progress in English* Victoria, Australia: Department of School Education

Victoria Department of School Education (1993) *Victorian Student Achievement Studies - 1992 Report.* Victoria, Australia: Department of School Education

Wiliam, D. (1993) 'Validity, dependability and reliability in national curriculum assessment' *The Curriculum Journal* 4, 3, 335-350

Chapter 11

Assessing reading in secondary schools: a Romanian perspective

Roxana Mihail
Institute of Educational Sciences, Bucharest, Romania

Introduction

In 1992/93, I developed a set of tests of Romanian language and literature for upper secondary schools in Romania. In 1994, on a study visit to the United Kingdom, I learnt about the tests of English used at age 14 in England and Wales in 1993, and about the feasibility study on monitoring reading standards in Northern Ireland carried out, also in 1993, by the Department for Education in Northern Ireland — the latter project included pupils aged 14 and 16. This paper deals with all three projects, describing the approaches and technical findings and concentrating on:

— the purposes for which reading is assessed nationally
— degrees of central control.

Devising literature tests in Romania: between the system and the process

At first sight it may seem a very banal metaphor to say that an educational system is like a beehive. But when you think that sometimes in the past the Romanian educational system was merely like 'an instruction machine', the metaphor seems to become an emblem for the ideal result of a 'Reform through Resubstantiation' (Mihail, in press), as we call it: from a mechanical to a 'living' image.

First let me give an outline of the Romanian educational system (see Romanian Institute of Educational Sciences, 1993). In Romania at present, children enter school at 6. Primary school lasts to age 10, and then comprehensive Lower Secondary Schools take pupils up to 14. Upper Secondary School begins at the age of 14 with an entrance examination; about 70 per cent of pupils go on to a Lyceum, and the rest to Vocational Schools or Complementary Schools. The Upper Secondary phase ends at the age of 18 with a Certificate of Secondary Education — which can be a Baccalaureate Diploma at the end of the Lyceum or other forms of certificate at the end of Vocational Schools and Complementary Schools. In all these schools Romanian Language and Literature is a compulsory subject, and the courses must follow the National Syllabuses. Until now, students had to follow the same text-book, without alternative. The idea of conceiving reading as a cross-curricular strategy for teaching and learning is still only a beautiful ideal of the linguistic research community, but it is strongly promoted by the Romanian Reading Association (RORA).

The political upheaval of late 1989 allowed some facts to emerge. In particular, it highlighted a deep gap between our examination system and our evaluation system. To give a typical example: we now find students who reach the Baccalaureate examination unable to handle properly the most basic tasks in reading or writing for a social purpose, who are, that is, functionally illiterate.

As researchers working in the Evaluation Department of the Institute of Educational Sciences (which is a public-sector institution wholly financed by the Ministry of Education, but has a degree of autonomy and is entitled to provide the results of its work to the decision-makers in the Ministry), we think that the situation just described persists because of the rigid existing system. In order to change it, we hope that our work will have at least two 'shock effects':

— at the level of Educational Theory, we intend to produce the scientific grounds to speed up the establishment of a reliable model of student assessment;

— at the level of Educational Practice, we intend to create the reference points of an alternative assessment system which is able to change the educational system from the inside.

Developing assessment instruments for Romanian literature

At the beginning of 1992 the need to have a national system of Standard Tests was accepted, in at least at the main subjects: Romanian literature, mathematics, physics, chemistry, biology, maybe foreign languages. But because of lack of funds, the establishment of such a system was postponed until the World Bank Project for Educational Reform funds the 'basic needs' of a National Assessment Unit or equivalent institution. Meanwhile, the main task for the few researchers working on process evaluation was to create a methodology of summative and formative evaluation.

In our Lyceum schools, the curriculum in Romanian is literature-centred. More than that, literature is seen chronologically, as the history of literature, and has as its main aim the maintaining of the cultural heritage. Theoretically, according to the general objectives of the curriculum, Romanian literature is to be used as a means of training the students in critical thinking, by instilling in them the habits of personal, individual criticism. But in practice, there are a lot of teachers who fail dreadfully in moulding skilful, critical readers. And this happens because our students learn *about* literature, not to respond to it, and not through reading as a global strategy (Mihail, 1993:5).

In 1992 our project had three complementary components relevant to literature assessment at the ages of 14 and 18:

1. devising and processing achievement tests;
2. devising a set of assessment instruments for a school year, in the form of Item and Test Banks;

3. collecting data on the individual and socio-economic characteristics of pupils.

The project was conceived as an action-research project and for the linked parts 2 and 3 we used the same sample of students (about 600) only from Bucharest, in our pilot-schools. Our main concern was to improve the objectivity of classroom assessment. It was not our intention at this stage to provide our teachers with absolutely valid, reliable standardised tests, but to show them some models of assessment in order to convince them that, sometimes, the current forms of classroom reading and writing assessment can be dangerously subjective. In doing this, we intended to provoke a rationally grounded debate on the topic of reading assessment. In the tests (two for 14-year-olds and two for 18-year-olds) we used multiple-choice items, short-answer items and some essay questions. Of these, only essay questions are commonly used in our secondary schools because the common 'philosophy' of our literature teachers is that students can demonstrate their knowledge and skills only by 'constructing an essay' which, as we know, is very hard to assess fairly.

There were a lot of interesting findings from our 1992 project, of which I have selected three:

1. A very high correlation was obtained between test scores and one measure of leisure time activity: students who mentioned reading as their favourite leisure time 'occupation' also obtained high scores in the Romanian Literature test.
2. Since the tests were conceived in a different way from the usual assessments, there were only moderate correlations between the test averages and the end-of-term and end-of-year students' averages (which are the 'active' forms of classroom assessment).
3. Similarly, only moderate correlations were found between the test results on the one hand, and the Lyceum's student profiles and students' future plans after the Baccalaureate exam on the other. For example, in our test one student obtained an average of 80 points (from 100 possible — which was a good result), but in the classroom assessment he was placed much higher (his end-of-term average was 10 — which is maximum), and his plans after the Baccalaureate examination were to go to the Faculty of Letters. After the test, he said to his teacher that he would prefer

to have this kind of test every week, rather than seem to be brilliant and nevertheless fail his faculty examination because of that.

Such findings and comments might seem very general and maybe unsound, but underlying them are the current problems of our educational reform movement: What should change and when? What is the proper balance between tradition and innovation? What can we do to move the usual way of thinking along faster? With what funds? And so many others...

In 1993 the pilot project continued. The intended hypothesis of this phase of the research was that if Romanian schools mould their students to make complex reactions through 'reading all kinds of signs', then as skilful readers they should:

a) efficiently process *different* kinds of content (knowledge and information) in different kinds of texts;
b) individually respond to any 'assessment incentive', in order to prove not only their mastery of reading strategies, but also their personal critical attitude towards the text.

(For more details about the 'Theory of Generalised Reading', see Mihail, 1993. The principal assumption of this theory is that the interpretive reading of the 'Environment', the 'Milieu' and the 'Surrounding' has to be the main aim of a cross-curricular education.)

This phase of the research had two main aims:

1. To create some Item Banks, make them available to teachers in the pilot schools to use, and so to improve them;
2. To apply a few tests using items from these banks, not to validate them, but to pre-test them.

Within these aims, three tests were developed and trialled at ages 14 and 18 (see Examples 1-3):

1. A very 'content-oriented' literature-based test of reading and writing. The novel aspect of this test was the very precise working tasks (May 1993);

2. An initial, diagnostic test, non-literature-based, for students at the beginning of the Lyceum. This was totally new, because diagnostic tests are not very well known among our teachers (September 1993);
3. A multi-level end-of-term test of reading, literature-based and intended as preparation for the Baccalaureate examination. The 'novelty' was the statement of the working task (December 1993).

Each of these tests was taken by about 400 students, drawn from Bucharest and two places in the provinces (one rural, one urban), but these were not nationally representative samples. Therefore we cannot generalise from the findings, but the fact that all the items in the tests were 'negotiated' with the teachers in the pilot schools, and that their opinions about the Item Bank were used for improving the instruments, entitle us to believe that, at least on a very small scale, one of our intended 'shock effects' — the creation of thought-provoking educational situations — had succeeded to a certain extent.

Among the other findings from this stage were the following:

1. The tasks in the tests covered the content of the National Syllabuses (in the first one, the literature test, they were deliberately too 'obedient'!), but we tried to change how classroom assessment was conceived and this surprised a lot of average students who declared that they were 'upset' by the tests.
2. Both students and teachers reacted positively to the idea of introducing tasks based on non-literary texts. This was seen as a means of liberating them from the overloaded syllabuses!
3. All three tests turned out to be 'tough', in the sense that they had lower mean scores than we usually consider desirable for assessment instruments in Romania. After discussions with the teachers, all of them agreed that 'the surprise' about the new form of the task meant that a lot of students (the average ones, mainly!) are not psychologically prepared to face tasks other than those they are used to, even when the content is the same.
4. We were not interested in proving the validity and reliability of the entire test as an instrument. But in the case of the diagnostic test the teachers found it truly useful, and we were surprised when

other teachers phoned us at the Institute and asked us to provide them with this test. Whether this is a good thing (considering the fact that at the moment we have no possibility of validating our instruments) or, on the contrary, a dangerous one, is still being debated.

5. Because our students' usual assignments are long essays and summaries, the very clearly-stated reading-writing tasks (in the third test) seemed to be very easy for them on first sight. But the big problem for them was to follow the instructions. (There were also very precise oral instructions.) More than 50 per cent of the average students gave 'unsuitable' answers — in terms of length and appropriateness to the task — and this was a surprise even for the students themselves.

6. As far as attitudes to reading are concerned, the principal finding (familiar in many other countries) was that, at the age of 14, girls read more than boys.

7. Although the teachers were not involved in marking the papers (they simply refused to do it, on the grounds that they had no time), when we discussed the marking scheme of the diagnostic test, for example, the objection was that it was too complex for them to apply it to all their students at the beginning of the 9th grade, although they had to admit that this way of conceiving diagnostic assessment was very efficient for them. The very unexpected conclusion of the discussions at this point was that external evaluation might be the solution to many assessment problems! ...

8. Even if there were no interference or pressure from the Ministry of Education or from the Local Inspectorates, we had to admit that the number of teachers eager to participate and truly interested in collaborating with us was disappointingly small (as a matter of fact, it was very hard to find them!). More than that, the 'negotiations' were based on the instruments we designed, although we made efforts to involve them directly in creating items or tests following the clearly-stated methodology. My personal perception has been that many teachers feel very proud of the general attitude to reading (mainly of literature), considering this

> to be 'a precious traditional feature of our education', which we have to keep at all costs. So it seems that the two intended 'shock effects' I mentioned at the beginning turned out to be too ambitious for research of the scale we were able to undertake.

All the data obtained from the three tests, together with the results of the discussions with the teachers and the responses to the questionnaires, were processed and the interpretations of the results were offered to the Ministry of Education. But, because between the research findings and their reaction there has been another gap, everything was shelved and no decisions were taken about further developments.

Therefore, in 1994, still aiming for the establishment of a National Assessment Unit able to provide standardised tests, we decided to design another alternative (informal) means to assess reading and writing, hoping that the impact on teachers' attitudes will be greater. So now the concept of Portfolio assessment is under discussion and the first reactions are encouraging.

In the meantime, we have learned that the first rule in a beehive is that, if you want to change the shape of the honeycomb, you have to change the bees' way of seeing the world!

National tests in English at age 14

As British readers of this paper will know, these tests were meant to occur in June 1993, to be taken by all Year 9 pupils in state secondary schools in England and Wales, and to deliver assessments of every pupil in the form of levels on the 10-level scale for reading and writing. There were three papers:

- Paper 1 was a test of factual reading and directed writing
- Paper 2 was a test of prior reading, based on literature, namely the anthology and either a Shakespeare play or a text from a set list
- Paper 3 was a test of extended writing.

Very little of this actually happened. Because of teacher opposition, only about two per cent of the 5000 secondary schools in the country both administered the tests and reported the results. Much of the teacher opposition arose from doubts about the quality of the tests, and a balanced summary of opinion about them might include the following:

— Some of the administrative arrangements (the tiers, some options within papers) were too complex;

— The tests provided adequate coverage of what the School Examinations and Assessment Council required;

— But they did not provide very broad coverage of the National Curriculum in English;

— The tests themselves were largely free from possible bias;

— But the anthology of literary extracts on which part of Paper 2 was based was not balanced;

— The tests of factual reading, which the pupils took unseen, were largely similar to familiar types of test paper;

— But substantial objections were raised against the other assessment of reading, namely the literature paper;

— A headteacher who put his pupils through both the middle and upper tiers of papers reported higher levels for them on the upper tier, which suggests that that tier was too easy, relative to the middle tier (Harding, 1993);

— Some teachers felt that questions which were options with each other were not of equal difficulty;

— The marking system was very complex;

— Some of the mark schemes seemed to some teachers to lack clarity;

— The assessment system as a whole, though operating within a framework designed to be criterion-referenced, was a compromise between criterion-referencing and norm-referencing.

This can be summed up by saying that there were problems with both the validity and the possible reliability of the tests. And from a Romanian perspective, the form of examination seemed to be of an eighteenth-century character in itself, and to be based on a curriculum which was more prescriptive than anything we had in Romania even in the 'bad old days'.

Monitoring reading standards in Northern Ireland

The 1993 study was by no means the first time monitoring had been carried out in Northern Ireland. The province took part, along with England and Wales, in the Assessment of Performance Unit (APU) surveys between 1979 and 1988 (Gorman *et al.*, 1988; 1991). This system of monitoring was, however, abandoned after 1988, and Northern Ireland decided to have province-wide tests based on its own version of a national curriculum. A start was made on the province-wide tests, but in 1992 the authorities there backed away from those tests, and became the first of the three areas previously involved in APU surveys to reintroduce monitoring.

The purpose of the tests carried out in Northern Ireland in 1993 was monitoring, that is, estimating the level of performance of pupils of particular ages overall; their purpose was not providing individual assessments. Also, the tests did not have to conform to any specified model of reading, or to any externally imposed list of texts. Therefore the tests had to be unseen, since they had to be feasible for pupils in many different schools who had not been taught about particular texts in advance. The six tests used in the surveys of 14- and 16-year-olds in 1993 had in fact all been used in APU surveys.

Comparisons and contrasts

In Table 1 I have attempted to draw together some of the major features of the tests I have been discussing, and to suggest some of the major parallels and differences that the analysis has revealed.

The features that all three sets of tests have in common are that they are for secondary students, that they address both literary and other forms of text, that they are not intended to yield cash value for students in the form of recognised certificates or qualifications, and that they do have at least a little learning value for students (beyond learning how to take tests). These features are admittedly obvious and ordinary, but they do suggest that the tests are sufficiently alike to make further comparisons between them legitimate.

Otherwise, the table reveals a set of features which tend to group the Romanian tests and the 1993 England and Wales Key Stage 3 tests

Table 1: Comparisons between tests in Romania and the United Kingdom

	Romania, 1992/93	England & Wales, 1993	N. Ireland, 1993
Ages of public exams	14, 18	16, 18	16, 18
Ages of tests	14, 18	14	14, 16
Degree of central control	high	high	arm's-length
Intended data	individual	individual, school, etc	group
Political purpose	changing system	raising standards	investigating standards
Educational purpose	summative, diagnostic	formative, summative, diagnostic, monitoring, etc	monitoring
Types of text	mainly literary, some factual	literary & factual	literary & factual
Backwash	intended to affect assessment practice	intended to affect and police curriculum	any backwash is incidental, but must not be harmful
Cash value to students	none	none	none
Learning benefit to student	a little	some	a little
Cost to students	very little - tests are short and cannot be taught to	teaching to tests takes time away from other teaching	very little - tests are short and cannot be taught to

together, and to set those two apart from the tests used in Northern Ireland in 1993:

— the N. Ireland tests were used to investigate standards and provide group data on them, were intended to have little backwash or other effect on the system, and attracted very little day-to-day involvement from the educational authorities;

— whereas in both Romania and England and Wales the tests were intended to yield individual data first (though data in England and Wales were also to be used for making group comparisons afterwards), were clearly and explicitly intended to affect the system and change it, and attracted a high degree of central involvement and control.

Finally, I venture to suggest that these groupings of features are far from coincidental. In Romania and in England and Wales, the tests were being used as the motor of change. It is therefore not at all surprising that the authorities kept a very close eye on them. But it is perhaps also not coincidental that both projects failed in their main purpose, in England and Wales because of massive teacher opposition, in Romania because the ambitious aims received insufficient resourcing from the government. Of the three initiatives discussed here, the only one that succeeded was that in Northern Ireland: this had the most clearly defined and specific purpose, perhaps also the closest match between aim and instrument, and definitely the lightest degree of central control. Perhaps the moral is not just that clear purposes are more likely to produce successful outcomes, but also that ambitious attempts to use assessment systems to change education systems run the risk of being stifled at birth if the authorities assume too much control.

Acknowledgments

I gratefully acknowledge financial support from the British Academy and the United Kingdom Reading Association which enabled me to attend the 1994 UKRA Conference and discuss this work further.

References

Gorman, T.P., White, J., Brooks, G., MacLure, M. and Kispal, A. (1988) *Language Performance in Schools: review of APU Language Monitoring 1979-1983* London: Her Majesty's Stationery Office

Gorman, T.P., White, J., Brooks, G. and English, F. (1991) *Language for Learning: a summary report on the 1988 APU surveys of language performance* Assessment Matters 4 London: School Examinations and Assessment Council

Harding, P. (1993) 'Reduced to tiers' *Times Educational Supplement* 25 June

Mihail, R. (1993) 'Problems of reading assessment' Paper presented at Romanian-British Seminar, Institute of Educational Sciences/National Foundation for Educational Research: Bucharest

Mihail, T. (1993) 'Why lectology?' *GRAAL* (Journal of the Romanian Reading Association) III 11-12, 2-11

Mihail, T. (in press) 'The Reform as a Curriculum. Eutropological premises; reform through resubstantiation' *Romanian Review of Pedagogy*

Romanian Institute of Educational Sciences (1993) *The Reform of Education in Romania: conditions and prospects* White Book, Bucharest: Institute of Educational Sciences.

Example 1

- — The first test (trialled in May 1993)
- — Age: 18
- — Type: achievement, end of term, summarising test
- — Content: Romanian Drama
- — Time: 2 hours

ANSWER ALL THE QUESTIONS

I. With reference to what I.L. Caragiale's work represents for Romanian Drama, *answer very briefly* the following questions and problems:

a) Name four methods or means by which humour is created in the comedies you studied. Give ONE example of each;

b) Identify the main four indirect methods of characterisation used by Caragiale in his comedies. Give ONE example of each;

c) Give four reasons in support of the statement: 'Romanian literary critics consider I.L. Caragiale to be the greatest Romanian playwright';

d) What relation or link can you find or establish between the world of Caragiale's comedies and the world of the comedies written between the two wars?

e) Explain briefly (in ten lines) the critical concept of 'caragialism' (introduced by G. Calinescu).

II. Through its subject the play *Raceala (The Coldness)* by M. Sorescu belongs to a long-standing form of Romanian Drama: the history play. Name three other plays (with their authors) from the same genre.

III. What is 'poetic and mythic theatre'? Give an example of an author and a play you have studied. Mention four of the main specific features of this kind of theatre by referring to:

- — the atmosphere;
- — the characters;
- — the language used by the author;
- — the relation between the literary genres;

IV. Marin Sorescu entitled one of his plays *The Coldness.*

a) Explain briefly (in ten lines) the meaning of the title;

b) Give at least three reasons why you think this title *is appropriate or is not appropriate* for the play.

Your answer must be a short essay (one page), and it will be assessed according to the following criteria:

- — direct quotation from the text of the play;
- — the relevance and the variety of your arguments;
- — the coherent structure of your arguments.

Example 2

— The second test (trialled in September 1993)
— Age: 14
— Type: diagnostic test
— Time: 3 hours

ANSWER ALL THE QUESTIONS

I. The following passage contains ten mistakes of spelling and punctuation. (Passage follows)

1. Punctuate the passage correctly and rewrite it with the correct spelling;
2. Why do you think the punctuation marks and spellings used by you in the passage are correct?

   Explain every correction you have made (by analysing it).
3. Select one of the punctuation errors you found in the passage, make up a similar one, and explain the role of the punctuation mark in this case.

II. Think about the following pairs of words:

— sacrifice - loss
— well - well
— cold - warmth
— imminence - eminence

1. What is the name of the terms in the above pairs?
2. What kinds of relations are there between the elements in each pair?
3. Find four similar pairs and make a phrase with each of the new examples.

III. Read the following sentences carefully:

Walking through the park, the flowers looked so beautiful! He said at home they have a garden flower which has a lot of exotic trees and flowers. I remember seeing him at his neighbours party last week. It was the coming of age party. He told them to come in before the beginning of the rain. Some were coming within and the others were resting without. But hardly anyone understood why this happened. No sooner had they been given the first piece of cake, then they felt asleep at once.

1. Are these sentences grammatically and stylistically correct? If not, rewrite them correctly.
2. Why did you correct the sentences in some situations? Explain each correction you made.
3. Choose one of the errors you found, construct a similar one, correct it, and give the reasons for your choice of correction.

IV. Read the first passage in this test again.

1. Draw the outline diagram of the syntactic structure of the passage.

2. Choose two clauses in the text and explain why the relation between them is as you stated it.
3. Construct a new sentence according to your diagram of this passage.

V. ANSWER EITHER (a) OR (b):

(a) In no more than 15 lines summarise the last book you read. Your answer will be assessed according to the following criteria:

— the type of language you use to explain the facts, the events, the relations between characters;
— the relation between the main elements and the details;
— the conciseness, clarity and structure of your summary.

(b) Think of your favourite character from *literature, film or theatre.* Describe him or her in *no more than two pages,* emphasising why this character is your favourite. Your answer will be assessed taking into consideration:

— the correct names of the character, the work and the author;
— the identification of the character's relations with the other characters in the work, and the attitude of the author and/or some critics to the character and the work;
— the presentation of some facts (data about the whole work);
— your own reflection about the elements presented.

Example 3

— The third test (trialled in December 1993)
— Age: 18
— Type: achievement, end of term test
— Time: 2 hours

ANSWER ALL THE QUESTIONS. EXCEPT WHERE THE QUESTION GIVES YOU A DIFFERENT INSTRUCTION, ANSWER EACH QUESTION IN NO MORE THAN THREE LINES.

Attention!

— Read through both the instructions and the questions two or three times before starting work!
— Answer on separate sheets of paper, and write your name, your class, and the number of the question on each sheet!

I. Thinking about the types of reading that can be applied to Mircea Eliade's text, read the following excerpt from his short story *La tiganci (To the Gipsy Women)* carefully:

(A page of the text follows.)

1. Who is Gavrilescu?

2. Who is Hildegard?
3. Where does Gavrilescu think his story begins? (In what place?)
4. What object has Gavrilescu lost?
5. What makes Gavrilescu suddenly remember the past?

   Stop and read the passage again!
6. What method does the author use to show us the conversation between the characters?
7. In what way do the sentences follow each other in the passage?
8. What do Gavrilescu's answers represent in the narrative structure of the passage?
9. The verbs of 'the authorial voice' accompanying the answers of the characters are the following:

   'exclaimed', 'whispered', 'tried to call out', 'continued

   to whisper', 'dwelled', 'stared in her eyes and sighed'.

   Considering only his outward behaviour, as explicitly stated in the passage, how does Gavrilescu's state of mind alter?

   a) upwards

   b) downwards
10. In what 'grammatical person' is Gavrilescu's dialogue?

    Stop and read the passage again!
11. What is the meaning of Gavrilescu's statement: 'It was a terrible day!'?
12. What role has Gavrilescu's hat in the narrative?
13. What role has the forgotten perfume in the narrative?
14. What is the meaning of the ale house in the whole story?
15. What is the meaning of the last sentence in the passage?

    Stop and read the passage again!
16. If you were the author and you wanted to cut out (for publishing purposes) one of the responses in the excerpt, which one would you cut out? In a few sentences, give the reasons for your choice.
17. What other elements in the text stress Hildegard's presence?
18. Give another title to this short story.
19. Supposing you were to change the last sentence in this excerpt, in what way would you change it? Pay attention to the role and the meanings of this sentence!
20. Any story has an infinite number of possible endings. If you had to write another ending for this story, how would you conceive it so that it would harmonise with the whole text? Rewrite the ending in no more than one page!

Section 4

Family Literacy

Chapter 12

Family literacy: ownership, evaluation and accountability

Anne Bentley*, Margaret Cook* and Colin Harrison**
*Sefton Local Education Authority
**University of Nottingham

What are the key issues?

This paper reports the background to and main strategies for evaluation of a large family literacy project funded by the UK government's City Challenge project in one area of a Local Authority in the north west of England. The paper begins, however, with a consideration of certain key issues in family literacy which the authors of this paper feel are of great importance. The issues are those highlighted in the title which we have given this paper, namely ownership, evaluation and accountability. We want to consider some questions which relate to these issues, questions which have caused us to reconsider some of our own positions and values. The concepts of ownership, evaluation and accountability may seem abstract or even remote from the practical issues of family literacy, but for us these issues are ones which impinge very directly upon the relationship between theory and practice, and in addressing them we are in good company; a number of colleagues in the field have also felt the need to address these issues in their own way (see, for example, Obrist, 1978; Thorpe, 1988; Beverton *et al.*, 1991; Morrow, Peratore *et al.*, 1993; UKRA, 1993).

The issues which we are considering relate to questions such as the following:

- Who owns a family literacy project? Is it the local authority, the grant awarding body, or the participants in the project?
- Who should decide how a family literacy project is evaluated? The LEA, the grant awarding body (in this case the government), or the participants?
- To whom are the project workers finally accountable in a family literacy project? To the LEA, the government, the project staff, the parents, or the children?

In our view, it is very important to consider these questions, and to consider them from the outset, rather than retrospectively. We have come to feel that, while it would be naive to assume that the grant-awarding body's perspective on such issues should be disregarded, it is also important to find room for other perspectives, particularly those of the participants. Why might this be difficult or problematic? The answer is that the perspective and value system of the grant-awarding body might be very different from those of other participants in a family literacy project. The value system of government or quasi-governmental agencies is sometimes (some would say inevitably) couched in terms of what is often called a 'deficit model' of literacy, and it is this which those working within a project find uncomfortable. If the term 'deficit model' sounds pejorative, one must accept that it tends to be used by those who find the discourse of the model difficult to accept. What, then, is a 'deficit model' of literacy, and of family literacy in particular? A deficit model of literacy is one which, implicitly or explicitly, makes assumptions such as the following:

- that illiteracy is widespread and probably increasing;
- that illiteracy leads inevitably to unemployment, to poverty, then to crime;

— that poor, undereducated parents lack the means and knowledge to introduce children to literacy.

Such a model usually has two other built-in assumptions, namely:

— that the model of literacy which is to be passed on within families is essentially that of school literacy;

— that the most appropriate evaluation model for a family literacy project is one which focuses on gains in reading ability, as measured by standardised reading tests.

The case against the deficit model has been argued eloquently through the ethnographies of Denny Taylor (1983; Taylor and Strickland, 1986; Taylor and Dorsey-Gaines, 1988) and the discourse analysis of Elsa Auerbach (1989), and we will not rehearse their arguments here, but we will make what is for us a crucial point, namely that, whether one likes it or not, it is the deficit model which is associated with large-scale funding for family literacy projects.

A deficit model is understandably the one which is associated with large-scale literacy projects, since it is anxieties at national level concerning standards of literacy which lead governments and multinational companies to intervene to alleviate what they see as a potentially disastrous problem, one which, left untreated, might lead to economic and social collapse. Why, then, should such a plainly benign set of intentions and apparently sensible assumptions come to be challenged? Why is the deficit model not attractive to literacy workers? One answer to this question is to consider the alternative, which we have called a 'wealth model'.

A 'wealth model' would argue the following:

— that illiteracy is not widespread, and is probably decreasing;

— that the link between illiteracy, poverty and crime is correlational, and not causal;

— that poor, undereducated parents have a great deal of knowledge which they use to introduce children to literacy.

In relation to assumptions concerning models of literacy and models of evaluation, those who subscribe to the 'wealth model' would tend to believe:

— that it is important to celebrate and give value to a range of literacies, including those of minority and sub-group cultures, of which school literacy is only one;

— that the most appropriate evaluation model for a family literacy project is one which is negotiated with the participants, and which may well not include standardised reading tests.

It hardly needs stating that this 'wealth model' would not be considered attractive by many groups which give funding to family literacy projects. Perfectly understandably, therefore, such a state of affairs implies at the very least a tension for those working within a family literacy project, between the 'deficit model' which brings the project its funding, and the 'wealth model' values and assumptions of the project participants. This tension has certainly been present in the project reported in this paper, and the authors suspect that such a tension is present within many other family literacy projects. In the present case, our intention has been to accept that such tension needs to be resolved in ways which are acceptable to the grant-awarding body and acceptable in relation to the participants. In many respects, the assumptions of the two models seem to be polar opposites, but the remainder of this paper offers an attempt to share an account of a practical attempt to resolve these ambiguities, and to do so in a manner which is pragmatic rather than adversarial.

Before doing this, however, it is perhaps appropriate to recognise that as authors we are conscious that the terms 'deficit model' and 'wealth model' are themselves highly charged, and that this terminology implies a very negative set of associations for the phrase 'deficit model', while making an implicit claim to the moral high ground with the term 'wealth model'. It is therefore appropriate to acknowledge that what we term the 'deficit model' could equally have been called (by authors favouring the alternative perspective) the 'high standards-rigorous research model', and our 'wealth model' would perhaps be characterised by those authors as the 'wishy-washy-liberal-anything-goes research model'. As Auerbach (1989) noted, choosing the discourse is as much a part of determining the issues of ownership, evaluation and accountability as choosing the research methods.

An attempt to live with the ambiguity

While it is easy to see that many school-focused literacy programmes are based on a 'deficit' model , the 'wealth' model should appeal to educationalists for several reasons, not least because it fits so well with the child-centred approaches to curriculum and pedagogy which are characteristic of good early childhood education. The model also gives parents positive roles so that they are not defined solely as the school's helpers and surrogate instructors. Instead, parents can be seen as bringing to the education of their own children and those of others, a richness and variety of experience which makes the traditional school curriculum seem wan and narrow. In this wealth model, families are makers and developers of literacies, not just the conduit for the literacy of others. Perhaps most importantly, the recognition of parents as having rights as the developers and conveyors of their own literacies, may ensure that their children, too, see these as their own and retain them into adulthood.

We are, however, a long way from even a partial recognition that, in the long-term, the imposition of an alien literacy is unlikely to be the best way of making children enthusiastic readers and writers. Moreover, unfortunately perhaps, the social and economic cost to individuals of failing to acquire 'school' literacy is seen as too substantial for radical approaches to literacy teaching to be contemplated. There is also the problem that, in current conditions, funded programmes are usually predicated on a deficit model of their clients and are mostly tied to specific 'educational' outcomes and achievements. The funding conditions also usually specify a short time-scale which gives little opportunity for bridging the gap between the literacies of home and school and, in particular, for supporting families in developing self-esteem and positive roles in literacy development.

These were all-important considerations for two of us when, in 1993, we began the planning for a large City Challenge funded educational project in one area of our Local Authority. City Challenge funding is essentially based on a deficit model but one based on an area, rather than a particular community within it. Funding comes from the Department of the Environment and is not primarily targeted at education but at the physical, economic and social regeneration of identified inner urban areas. These areas are defined geographically by a range of indicators which include educational and training factors usually related to quantitative measures such as examination and testing results, truancy rates, entry into further and higher education and so on.

Essential to the City Challenge philosophy is that the success of the programme is determined by the progress of the area as a whole according to a range of specified outputs which, for education and training are usually couched in recognised quantitative measures of the kind mentioned earlier. In practical terms, this meant that we had to present our families and schools as failing in literacy development as against LEA and national norms if we were to secure and retain the funding on offer. Since this funding amounted to about £0.75 m over five years, including the provision of parents' rooms in the fourteen schools in the programme, the Authority was obviously anxious for our schools to benefit from the programme. Since both the schools and ourselves recognised the potential of the area's families, it became imperative that the way in which we planned our own project would resolve the tension between the deficit model underpinning the programme funding and our own beliefs about family literacy, while satisfying the funders' requirements for outputs related to recognised measures of education and training. Essentially this meant that success in the development of literacies which would support, or lead into, school literacies, had to be an important part of any evaluation.

Our own strongly held beliefs were those lying behind the 'wealth' model: that no homes are 'illiterate' and that all families already educate their children in some forms of literacy without, however, necessarily recognising or valuing the significance of what they are doing. We also believed that most parents would welcome more information about how literacy works and how it is acquired. If we were to intervene in this area, we thought it essential that this information should be gained in ways which gave families ownership of knowledge about literacy so that they, rather than schools, continued to generate and build on opportunities for literacy learning in the home. In all this we were strongly influenced by ethnographical studies of community literacies, by current approaches to the development of emergent literacy, and by interventionist pedagogies based on modelling and scaffolding rather than on direct instruction. In the planning of the home visits which were to form a substantial part of the programme we were most indebted to the work of Peter Hannon, Jo

Weinberger and Cathy Nutbrown and especially to their model of family literacy support, to which we shall return later in this paper.

We were also influenced by much current thinking on the intergenerational influences on literacy development and in particular, on the association which is increasingly claimed for the effect of parental levels of education on children's literacy. We already had a very successful Parents As Educators programme, accredited by the Open College in the area, and the parents involved were increasingly telling us how much their confidence and self-esteem had grown. Indeed, we could see for ourselves how this was likely to enhance the way their children valued education.

Lastly, in these early stages, we were acutely conscious that although the fourteen schools to be involved in the project were strongly committed to increased parental involvement in their schools, and to beliefs similar to our own about the development of family literacy, all of us were conscious that there were very differing perceptions about how these might be implemented. Also, everybody was, in any case, at a different point in their own journey towards effective parental involvement with schools.

What we came up with was an integrated programme with three clearly identified strands and a participant management structure reflecting these and aimed at developing self-esteem and effective decision-making for all the participants. The first strand supported work on the development of children's literacy at home and at school. A team of four outreach workers was trained in emergent literacy practices and the use of the Hannon/Weinberger/Nutbrown model of family literacy support mentioned earlier. This is a four-fold model which consists of:

1. the recognition by parents of existing literacy opportunities in the home
2. the modelling of literacy activities by parents
3. appropriate intervention/instruction
4. the provision of feedback by parents to children.

Books from the project's large resource collection are left in the home between visits, and there is a strong emphasis, more so than in the original model, on the use of toys and the development of representational play. Parents are strongly encouraged to engage in the play themselves and to link it with book characters and events. A record of achievement is kept by parent and child and the parent is encouraged to comment on the literacy opportunities she provides for the child and how the child reacts to these. Families are encouraged to follow up the visits by attending workshops on early literacy run by the outreach workers in the parents' rooms attached to the schools. A planned programme of INSET, which parents and teachers often attend together, ensures that the same messages about early literacy are taken up by school and home. In order to ensure continuity, a further INSET programme supports teachers at Key Stages Two and Three in developing an understanding of literacy processes.

The Programme's second strand is concerned with the development of climate setting and management strategies in schools which will support parental involvement. Every school has a teacher with responsibility for parental involvement, the extra point on the scale being paid for from the project's budget. Again, INSET is provided by the project and climates are assessed using a prototype instrument (Weinberger, 1994).

The third strand is solely concerned with the development of parents' own education, training and self-esteem through the extension of the existing Parents As Educators programmes, and the provision of adult education courses together with a range of other activities in the parents' rooms.

What we hope is distinctive about this project is the underpinning of these strands with a philosophy of ownership by families of both literacy and the project itself. Central to the project is the group of parent representatives from each school who are responsible for communicating with their own school and its parents, for the joint planning with their own school of the parents' rooms activities and for the management of their consultative group and its representation on the appropriate City Challenge management and evaluation groups. This involves these parents in a constant high level of activity and they have become both sensitive and knowledgeable about a wide range of issues from matters concerning insurance and codes of conduct to the use of IT and knowledge of literacy development. They are certainly now at the heart of the programme's day-to-day operation as the home visits are at the heart of its beliefs about the development of literacy.

Tentative Conclusions

It is far too early to see whether the project will succeed in all its aims. So far we have easily exceeded our funders' output requirements and we hope to continue to do so. We seem also to have moved substantially towards developing in some parents at least the kind of confidence and knowledge which will enable them to become equal partners with their schools in the development and management of their children's education. The crux of the matter will be whether we can also achieve our major aim of enabling parents to gain ownership of their own and their children's literacy. We feel that both these kinds of ownership — of literacy and of the means by which families and schools communicate — are essential if the literacy of home is to carry over into school, and be supportive of the development of school literacy, without being eroded in the process. Any evaluation of the project will therefore, in our view, have to establish the relationship between the three strands of the project, as well as recognising the effects of the management structure on the effectiveness of the participants. If we have been right in our thinking and planning, it may be that it is, after all, possible to use funding based on a deficit model of achievement to serve the purposes of a wealth model of family literacy.

References

Auerbach, E.R. (1989) 'Toward a socio-contextual approach to family literacy' *Harvard Educational Review* 59, 165-181

Beverton, S., Hunter-Carsch, M., Stuart, A. and Obrist, C. (1991) *Family Reading Groups Project Report* Ormskirk: United Kingdom Reading Association

Morrow, L., Peratore, J., et al. (1993) 'Family Literacy: perspectives and practices' *The Reading Teacher* 47/3, 194-200

Obrist, C. (1978) *How to Run Family Reading Groups* Ormskirk: United Kingdom Reading Association

Taylor D. (1983) *Family Literacy* London: Heinemann Educational Books

Taylor, D., and Dorsey-Gaines, C. (1988) *Growing Up Literate* Portsmouth NH: Heinemann

Taylor, D. and Strickland, D. (1986) *Family Story-book Reading* Portsmouth NH: Heinemann

Thorpe, D. (1988) *Reading for Fun* Cranfield, England: Cranfield Press

United Kingdom Reading Association (1993) *Running Family Reading Groups: Guidelines for Teachers* Widnes: United Kingdom Reading Association

Chapter 13

Parents' contribution to children's literacy learning

Jo Weinberger
University of Sheffield

Recent work has shown the importance of family context for literacy learning (Heath, 1983; Teale, 1986; Saxena, 1994). This paper is specifically concerned with the part parents play in their children's literacy development. Highlighting this aspect of social practice can, in Taylor's (1983) words, help to make 'the customary visible', and so lead to greater understandings about the contribution of parents to literacy learning. These insights have implications for schools.

This paper is based on a longitudinal study of children's literacy at home and at school. Data here concerns parents of 42 children aged seven, who attended eight schools, from a wide cross-section of social class groupings. Particular findings discussed here focus on the home, and on interaction with school. They show how the parents were involved in children's literacy learning as part of everyday life, their sources of information and advice, and their own childhood experiences of parental involvement. In addition, parents' views on hearing their child read, and their contacts with teachers are explored. Fuller details of the study can be found in Weinberger (1993).

Key findings from the study: at home

Parents' views of literacy learning in everyday activities

Teaching and learning occur in very different contexts at home compared with school. Some parents in the study were uneasy with the term 'teaching' to describe what they were doing with their children. They commented for instance,

> 'Not so much teach him. We'd look at books. He'd say, 'What does that say?' I think that's part of learning.'
>
> 'Teaching, maybe I was, unconsciously, by looking at books.'
>
> 'I didn't sit down and teach a-b-c. I did it gradually, at his own pace.'

Most parents were involved in activities which taught the children about the content and purpose of literacy. These often occurred as a natural part of a more general activity. Much of this teaching and learning was effectively 'invisible' in that it occurred so naturally and was so much a part of day-to-day living, that it could go unnoticed. As Clark (1976) commented of parents in her study, their literacy encounters were 'casual' rather than 'systematic', and part of daily life as opposed to being separate from it. Similar findings are reported in Atkin and Bastiani (1986), in their study of parental perspectives on teaching. All but four parents described a variety of situations connected with family life in which literacy learning took place. As they talked, some parents had a sense of just how much they were actually doing. As one said,

> 'I suppose until you think about it you don't know how much you do.'

Similar comments by parents were noted in a project which aimed to increase their awareness of their role in their children's literacy development (Weinberger, Hannon and Nutbrown, 1991). Here, the children whose parents could not supply examples of naturally occurring literacy activities in day-to-day life were having literacy difficulties at age seven.

Parents of the majority of the children (38), however, were able to provide examples.

Some of the parents mentioned going on journeys as opportunities for literacy learning, for instance,

> 'She asks what the signs say on the road.'

> 'We read things on buses. When we go out for the day, they pick out road signs — they have to look out for road signs.'

A number of parents described other occasions when they were involved in everyday activities outside the home as times when they incorporated literacy learning into what they did with their child, for example,

> 'When we're in the supermarket he knows which is soap powder and Comfort and margarine and that.'

> 'I point things out like car park, the signpost for the toilets...'

> 'We look at the hymn book and sing hymns at church.'

Several parents gave examples of special outings and going on holiday as times that gave rise to literacy related to the activity, such as going to local places of interest, going to a zoo or farm, and going on holiday, for instance,

> 'We went to visit (a local historic house). If you take them to places like this they understand better — there's things to read in all the rooms.'

> 'We went to London for her birthday. We went to the tube and she was wanting to know all the different stops.'

One family went on holiday to Butlins. The child wrote a postcard to the teacher and children at school, and it was later pinned on the class noticeboard.

At home, parents mentioned writing letters, cards and invitations together, writing shopping lists, doing crosswords and wordsearches together (including one family where the child and parent actually sent off the results of a wordsearch to a newspaper, and won tickets to Blackpool), reading items together from the television, reading the back of cereal packets and sending off for things, reading recipes together for baking, and selecting a holiday destination from brochures. Two parents, both middle class, explicitly aimed to show their children how you could use reading to gain information. They commented,

> 'I teach her she can get more information by using reading, like looking in a catalogue for something she wants like a sleeping bag, or looking for a television programme — that it's an information giving thing'

and

> 'If I came across anything like tadpoles at nursery, or Martin's been on a walk collecting conkers, we'll look it up in the encyclopaedia.'

In some cases, the parents' work generated literacy activities for the child, for example one parent mentioned doing the books for a family business, and her child wanted to be involved,

> 'She'd want to do the same. She says, 'Oh, I'll do a letter mummy.'.'

Another two parents studied and wrote at home,

> 'Sometimes if I'm doing my work she'll sit alongside me, but she's writing independently.'
>
> 'If Mick's sat at the table drawing or writing, he'll want to join in with him.'

Because these types of activity are sometimes hard for parents to disentangle from the day-to-day business of everyday life, there is likely to be under-reporting of what was happening with the parents and children. However, these examples give a flavour of the types of situationally embedded activities involving literacy that parents and children engaged in together.

Sources of information for parents about children's literacy

Over half the parents felt that most of the information they had received about how children learn to read and write came from sources other than school, through family and friends, printed matter and the media. Of the parents who received information from school, 15 also mentioned other sources of information as well. Most frequently mentioned was what parents learned from children showing them and telling them about literacy (15 parents). For 10 parents, their primary source of information was from members of their family, and from other parents, saying for instance,

> 'I ask my mum.'

or

> '...probably within the family, with my other sisters having older children.'

Ten parents gleaned information on literacy from books, and five from magazines. Eight parents mentioned information from television, both from documentary programmes such as *'Help your child to read'* and *'40 Minutes'*, and from children's television programmes with a literacy content, such as *'Sesame Street'*. Two parents could not suggest sources of information on literacy because they felt they did not know about it.

These findings show that only some parents receive information from school, and that, for most parents, information comes from informal channels of communication.

Sources of advice to parents

Parents were asked if they had ever been given specific advice about children's reading or writing. Only seven parents said that they had. Most used their own experience and ideas to inform how they interacted with their child on literacy. As one parent expressed it,

> 'What I know is because I've used my own initiative. I've always thought it was important that they should read and write.'

Five of the seven parents who said they received advice said this was from teachers. Four were parents of middle-class girls — the group of children least likely to be having problems with literacy. The fifth was the parent of a child who attended a school that was pro-active in enlisting the help of all parents in school-initiated literacy, sending reading books home each night, and arranging meetings with individual parents to explain aspects of literacy to them. The remaining two parents, as when the children were aged three and four, mentioned advice from other family members (who were themselves teachers). These were also parents of middle-class girls.

It is quite likely that there was some under-reporting of advice received, as it could well have been given informally, and may not have been consciously acknowledged. Nonetheless, these replies illustrate parents' perceptions of the low level of advice given about children's literacy.

From parents' responses to the question about advice, it seems that on the whole they were using their own initiative in the way they worked with their children on literacy, with little help, guidance or information either from printed materials or from other people. School was generally not seen as offering advice or information about literacy. Similar findings have been reported elsewhere (Hall et al., 1989).

Generational patterns of literacy

Currently, interest in parental involvement in literacy seems to be increasing. While all the children in the sample were helped with literacy in some way by their parents, and the majority were read to, only half the parents (21) recollected having had these experiences themselves as children. When they did, it may well often have been to a lesser extent. Parents commented, for instance,

> 'My mother read to me. Not like we do it with them, not to the same extent. When I was at school, parents weren't consulted. If anybody's mother came up to school it was an event.'
>
> 'Not as much as we do. I don't think they did at that time.'

Parents provided a range of examples of the literacy activities undertaken with parents and other family members, such as,

> 'I was read to a lot, including at bedtime.'
>
> 'I suppose my mum read to me, but not writing. I can remember writing stories with my grandparents every weekend. My grandfather gave encouragement with story writing. He pointed things out — this could be better, and he would buy a new exercise book and pencil.'
>
> 'Yes, with my mother, She used to sit hours. She had ten kids and she'd leave her work and sit with us. My mother used to like to read and write. I think that's where I get it from.'
>
> 'I used to read a lot with my father. We read newspapers back and front. Mum was the one who played games to do with reading.'

> 'Grandad looked at Rupert books with me. I can remember when I was three, the books had things to do in them. My grandfather made a cage out of straws for me out of my Rupert book.'

> 'Yes, with my dad more than my mum, and three older sisters. They used to read a lot.'

Many children in the sample had similar experiences at home.

In contrast, there were many parents who could not remember any involvement in literacy activities. Where explanations were suggested, these were that large families implied lack of time, and made interaction with individual children difficult (two families had seven children, one nine, and one eleven; none of the children in the sample were from such large families), and parents being busy at work (three instances). In addition, the Chinese mother could not remember literacy activities at home, and explained,

> 'My parents couldn't read or write in English.'

Parents were not asked whether they had literacy difficulties themselves, but four of the parents volunteered that they had problems with reading and writing. All their children were amongst the group experiencing difficulties with literacy.

Highlighting these generational patterns of family literacy helps to show the extent of change and replication in patterns of behaviour, and also gives an indication of where support might usefully be given.

Key findings from the study: interaction with school

Parents' knowledge about literacy teaching in school

Only a minority of parents felt they knew how reading and writing were taught in school: uncertainty was the norm. However, more information would have been welcomed, for instance parents made comments like,

> 'They don't tell us about what our kids are doing. If they'd tell us more, we'd be able to help them better.'

> 'I think parents ought to be a lot more involved. I think parents should be told a lot more exactly how they teach them, then they could help them a lot better at home.'

The high proportion of parents who felt they did not know how their child was being taught to read or write in school reveals a gap in basic communication from schools to parents (this has been reported at nursery level by several studies, for instance, Tizard *et al.*, 1981; Hannon and James, 1990). Those parents who themselves initiated contact with teachers, or elected to be on the premises at some time during the week, were the group of parents with the most knowledge about what their children were being taught in school. This group of parents included disproportionate numbers of middle-class mothers who do not go out to work, and other mothers for whom the school as an institution fulfilled a social function. This meant that a sizeable majority of parents were excluded.

Parents' views of hearing children read from school books

In all the schools that the children attended, reading books were sent home, but, for all but one school, this was not done systematically, and little information was given by the schools to all the parents.

The parents were asked if they knew what was expected of them when a school reading book came home, or if their child read aloud to them. The majority (27) did feel confident they had an idea, and made comments like,

> 'I sit and listen to her read and try to help her with words she doesn't know.'

However, many parents said that they had to make assumptions, as this was never discussed with the staff, making comments such as,

> 'I think we're expected to read to her and her to read back to us, and put her right on her mistakes. I just assume that — we've never been asked to do that.'

> 'Nothing's said, but I'm happy about what I'm doing. He brings his book home — but no folder and no information.'

Over a third of the parents (15) did not feel they knew what was expected of them, because of lack of information and feedback. Thus while the majority of parents were able to use their initiative and felt reasonably confident in the way they supported their child's school-initiated reading, a sizeable proportion of parents felt unclear and unsupported. Similar findings were reported by McNaughton, Parr, Timperley and Robinson

(1993) in their interview study of parents and teachers in New Zealand. In the current study there seemed to be an information gap between parents and schools for some of the parents who could most have benefited from such information.

Half the parents were happy about the frequency with which their child brought their book home from school. The flexibility of the system, whereby children and parents could choose when to take books home, was generally welcomed, for instance,

> 'It's just right — it's left to you.'

> 'You can set the pace. The reading books are always available to come home. The relaxed atmosphere makes it much easier.'

Whilst these parents seemed happy to 'set the pace', other parents were less happy about the arrangements. They implied they would have liked a more pro-active approach by the school. More than a third of parents (15) thought that reading books did not come home often enough, making comments like,

> 'I don't think they're encouraged enough. I'm waiting in the car, I don't always go in.'

> 'His teacher doesn't encourage it. I get his folder out of his drawer.'

A flexible approach was creating gaps in the system. But a more rigid policy had its problems too. The one parent who thought her child brought books home too frequently, had a child who attended the only school where books were systematically sent home every night. His mother commented,

> 'I think every night is a bit much. It feels as if they've got to do it. Sometimes you feel you don't want to do it. If you push Adam to do something, he'll not do it.'

It seems a compromise would be helpful; regular encouragement from the school, backed up with seeing if particular children are missing out altogether, but without the insistence that reading has to be done every night by every child. Dialogue with parents about this would be helpful.

Contact between parents and teachers

Parents were asked whether they talked with their child's teacher specifically about reading and writing. This was in addition to biennial, formal, parent-teacher consultations. The majority of parents (29) did talk with the teacher about literacy at other times. Of those that did not, most said they were not involved in some way at school. It appeared that lack of regular contact within school lessened the likelihood of dialogue between parents and teachers concerning children's literacy. Such dialogue between parents and teachers is important for children's literacy development, since increased contacts have been shown to have positive consequences for children's literacy performance (Iverson *et al.*, 1981).

Teachers tended to wait for parents to take the initiative in talking about literacy (apart from formal consultations, made a legal requirement of schools, Department for Education, 1992). As a result, some parents received a great deal more information than others. Many of the parents who could have most benefited from information were the least likely to receive it (Toomey, 1989). This reliance on parental initiative was also reported in a number of studies of preschool education, (for example Pinkerton, 1978; Tizard *et al.*, 1981). Typical comments from those parents who did talk with the teachers concerned their need to 'ask in order to find out' any information,

> 'I think they let me get on with it... If it weren't for parent's day I don't think we'd really get to know much — unless you ask, which I do.'
>
> 'If I've got any questions, I ask.'

This form of contact relies on a level of confidence and some understanding of literacy learning, on the part of the parents. It appears that those parents who could have benefited most from a dialogue with teachers on literacy were the least likely to receive it.

Teachers too reported that talk was usually initiated by parents, and often in response to problems perceived by the parent, for instance,

> 'She asked me why he wasn't reading.....'
>
> 'When we have a chat, she asks about her handwriting.'

Those parents who did not have contact with the teachers concerning literacy expected that they would be told if there were any problems,

> 'They invite you to go in if you've a problem. I don't seem to, so I don't seem to bother them.'

However, even for some children experiencing problems, dialogue between parents and teachers was limited, and often instigated by the parent. The underlying assumption for both teachers and parents was that if there were problems they would be addressed. Silence implied that everything was satisfactory. However, in reality, parents and teachers did not necessarily communicate much even if there were problems.

Parents of some children whose teachers thought they were having problems with reading and writing, seemed unaware that this was the case. It may well be that some children could have been offered more support at home had their parents been made aware of the problems the children were facing in school.

Communication between parents and teachers tended to occur with regular contact. In this way, a select group of parents, often those who had the most confidence and knowledge about literacy in the first place, had the most frequent discussions about literacy with the teachers in school.

A more consistent flow of communication with all parents could have helped with parents' confidence and also alerted teachers to some of the literacy learning occurring at home which might otherwise have been overlooked.

Implications for practice

To allow schools to build effectively on the extensive literacy learning that children do at home, and to support those children experiencing difficulties, literacy learning that takes place in homes needs to be made more visible. It would be beneficial for children's literacy for teachers to talk with parents about literacy occurring as a part of day-to-day family activities at home and to exchange information about children's literacy learning.

It would be helpful if schools could find a variety of methods for explaining to parents how literacy is taught in school. In encouraging reading books to go home, it would be useful if teachers could check that parents knew what their role was, and ensured all children were reminded that they could take their book. Many parents in this study would have liked their child to bring a book home more frequently.

This study shows that it would be beneficial for children's literacy development if schools found ways of increasing dialogue between teachers and all parents. Teachers need to initiate communication about literacy with parents in a number of different ways, through printed information, and most importantly, discussion, so that all parents have the opportunity to find out how literacy is taught in school, and are able to tell teachers about the literacy learning at home.

Summary

Data from this study suggest that most of the ways in which parents interact with their children on literacy are intuitive and come from well-embedded child-rearing practices within homes and social networks. Some information about new methods of literacy teaching had penetrated into children's homes from school, but this was by no means uniform, nor was information always fully understood.

Parents tended to be keen to help their children with literacy. They were, however, fairly unsupported in this by schools, often with children with the most difficulties receiving the least support at family level.

References

Atkin, J. and Bastiani, J. (1986) 'Are they teaching? An alternative perspective on parents as educators' *Education 3-13* 14, 2, 18-22

Clark, M.M. (1976) *Young Fluent Readers* London: Heinemann

Department for Education (1992) *Reporting Pupils' Achievements to Parents* Circular 5/92 London: Her Majesty's Stationery Office

Hall, N., Herring, G., Henn, H. and Crawford, L. (1989) *Parental views on writing and the teaching of writing* Manchester: School of Education, Manchester Polytechnic

Hannon, P. and James, S. (1990) 'Parents' and teachers' perspectives on pre-school literacy development' *British Educational Research Journal* 16, 3, 259-272.

Heath, S.B. (1983) *Ways with words: Language, life and work in communities and classrooms* Cambridge: Cambridge University Press

Iverson, B.K., Brownlee, G.D. and Walberg, H.J. (1981) 'Parent-teacher contacts and student learning *Journal of Educational Research* 24, 6, 394-396

McNaughton, S., Parr, J., Timperley, H. and Robinson, V. (1993) 'Beginning reading and sending books home to read: a case for some fine tuning, *Educational Psychology* 12, 3 and 4, 239-246

Pickerton, G. (1978) 'Where do you come in at the nursery?' *Nursery World* 19 October

Saxena, M. (1994) 'Literacies among the Punjabis in Southall' in M. Hamilton, D. Barton and R. Ivanic (eds) *Worlds of Literacy* Clevedon: Multilingual Matters

Taylor, D. (1983) *Family Literacy: Young children learning to read and write* London: Heinemann

Teale, W.H. (1986) 'Home background and young children's literacy development' in W.H. Teale and E. Sulzby (eds) *Emergent Literacy* Norwood, NJ: Ablex

Tizard, B., Blatchford, P., Burke, J., Farquhar, C. and Plewis, I. (1981) *Young Children in the Inner City* London: Lawrence Erlbaum

Toomey, D.M. (1989) 'How home-school relations policies can increase educational inequality' *Australian Journal of Education* 33, 3, 284-298

Weinberger, J. (1993) *A Longitudinal Study of Literacy Experiences, the Role of Parents and Children's Literacy Development* Sheffield: University of Sheffield (Unpub. PhD)

Weinberger, J., Hannon, P. and Nutbrown, C. (1991) *Ways of Working With Parents to Promote Early Literacy Development* USDE Papers in Education 14 Sheffield: University of Sheffield

Chapter 14

Connections and negotiations: early literacy learning at home and school

Kathryn Kohl
University of Sheffield

Introduction

Many research studies in the United States and Britain have highlighted the central role of parents in children's reading and writing development (Taylor, 1983; Weinberger, 1993). Parents encourage children's literacy development at home by modelling writing and reading themselves; by providing opportunities for meaningful literacy experiences; by recognising children's literacy achievements; by pointing out environmental print; and by reading to their children (Harste, Woodward and Burke, 1984; Weinberger, Hannon, and Nutbrown, 1991).

Studies have confirmed that children already know a lot about literacy by the time they start full-time schooling, whether or not they have been formally taught at home or in a preschool setting. Children actively construct their own literacy — during their preschool and school years — at home, within their own communities, in meaningful, everyday activities (Ferreiro and Teberosky, 1982; Wells, 1986; Schickedanz, 1990). It has also been shown that teachers are sometimes unaware of, or underestimate, children's preschool, home literacy experience and knowledge. Some children fail to become, in the school's eyes, readers and writers, even children who are readers and writers at home (Heath, 1983; Taylor and Dorsey-Gaines, 1988.)

School literacy activities that fail to build on children's previous achievements may not offer the same degree of autonomy and authenticity that children experience in their home- and community-based literacy learning. The results may range from missed opportunities for meaningful literacy experiences in the classroom to a dramatic discontinuity between home and school literacy learning that hinders a child's development.

Background to the study

This paper draws on literacy research carried out between 1990 and 1991 into children's transition from home to school. The study began as an attempt to understand apparent differences between my own child's early home and school literacy learning. I had encouraged my daughter in her home, preschool literacy pursuits by reading to her daily, by providing drawing and writing materials, and by offering help (for example, acting as scribe for her stories) when she asked for it. I did not ever set out to instruct my child in reading or writing. Nor did her nursery school overtly seek to develop literacy learning. Indeed, I was struck by the degree to which she seemed to be self-taught at home. She spent a great deal of time drawing and writing in the course of her self-directed activities, incorporating increasingly mature notions of the forms and functions of print in her dramatic play. For example, she might play restaurants with friends and dolls, making menus and play money, writing down orders and writing out bills.

I was interested to see what would happen when someone set out deliberately to teach my daughter to read and write at school. At the age of four years and eight months, she entered a large class of four-to-six-year-olds in the Summer Term, already an active participant in sharing books at home and, as I have said, highly productive in directing her own writing activities.

Once she started school, she seemed to undergo a kind of regression in her home literacy activities. Now bringing home reading scheme books, in which she quickly lost interest (vividly demonstrated when she threw Roger Redhat across the room, saying, 'I'm not reading this rubbish anymore!'), she also lacked the confidence which she had previously shown in our shared reading of her own books. She no longer considered herself to be a *reader.* Likewise, in her home writing, she became anxious and came to me for spellings of most words, whereas before she was happy to try her own spellings or to produce writing-like forms.

At school, the teacher controlled the children's writing production by directing them in dictating stories and then over- and under-writing the teacher's writing. Oddly, I thought, the stories my child dictated to the teacher in that first term began as only a few words ('Mummy and me'), and gradually lengthened ('Mummy and me in the garden'; 'Mummy and me on the boat going to Legoland') in what seemed a very controlled meting out of diction and syntax. Indeed, there seemed to be similarities between the language in her stories and the language of Roger Redhat! Her home writing, by comparison, included diction and syntax which were varied, complex, conversational and unpredictable.

My child's notions of print, and of herself as a writer and reader, were certainly being challenged at school. Her preschool, home experiences had seemed central to her literacy development yet they seemed in conflict with what she was asked to do at school. It was that discontinuity which I saw in her transition from home to school that led me to widen my inquiry into the differences between home and school literacy development. My goal was to find out more about similarities and differences between literacy learning at home and literacy *teaching* at school: where children are able to make connections, and where they might have to negotiate their way in conflicting settings.

Main study

The main study investigated the home-to-school (and back home again) literacy experiences of 18 four-to-five-year-old children who formed the Summer intake of a nursery-first school. I collected home-based literacy data during the two terms prior to the children's school entry; and home-

and school-based literacy data during their one term in Reception class. The children's mothers (and in one case, a father) assisted me, in their homes, in the collection of home-based data. Data collected from home visits included taped talks with the parents, parent diaries of their children's home (and later also school) literacy experiences, and drawing and writing samples. In addition, when the children were at home during my visits, and engaged in literacy pursuits, I made observation notes. For example, children and their younger siblings often sat at the kitchen table with their parent and me, drawing and writing as we adults talked and watched. A greater number of visits were made to the homes of nine of the children, and these visits were continued once the children started full-time school. I returned to the homes of the remaining nine children once during the Reception term, at the end of the school year.

When the children entered school, I observed them throughout the term in the two Reception classes which they joined. It was essential to define my role in the classrooms as a non-helper, and I seldom deliberately interacted with the children. Instead, I recorded anything and everything that seemed of interest, particularly on the subject of literacy. For example, I made notes of the children's free play in the home corner, and of their 'news' writing and letter writing practice. Data collected from school included extensive observation notes, copies of most written work, and interviews with the teachers and the Head teacher.

By the time the children entered school, I was already familiar with their home literacy achievements. Likewise, as I continued my home visits during the school term, I saw evidence of the children's post-school home literacy achievements. I was thus in a position both to assess the differences between what the children had accomplished at home before school entry and what they were enabled to do in their first term of school; and to make on-going comparisons between their concurrent home and school literacy experiences. Sometimes a child demonstrated what I would call low-level literacy strategies at school (for example, restricting writing output to dictating a story and then under-writing the teacher's writing) on the very same day that he or she demonstrated higher level strategies at home (for example, independently copying — or, indeed, writing from memory — print from books or environmental print on to pictures to make stories).

The data reflect the complexity and individuality of the children's literate lives, and suggest gaps between their home and school experiences, which in some cases were quite marked. The flexible research design allowed me to identify emerging themes in the course of data collection as I moved toward as detailed an understanding as possible of each child's highly individual early literacy experiences. Incorporating both emergent literacy and social construction perspectives, I have sought to understand both general similarities and differences that appeared between the children's home and school literacy learning contexts, and the individual children's construction and reconstruction of their own unique literacy in both settings: in other words, the observable connections and negotiations made by each child in his or her early literacy learning at home and school.

Case study: Tom

Major themes from the study include the children's relative autonomy as writers and readers at home and at school; and the relative degree of authenticity, integration, and social interaction of their literacy experiences in the two settings. To illustrate, one of the study children was a boy named Tom. Early in the study, Tom demonstrated a unique and highly cultivated approach to his writing at home. His mother often said that Tom did not like to be 'pushed'; that when she tried to help him, for example, with letter formation, he became anxious. She thus learned to leave Tom to his own devices when it came to his writing. He was very active in integrating drawing, writing and play — on his own and with his younger sister, friends and parents. His main strategy seemed to be to copy print from his environment — from packaging, clothes, books and toys — on to his drawings, and to practise it repeatedly until he had learned it. His independent writing repertoire, at age four, included the words *Lego, ambulance, police* and *turtle,* which he usually wrote in capital letters, as they appeared to him. He incorporated these words in his pictures and stories many times a day. In this way, by the time he started school, Tom had taught himself many words and had the means to teach himself new words whenever he wished. Sometimes he would ask his parents how to write a word. Sometimes his mother was unsure where he had learned a word; for example, one of his words was *'dance'*.

It was clear that Tom was highly aware of language appearing in different forms in his environment, and that he actively reconstructed that language in ways that informed and pleased him. At home, Tom was a literacy *learner,* observing and manipulating print. In the context of his everyday life, within a small circle of family and friends, Tom's literacy experiences were active and autonomous; the learning, *per se*, was almost incidental. He moved fluidly between drawing, writing and play; whether he was reading to his little sister from a familiar story book; playing schools with a friend; writing a shopping list while his mother wrote hers; or playing a board game, which he had invented and made on his own, with his parents. His home literacy experiences could be said to have a high degree of autonomy, authenticity, integration, and social interaction.

My observations of Tom during his term in reception class suggested that his teacher was not aware of the many ways in which Tom's literacy learning manifested itself at home. Indeed, how could she be, when Tom did not fully demonstrate his home literacy achievements at school. The teacher had the children dictate stories to her and then under-write her writing. Tom seldom did free writing though there was paper for this purpose in a drawer, which I saw a few older children make use of. In the home corner, where Tom played regularly with the very children from his neighbourhood with whom he played and wrote at home, there were seldom paper and pencils. When there were writing materials, Tom and the other children enthusiastically wrote telephone messages and shopping lists, as Tom did at home. In the class cafe, there were no writing materials at all, and children were instructed to take orders verbally.

Sometimes, at school, Tom made words with magnetic letters: his name, or his mother's and sister's names. He wrote his name on his work. He would sometimes sit and look at a book in the book corner — a free activity which the teacher encouraged. With the teacher, he practised letter formation and dictated 'news'. But his central writing strategy — incorporating environmental print in his drawings and stories — did not make the transition with him from home to school, either in free-writing or teacher-led activities. Tom neither copied words from the classroom word bank, nor wrote any of his own long-practised words. At home, Tom continued using his favourite writing strategy to find and use new words in his stories. At the end of Tom's term in reception class, his mother told me that he had said to her, 'I haven't told my teacher I can write'. In spite of the fact that both the school's language policy and the National Curriculum called for children's previous knowledge to be extended through authentic literacy experiences, this did not happen for Tom. His school literacy experiences could be said to have a low degree of autonomy, authenticity, integration, and social interaction.

Implications for schools

In a study of this nature it is all too easy to criticise teachers, and it is important to remember that my research focus was the children and not the teachers. Indeed, it was the teachers' generosity in permitting me to observe in their classrooms which enabled me to follow Tom's transition from home to school. My privileged information about Tom's preschool literacy achievements put me in a very unusual position in the classroom. I could not discuss my knowledge with the teacher — nor my classroom observations with the parents — without jeopardising my study. Further, it must be acknowledged that Tom's teacher made her own assessments based on what Tom did demonstrate in class and, even had she known of his home literacy strategies, she might well have wished to encourage him to be more flexible and to widen the range of writing strategies which he could comfortably use.

Clearly there are implications for parents, teachers and schools. It is difficult to imagine, in present circumstances, an extensive exchange of information between parents and teachers about children's home literacy experiences. As it is, many parents, including those in this study, feel they have inadequate information about how reading and writing are taught in their children's schools (see also Hannon and James, 1990). There is little scope for parents to communicate fully and continually with teachers about their children's home literacy achievements, but the onus must be on schools to facilitate such communication.

Tom's story may suggest, in addition to the need for greater communication between home and school, priorities for classroom organisation and making clear to children what their options are at school. For example, the teacher-led writing activities did not build on Tom's existing strategies. But neither did Tom seek writing materials, or draw on classroom environmental print, to employ his own strategies in free-choice or play activities, both of which the teacher made space and time for. Admittedly, we may not want school to mirror home exactly, but this study suggests it may not be easy to make home and school literacy environments as *explicitly* compatible as we would like them to be.

Summary

Teachers who do not have vital information about children's home literacy achievements cannot hope to build on those achievements at school. For the teacher, there may be missed opportunities to consolidate and extend what the children already know, and misconceptions around what they think the children do not know. The message to children about the nature of print, and about themselves as writers and readers, may well be quite at odds with the children's existing notions. The result may be the creation of a *school literacy* which leaves the child feeling confused or alienated from an early age. This study suggests there is a case for restructuring the notion of authenticity in school literacy activities with a greater sensitivity for the individual child's needs and prior experiences. In this way, the gap between home and school literacy learning may be bridged, to the benefit of children, parents and teachers.

References

Ferreiro, E. and Teberosky, A. (1982) *Literacy before schooling* Portsmouth, N.H.: Heinemann

Hannon, P. and James, S. (1990) 'Parents' and teachers' perspectives on pre-school literacy development' *British Educational Research Journal* 16, 3, 259-272.

Harste, J.C., Woodward, V.A. and Burke, C.L. (1984) *Language stories and literacy lessons* Portsmouth, N.H.: Heinemann

Heath, S.B. (1983) *Ways with words: language, life and work in communities and classrooms* Cambridge: Cambridge University Press

Schickedanz, J. (1990) *Adam's righting revolutions: One child's literacy development from infancy through grade one* Portsmouth, N.H.: Heinemann.

Taylor, D. (1983) *Family literacy: young children learning to read and write* London: Heinemann

Taylor, D. and Dorsey-Gaines, C. (1988) *Growing up literate: Learning from inner-city families* Portsmouth, N.H.: Heinemann

Weinberger, J. (1993) *A Longitudinal Study of Literacy Experiences, the Role of Parents, and Children's Literacy Development* University of Sheffield: unpublished Ph.D. thesis.

Weinberger, J., Hannon, P., and Nutbrown, C. (1991) *Ways of Working With Parents to Promote Early Literacy Development* USDE Papers in Education, No. 14. Sheffield: University of Sheffield.

Wells, G. (1986) *The meaning makers: Children learning language and using language to learn* London: Hodder and Stoughton

Chapter 15

Family matters: adults reading aloud to children at home and at school and its implications for language education

Julie Spreadbury
Queensland University of Technology

Introduction

With two sons of my own who had been read to from birth by our extended family and the belief that families do matter in children's literacy development, I began a PhD study of 25 Brisbane families reading aloud to their children in the home.

This study examined the complex three-way interactions that take place when a parent and a child share a text. It endeavoured to tease out the particular variables in this interaction that facilitate the child's later reading ability. As part of this, the study also investigated parent styles in such book reading episodes and how these changed from when the child was a dependent reader to when the child was an independent reader, i.e. the transition period from the end of the child's Preschool Year to the end of the first year in Primary School — a period neglected by researchers in early literacy.

Reading Aloud at Home

The subjects were 25 children drawn randomly from the two Year 1 classes at a State Primary School in Brisbane. This school was chosen because it has varied socio-economic levels. 15 were boys and 11 were girls. One of the girls left the study in March of her Grade 1 as her family moved to seek employment. At the beginning of Grade 1, the majority of the children had turned six (16), nine were five year olds and one child was slightly older at seven.

The fathers' occupations ranged from medical doctor, research scientist and engineer to three fathers being unemployed. On the other hand, the occupations of the mothers who worked outside the home were not as varied, ranging from a bank officer through secretarial work and shop assistant to a nursing home aide.

At the end of the child's preschool and at the end of Year 1 at school, I went in to each child's home and interviewed the parent about demographic aspects of the family, the family's literacy practices and parents' attitudes and ideologies about literacy. On both occasions, the parent and child were videoed reading the picture book, *Sloppy Kisses* (Winthrop, 1986) which was chosen because it had just been published and so was an unknown text to all the families. By videoing all the dyads of parent and child reading the same text there was a basis for comparison. In most homes only one parent read to the child, in others both mother and father read the texts. I also interviewed the children's teachers at both Preschool and Year 1 and videoed them reading to groups of the children as part of their daily routine .

Throughout Grade 1, various standardised tests were conducted on the individual children in the project. Children were tested early in the year for their concepts of literacy using Kemp's *Children's Understanding of Reading Language* (1982) test, then at various times throughout the year for language and reading abilities, using the *Test of Early Language Development* (Hresko, Reid and Hammill, 1981) and the *Test of Early*

Reading Ability (Reid, Hresko and Hammill, 1981) respectively. Towards the end of Grade 1 they were tested using the *Revised Peabody Picture Vocabulary Test* (Dunn and Dunn, 1981) and the Piers-Harris *Self Concept test* (1969). Running records on whether the children were dependent or independent readers were also carried out at the end of Grade 1 and, because the findings of the study were so similar to those of Wells ' Bristol study (see Wells, 1981a; 1981b; 1982; 1985; 1987; 1988), Holdaway's *Informal Prose Inventory* (1979) was used at the end of Year 3 to assess the children's reading ability at age 8 and the *TORCH* test (Mossenson, Hill and Masters, 1987) was used to assess the children's reading ability at age 10. At these times the children were also interviewed about how they had learnt to read and their reading strategies.

The videos of the parent and child reading *Sloppy Kisses* were transcribed and coded using various different analyses (see Spreadbury, 1993).

Some of the results of this study are discussed below.

During both readings parents showed great variation in individual style of reading *Sloppy Kisses*. It is interesting to note that, contrary to Flood's (1977) research, no parents discussed the cover of the text but a few parents contextualised the narrative by linking it to their child's past experience, as Brendan's mother does in this Preschool reading —

Mother:
We'll read *Sloppy Kisses* first.
Sloppy Kisses
Brendan, that's like the kids don't like me kissing them with my lipstick on, eh?

Brendan:
(laughing) Yeah!

During the reading, parents focused on the story meaning, not on word meaning. Only one parent explained a word meaning to her child —'papa' for 'daddy' or 'father' — a word only used by one family in the study. There was no discussion in either the Preschool or the Grade 1 reading about letters or indeed 'print'.

Several parents focused the discussion on the illustrations in the text as in this Preschool reading by Samantha's mother —

Mother:
Emmy-Lou kissed Papa goodbye
when she went to school.
And when they came home,
it started all over again.
Emmy Lou's family just loved to kiss.

Mother:
There's Papa going to work.
They're a funny family aren't they?
They look like piggies.

Sam:
They are! (laughs)
Oh look at that! (points to illustration)

Mother:
Have you ever seen a piggy kiss?
I reckon they grunt (makes grunting noise)

Sam:
Yes! (Mother and Sam both laugh)

There are also frequent examples in the transcripts of children modelling questions on those of the parent reading to them, for example, in the Preschool reading of *Sloppy Kisses* after 'Emmy Lou snuggled down under her covers. It took her a long time to get to sleep', Alice's mother asked 'I wonder why?', an inferential question that Alice did not answer. Later during the same reading after 'One night Emmy Lou couldn't get to sleep ... No matter what she did she could not get to sleep' Alice asked the same question 'I wonder why?' Her mother answered 'I don't know. Let's read on.'

During both readings parents asked many inferential questions which their children did not respond to. Alice's mother's, 'I wonder why?' was asked by 10 parents over both readings and was mostly allowed to 'plop' or be ignored by the child. In some readings where the child was unable to answer the question, the parent 'scaffolded' or helped the child succeed by providing more information, as in this interaction with Sean and his mother during the Grade 1 reading:

Mother:
It took her a long time to get to sleep.

Mother:
Why do you think it took her so long to get to sleep?

Sean:
'Cos she was thinking.

Mother:
She just had a pat on the shoulder instead of her usual kiss goodnight, didn't she?

Here, Sean's mother provided him with the necessary information in the form of a confirm — verify — reassure type question, a tag question which threw the conversation over to him. He responded nonverbally by nodding his head to show he understood.

When a child could not answer an inferential question, some parents provided more information as Sean's mother did, but then dropped the level of comprehension required by asking a determinate comprehension question as in this interaction between Brian and his mother during the Grade 1 reading —

Mother:
Why do you think it took her a long time to get to sleep?
(INFERENTIAL)
She's thinking about what they said about kissing.
(PROVIDING INFORMATION)
You find it easy to get to sleep, cause you always have a kiss goodnight, don't you?
(DETERMINATE)

In the highly interactive dyads, many parents 'uped the ante' during the Grade 1 reading by asking questions that demanded a higher level of comprehension from their child. The parents were unaware of doing this, that is, they were interacting with their child during the reading, not consciously teaching the child. This is similar to the parent using simpler lexis and grammatical structure in language to converse with a baby, or how they scaffold the child's language or tasks in the early years. This is in keeping with the research findings of Snow, Perlmann and Nathan (1986).

During the readings of *Sloppy Kisses* some parents even focused their discussion at a deeper level on the ideology of the text. An analysis of the discourse between two dyads during the reading of *Sloppy Kisses* shows that both mothers used similar strategies to transmit the ideology of the text. Both used tag questions i.e. confirm — verify — probe or confirm — verify — reassure questions to include their child in the conversation while directing attention to the ideology by explicit information providing statements. They also linked the ideology included in the text to their child's own everyday experience thus making it real and powerful for the child.

Unlike Flood's (1977) research, no parent asked any comprehension questions at the end of the text at either Preschool or Grade 1 levels. They did, however, frequently comment on their own enjoyment of the book or ask if the child enjoyed the text . Although the parents had more utterances overall than the children, in the highly interactive dyads, the power was shared by parent and child, with the child contributing questions and comments, not merely responding to the parent's questions and comments. This was in contrast to the Grade 1 teachers' readings where the teacher alone controlled the interaction.

There was great variation in parent reading style, ranging from those who were highly interactive with their child during the reading to those who had little or no verbal interaction. The decrease in interaction from the Preschool reading to the Grade 1 reading can be seen at the non-interactive end of this continuum where there were three dyads with no interaction at the Preschool level but ten dyads with no interaction and five with only one or two utterances at the Grade 1 level. This is in keeping with Heath's (1980) findings that interactive behaviour during story reading episodes in the home changes as the child gets older. Initially, parents encouraged interaction but by the age of three [in this study age six] parents expect the child to sit still, listen quietly to the text, and gain information from it as they are expected to do in many classrooms.

The amount of child comment at the Grade 1 reading fell to a highly significant degree which may suggest that even after one year of formal schooling children have learned to be passive listeners of stories, not actively interacting with either the person reading the text or the text itself. This may be because at Grade 1 level these children had been read to as a whole class of twenty children, not individually or in small groups as they had been at Preschool and in the home, and although there was some interaction between children and teacher during Shared Book reading sessions, children's comments or questions were discouraged and regarded as 'interruptions' at other times when the teacher read aloud to all the children. These reading aloud sessions were more performance oriented than interactive.

Children's Understanding of Reading Language, which tested the children's understanding of literacy, correlated not only with the other tests but highly correlated with the children's reading scores at six and eight and ten years of age. This is in keeping with Wells' Bristol Project findings.

The correlations of greatest significance in the study were found in the fact that the number of parent utterances correlated with the child's reading at six, eight and ten years suggesting it is not merely reading to the child which facilitates their reading but the amount of interaction between parent and child; not merely the amount of talk but also the type of talk. This is shown by the correlation of the child's reading at age six , eight and ten with tag questions which, as Snow (1977) suggests, pass the conversation over to the child, thus affirming the child and also increasing the interaction between the two. There is also a correlation of 'Confirm — enquire — ask' questions where the verbal process comes first as in 'Did you see the mother?' and 'apprise — precise— specify' questions — the 'wh' questions that require specific information also correlate with the child's reading ability. This may highlight the particular parent language behaviours which expedite the child's reading. Many parents use these unconsciously during reading aloud interactions.

Overall, the number and level of correlation between the variables strongly suggest that reading aloud in the home is of great influence on the child's reading ability at school.

This study has revealed that parent, child and text reading aloud in the home changes in the transition period from preschool to Grade 1, from when most children are dependent readers to when most are independent readers, at least on suitable text. It shows that reading is a social process, learned in interaction with other people. Family story-book reading is seen as a vital social construct for the child's later independent reading.

Parents and Literacy (PAL)

As a direct result of this first project, I devised an intervention program for parents to both support them in their role as their child's first teacher and inform them of the changes in literacy teaching since they were at school.

This Parents and Literacy Project focused entirely on low socio-economic families in the Logan area of Brisbane. Parents, especially from low socio-economic areas where self-esteem may be low, often do not recognise their significance to their children's literacy learning. No known research of this kind has been carried out in Brisbane on family literacy practices in low socio-economic families, although research overseas (e.g. Heath 1983; Heath and Thomas, 1984) has shown important socio-economic differences in families in the USA. Heath comments on the need for more in-depth analyses of different individuals in the same cultural conditions so that 'we can identify the habits of perception and conceptualisation which are the unconscious supports behind the sustained symbolic structures of literacy in varied societal contexts' (Heath and Thomas, 1984:71).

Parents and Literacy Project was originally trialed with a small group of parents from Woodridge Catholic Primary School who had a child in Year 1 in 1992. In 1993 PAL was extended to include twenty Crestmede mothers. Crestmede is a low socio-economic suburb where the parents were young, only educated to the compulsory Year 10, and most only had each other as a support system.

PAL is practical action research based on the proven fact that parents play a critical role in children's literacy learning. The Intervention Program differs from any in Australia in that, far from trying to make parents more skilled 'teachers', it endeavoured to help parents and children escape from the 'non-literary trap' by firstly supporting parents and literacy in the home and secondly by informing them of how home literacy practices foster literacy learning in children at school. It included practice in communication skills such as self-esteem building and positive appreciation of others and emphasised that the attitudes and skills gained in a warm and interactive family constitute a resource that is just as real as economic resources and security. Indeed, it may be the key to giving their children a brighter future.

The aims of the programme were:

- To investigate family literacy practices in a low socio-economic suburb of Brisbane
- To run a Parents and Literacy Programme for parents in this area with a child in Year 1
- To evaluate the programme to improve its ability to support and educate future low socio-economic families.

Parents and Literacy Programme was trailed over a 4 week block of 2 hours a week. It was held on Tuesdays 12.45 — 2.45 in the community hall of the school. The programme was as follows:

WEEK 1
Fostering Learning in the Home
Self-esteem for parents and children
Listening to and affirming your child
How children learn to speak

WEEK 2
Reading at Home and at School
Parents reading aloud to children in the home
What is reading? Where does it start?
New teaching approaches to reading
How to help your child with reading aloud

WEEK 3
Writing at Home and at School
What is writing? Where does it start?
New teaching approaches to writing
How to help your child with school written work

WEEK 4
Technology and Literacy
Films, video games and computers at home and school
How to continue to support your child in literacy learning
Parents are important!
Evaluation of the course.

Evaluation of the Programme

A highly interactive workshop approach was used and this worked well with the number of parents involved. Parents were encouraged to see themselves as equal participants in the programme with the facilitator as they were the 'experts' on their own children. There was some attrition in that only 12 parents out of the original 20 attended all 8 hours of the course. This was attributed to sickness in the family and other family commitments. Those who attended all of the course were asked to complete an evaluation form. All rated PAL as either 'good' or 'excellent'. Their evaluation comments were very positive with almost all saying the programme could be improved by either lengthening it or by having all parents attend the sessions! All reported learning from it and most said they also found the sessions 'enjoyable'.

All parents were videotaped reading a narrative and a factual text to their Year 1 child before PAL began. Those who attended all sessions of PAL were also videotaped reading the same texts to their child three months after completing PAL. These videos were transcribed and analysed. A comparison showed there was twice as much interaction between parent and child during reading after completing PAL. As the amount and quality of interaction between parent and child correlated significantly with the child's reading ability at age 6, 8 and 10 from my first study, this may help with literacy achievement in the children whose mothers attended PAL.

The programme's value lies in that it seeks to update parents on school literacy teaching, support what parents are doing with their children in the home, and in turn encourages parents to support teachers in the school. All parents involved in the programme felt it was time very well spent. They regretted that more parents had not attended to gain the same insights that they had learned from it.

Collaboration for Successful learning —A Partnership of Parents, teachers and students

The third project is one that has been funded by the Australian government for the Australian Parents Council. This project has two parts. The first, for which I was responsible, was to access and document the literature and information about programmes that involve parents in their children's schooling with a view to identifying best practice. I found this to be quite a difficult task as most parent programs originate in individual schools usually conducted by innovative teachers and are rarely written up or evaluated in any way.

The second part of the project was to develop and pilot a programme of parental participation as an integral part of school organisation. The programme which was jointly written by an experienced primary teacher and parents, was piloted in twelve primary schools in three states of Australia. What was different about this programme was that parents conducted it in schools, not teachers or university educators. Parents responded very positively to the programme and there has been widespread support from both school administrators and classroom teachers.

Implications for Language Education

From my first study, parents showed they facilitate their child's literacy learning long before the child begins formal schooling. Parents do this across all educational and socio-economic levels. Instinctively they adapt the language they use in interactions with their child to suit the language level, including the reading level, of the child:

> Learning to read is a gradual process that begins early in the child's life, not a sudden happening that comes about when the child enters school. The roots of literacy are anchored within the social network of the family. (Chapman, 1986:11)

It is the interaction between parent and child that takes place when a parent reads to a child that facilitates this child's reading. In particular, reading is aided by the types of questions that the parent uses. These not only make the child responsible for his/her own learning but also, and perhaps more importantly, appear to strengthen the relationship between parent and child. Heath (1984) found that when a black teenage mother was encouraged to read to her young son she grew to know him better and many discipline problems disappeared —'When parents and children read stories together, they learn about themselves and gain a deeper understanding of one another' (Taylor and Strickland, 1989:1).

I would encourage every parent to make time to read individually with their children. Often this is the only time in a busy day where parent and child can really talk to each other. Try to read your child something beyond their own level of reading yet within their understanding. When my older son was eleven, we cried together over *Bridge to Terabithia* (Paterson, 1978) in which Leslie, the 12-year-old friend is drowned. Often he would go to sleep with the sounds of Dylan Thomas' poetry echoing in his ears—

> Now as I was young and easy under the apple boughs ..
> Time held me green and dying
> Though I sang in my chains like the sea.

My younger son and I have laughed at the antics of Fudge in Judy Blume's books *Tales of a Fourth Grade Nothing, Superfudge* and *Fudge-a-Mania.* We have discussed the birth of a baby by reading Paul Jennings' latest popular book *Undone.* Try looking at the ideology and values that come through different books with your child. We can thus make children aware of prejudice and bias in books so they can judge better for themselves not only in books but also in the videos and television programmes that are a very important part of their world in 1994. Above all, reading aloud to your child should be an enjoyable time for both of you —a time of caring as well as sharing.

Parents matter! Parents need to be told that they are most important to their children's intellectual growth, not least of all because of these close affective links between parent and child. The importance of the parent-child relationship in literacy learning must not be under estimated:

> The years before a child reads are replete with the impact of environmental experiences which present him to the reading teacher with certain skills, concepts, feelings and knowledge which form the pre-reading base from which she will need to build ...The role of 'parenting' is so vital to the arranging of such accumulations that the role of being 'the first teacher of reading' is unmistakable. (Ward, 1970:756)

From my third study, a collaboration of parents, teachers and schools, I made these recommendations. Firstly, parents do indeed teach literacy to their children and to do so, they often use different strategies from those used by teachers. Both parents and teachers need to accept that they each bring the child special attitudes, skills and knowledge necessary for success in reading. Both parents and teachers need to value the contribution of the other and work together as partners in children's learning.

Secondly, parent and literacy programmes should aim to be on a continuum from home based learning to school based learning.

HOME...	SCHOOL
parents as literacy tutors of their own children in their home	parents as literacy tutors of their own and/or other people's children in the classroom

Programmes at the home based learning end should be taken by parents while those at the school based end, where the end product may be to train parents as literacy teacher-aides for in-school literacy sessions, should be taught by qualified teachers.

Within these two contexts of home and school there needs to be a wide variety of parent and literacy programmes offered to parents, ranging from the informal to the more formal. Perhaps the more formal of these may be offered from outside organisations such as local universities and such courses would be counted as credits for degree courses such as Education in general and more specialised courses such as Adult and Community Literacy.

Thirdly, there is a great need for parent programmes in literacy to be taught by *parents*. It is significant that the research of this project did not find any parent and literacy program in Australia conducted by parents for parents. Instead of always relying on the professional teachers, parents must educate themselves and each other in how they teach their children literacy and how they can do this better.

Fourthly, parent and literacy programmes emphasise the importance of a balance in power between parents and teachers. In the past, teachers have been reluctant to relinquish their power over children's learning by even acknowledging the important educative role of homes and parents. On the other hand, there are those groups in our community who wish to redress this balance by giving parents great power in formal education settings. It is time to stop this power broking which emphasises competition instead of co-operation, and isolation between homes and schools instead of building bridges between the two.

Parents and teachers need to see the unique contribution they each give to children. Parents and teachers need to see each other as *partners* in children's learning —as collaborators, communicators and people who make connections between the different contexts of home and school.

Children who have been read to by parents in the home will continue to pass on their love of books and reading to younger children. As parents of the future they will know that families matter and that

> the attitudes and skills gained in a family with warm and secure relationships within the family and supportive, reliable relationships with extended family, friends and wider community constitutes a resource that is just as real as economic resources and security. (Eastman, 1989:45)

If parents were to interact more with their children they would realise the great enjoyment and satisfaction to be found in sharing a text together. Families would grow closer together. This may have profound social implications resulting in not only a more literate society but also a more emotionally stable one.

References

Blume, J. (1981) *Tales of a Fourth Grade Nothing.*St. Ives: Piper

Blume, J. (1983) *Superfudge* St Ives: Piper.

Blume, J. (1990) *Fudge-a-mania.*New York: Yearling

Chapman, D. L. (1986) 'Let's read another one' in Tovey D. and Kerber, J. (eds) *Roles in Literacy Learning —A New Perspective* Newark: International Reading Association

Dunn, L. and Dunn, L.M. (1981) *Peabody Picture Vocabulary Test — Revised* Minnesota: American Guidance Service

Eastman, M. (1989) *Family: The Vital Factor* Melbourne: Collins Dove

Flood, J. (1977) 'Parental styles in reading episodes with young children' *The Reading Teacher* May 864-867

Heath, S. B. (1980) 'The functions and uses of literacy' *Journal of Communication* 30 123-133

Heath, S. B. (1983) *Ways with Words: Language, Life and work in communities and classrooms* Cambridge: Cambridge University Press

Heath, S.B. with Thomas, C. (1984) 'The achievements of preschool literacy for mother and child' in Goelmen, H., Oberg, A. and Smith, F. (eds) *Awakening to Literacy* London: Heinemann

Holdaway, D. (1979) *The Foundations of Literacy* Sydney: Ashton Scholastic

Hresko, W., Reid, D. and Hammill D. (1981) *The Test of Early Language Development* (TELD) Austin: Pro-Ed

Jennings, P. (1993) *Undone* Middlesex: Penguin

Kemp, M. (1982) *Children's Understanding of Reading Language* (CURL) Melbourne: Nelson

Mossenson, L., Hill, P. and Masters, G. (1987) *Tests of Reading Comprehension (TORCH)* Melbourne: Australian Council for Educational Research

Paterson, K. (1978) *Bridge to Terabithia* Middlesex: Penguin

Piers, E. and Harris, D. (1969) *The Piers-Harris Children's Self Concept Scale* Tennessee: Counsellor Recordings and Tests

Reid, D., Hresko, W. and Hammill, D. (1981) *The Test of Early Reading Ability (TERA)* Austin: Pro-Ed

Snow, C. (1977) 'The development of conversation between mothers and babies' *Journal of Child Language* 4, 1-22

Snow, C., Perlmann, R and Nathan, D. (1986) 'Why routines are different: towards a multiple-factors model of the relation between input and language acquisition' in Nelson, K. (ed.) *Children's Language* Hillsdale: Lawrence Erlbaum

Spreadbury, J. (1993) *Parents, child and text factors in reading aloud in the home.* Unpublished PhD Thesis. Brisbane: University of Queensland

Strickland, D. and Taylor, D. (1989) 'Family story-book reading: implications for children, families and curriculum' in Strickland, D. and Morrow, L. (eds) *Emerging Literacy: Young Children Learn to Read and Write* Delaware: International Reading Association

Ward, E. (1970) 'A child's first reading teacher —his parents' *The Reading Teacher* 23, 756-760

Wells, G. (1981a) *Learning through Interaction* Cambridge: Cambridge University Press

Wells, G. (1981b) 'Some antecedents of early educational attainment' *British Journal of Sociology of Education* 2, 181-200

Wells, G. (1982) 'Story reading and the development of the symbolic skills' *Australian Journal of Reading* 5, 142-152

Wells, G. (1985) 'Preschool literacy related activities and success in school' in Olson D., Torrance, N. and Hilyard, A. (eds) *Literacy, Language and Learning* Cambridge: Cambridge University Press

Wells, G. (1987) 'Apprenticeship in literacy' *Interchange* 18, 109-123

Wells, G. (1988) 'Creating communities for literacy development' *Australian Journal of Reading* 11, 84-95

Winthrop, E. (1986) *Sloppy Kisses* Middlesex: Penguin

Chapter 16

The ALBSU family literacy initiative

Annabel Hemstedt
Adult Literacy and Basic Skills Unit

Background

ALBSU [the Adult Literacy and Basic Skills Unit] is the national developmental agency for basic skills work with adults in England and Wales (ALBSU, 1992). With funding from the Department for Education and the Welsh Office we work, independently, to achieve the aims of improving the quality of basic skills programmes and encouraging an increase in the scale of provision.

Our research shows that one in six of the adult population has a problem with basic skills and some half a million of those whose mother tongue is not English need help with language. Contrary to the apocalyptic claims of newspaper headlines it does not show that we are 'a nation of *illiterates*' [a term never used by ALBSU]. A very small proportion of adults has profound literacy difficulties that mean that they are unable to read or write at all. However, it is true that large numbers of people have a shortfall in the literacy and communication skills they need, both in everyday life and at work.

This paper outlines the initial stages of a four year developmental initiative led by ALBSU that focuses on family literacy (ALBSU, 1993a; 1993b). There are a number of starting points for this work. Every analysis of the reasons why adults enter basic skills programmes identifies two dominant sets of motives (ALBSU, 1993c). One set relates to employment, the other to being a parent. 62% of those joining programmes are aged between 21 and 40. Typically they say that they want to improve their skills so that they can help support their children's education and ALBSU has funded many projects that focus upon this. In 1992 we commissioned City University to examine possible correlations between parental literacy and the early reading achievements of children, based on data in the National Child Development Study (Ekinsmyth and Bynner, 1994). Their findings showed that 54% of children from families where parents had reading problems and no school leaving qualifications were in the lowest reading score group.

There has, of course, been a host of educational interventions in this country and abroad that have sought to increase children's early reading achievement by involving their parents (Birmingham, 1993; Hannon et al, 1991a; 1991b; NFLC, 1993; Nickse, 1989; Taylor, 1983; Tizard and Hughes, 1984). Many of these begin with an examination of the characteristics of the 'good' or 'successful' reader, at an early stage or when more advanced skills are established. They pin-point a wide range of factors from high parental involvement, experience of pre-school education, a literacy and language rich home environment, frequent story reading, interactive, dialogic or paired story reading, to position in the family or social class. Interventions are then designed which seek to reproduce [where possible] the conditions associated with success, in contexts where they may not be present. As research on these programmes has shown, certainty about which are the salient variables is elusive and there can be disappointments as well as successes when the results of supplementary programmes are analysed (St Pierre and Swartz, 1993).

Our approach to family literacy starts from the recognition that parents are the first, most influential educators of their children and that they have a continuing role alongside the changes in teachers and schools that their child will experience. The aim of the initiative is to provide learning opportunities for parents with literacy difficulties, and their children, so as to enhance skills in both generations and empower parents by exploring with them the strategies they can use to support their children's literacy development. Whilst the number and range of learning opportunities in basic skills for adults has grown beyond recognition since the mid seventies, almost none of them offer joint learning opportunities. Adults do make considerable progress. However, no one who has worked in the field would claim that it is the model of first choice. Through family literacy we are engaged in exploring alternatives. Alternatives that may prevent failure, harness the interest and motivation of parents in assisting their children and offer programmes that deliberately bring together the expertise of adult and early years tutors rather than having separate and largely unconnected provision.

What is distinctive about our approach is that it targets parents with difficulties in literacy and communication skills, and their children. Much of the research on wider parental involvement programmes shows that this group either does not participate, or is not in a position to take full advantage of different programmes. Highly literate parents do not have the monopoly on interest and concern for their children's education. But they are quite skilful in monopolising programmes. Family literacy deliberately discriminates in favour of those who do not have, or do not perceive themselves as having, a 'surplus' of confidence and skills in literacy.

Preparatory work, over nine months, included a study of work in the USA and Europe, examination of previous and existing work in the UK from the adult and early years perspectives and consultation with numerous experts (cf. Topping and Wolfendale, 1985). In 1993 ALBSU gained additional funding for the initiative.

The Initiative

Our priorities are to stimulate, fund and support the delivery of family literacy and to explore its impact through research. The principal areas of work are:

- Four Demonstration Programmes piloting an intensive delivery model
- A Small Grants Programme funding local work based upon partnership models
- In depth and action research evaluating impact and highlighting lessons
- Publications, promotion and staff development
- A major collaboration with the BBC.

Underlying all the work are a number of assumptions that we see as important if family literacy is to meet those needs it aims to meet. It is about writing, talking and listening, not just reading (Dickinson, 1994). It offers parents learning for their own sakes [supported by accreditation] and does not view them solely as conduits through which their children's literacy may be improved. It recognises and values the range of home literacy practices which may be distinct and different from those which prevail in school (Sticht, Beeler and McDonald, 1992). At the same time it should respond to the obvious interest which parents have in understanding the methods and approaches used in their child's school. It opens up and illustrates ways in which parents can have multiple roles in supporting their children, including those of role model, provider of opportunities and encouragement and teacher. It gives examples and opportunities to model ways in which everyday, inexpensive activities contribute to emergent literacy, like those identified by Hannon, Nutbrown and Weinberger (1991). It also provides insights into the underlying theory, so that parents have confidence, authority and an extended repertoire of support (Clay, 1979; 1987). It is complementary to other programmes, such as Reading Recovery. It should not be based upon extravagant claims that suggest universal, quick and easy solutions.

There are also practical, good practice issues that we see as contributing to effective programmes. For example the staff team should include people with expertise and qualifications in adult and early years work. However, they also need time and opportunity to develop a truly joint programme rather than two parallel offerings or a course with either parents or children added on as an annexe. One of the potential strengths of family literacy is that it is multi-dimensional and draws upon the knowledge of many agencies and disciplines — schools, LEAs, colleges, voluntary organisations, libraries, social services, advisers. However, unless structures are established which constructively guide the different contributions, there can be frustration and misunderstanding over 'turf' issues. At the delivery level it is, of course, important that the aims of the programme are clear and that this is reflected in learning plans, negotiated with parents. Materials and teaching and learning approaches should be stimulating and appropriate for both children and parents.

Demonstration Programmes

The four demonstration programmes in Cardiff, Liverpool, Norwich and North Tyneside are all working to the same overall framework and testing out an intensive delivery model. The features they share are:

- Free 12 week courses with 6 hours separate and two hours joint tuition each week
- Target audiences of parents at Foundation or Level 1 of the ALBSU Communication Standards and children aged 3 - 6
- Creche or child care support for younger children and support with transport
- Location in disadvantaged areas
- Staff teams led by full time adult basic skills and early years workers
- Inter agency partnership.

All the courses are based in, or on premises close to, infant or primary schools. The lead agencies are a Community College, an LEA, a County Council and a Metropolitan Council. The programmes offer two or more courses at the same time, and aim to recruit up to twelve parents and children on each course. They are based in places where there is a reasonably extensive range of adult basic skills provision, and guidance on further learning opportunities is built into the courses. The context for work with children under five contrasts sharply across the sites: in Norfolk nursery classes are exceptional whereas in Liverpool they are almost universal.

Each course is different, depending on the group which attends and their priorities. On one of the first two courses in Norwich sessions with parents and children included these topics: children's pre-reading skills, reading together, children's drawings, stimulating children's writing activities, phonics, making a sound game, print in the environment, making a shopping precinct, children's diet and nutrition, using computers together, visiting the zoo, sharing a story-telling session, making puppets and sharing a puppet show. The children participated in a wide range of activities designed to develop language and literacy, suited to their ages (Minns, 1990; Littlefair, 1994).

Sessions for parents alone also vary according to the interests of the group. The opportunity to gain accreditation is proving a strong motivation for parents. Staff teams therefore build in opportunities to extend communication skills within sessions where the content may be aspects of child development or the growth of literacy. So, for example, part of a session in Liverpool included viewing and taking notes on the video 'Leading to Reading' which illustrates positive, everyday ways of building early literacy skills. After this the tutor gave out four short 'Agony Aunt' letters, all based upon issues raised by members of the group earlier in the course. For example:

> Dear Liz,
>
> My son is nearly two and my sister tells me that I should be starting to help him read. I've bought some books but all he wants to do is chew them. I think I'd rather he was playing with his toys and enjoying himself rather than stuck in the house with books. He's too young. I want to leave reading until he starts school. What do you think?

Working in pairs the parents drafted replies, which were then discussed in the whole group. They showed confidence and authority in reviewing what positive advice they would give. After this a parent with quite basic writing skills worked individually with the tutor to produce a fair copy of one reply whilst another more advanced parent went straight to the word processor to produce final versions of four replies. Each activity combined: content that interested the parents, scope to extend skills and the opportunity for accreditation through a portfolio based on the elements of Wordpower. Also, and this has been true of all the courses so far, people enjoyed it.

Teaching is in small groups and 1:1. Some programmes work with volunteers. Programmes are not entirely classroom based: visits [for example to St Fagan's museum in Cardiff] have been popular and a rich source of ideas. 'Toolkits' [with paper, scissors, glue, pencils] support literacy activities at home.

In designing the framework for the Demonstration Programmes we gave considerable thought to format and length — both the number of weeks and the number of hours each week. Twelve weeks is, of course, very brief when one considers the magnitude of the task. Attending for eight hours a week is a major commitment for parents who have usually not studied since leaving school. Most of the programmes have now offered four courses, so it is too early to draw any firm conclusions. However, the fact that both attendance and retention rates have been over 90% suggests that the length and content of courses have suited the participants.

In order to evaluate the impact of the programmes the NFER is undertaking in depth research. This will look at gains in literacy for both parents and children. Assessment instruments have been devised and are used at the beginning and end of each course, after a period of twelve weeks and, for sample groups, after nine months. The research will also seek to capture the array of other information that could be relevant. How satisfied are parents with the courses? Do they gain accreditation? What do they do after the course? What impact is there on literacy practices at home? Are other family members affected? What are the views of the staff team and project partners on its impact? What changes have teachers noticed where the participating child is already in school? Are parents more involved with the school?

We have to wait for answers to these and other questions. So far there are positive signs. Accreditation and satisfaction rates are high. Parents who finish courses actively recruit for subsequent courses, give interviews on TV and radio and set up continuing activities. Many are taking on a regular role of helping in their child's school. In North Tyneside one group of graduates formed themselves into a charity 'MUMS — Mothers United May Study' and gained a grant so that a creche could be added to a computer course they wanted to attend. In her end of course evaluation, one Liverpool parent wrote:

> Before this course I was completely confused as to how children learn and how I could help at school. Now I am very clear about all these points and I am very glad I decided to enrol as it has really put me in a good position to help my child and hopefully give my child a better start to his education.

It would be a mistake to suggest that the development process so far has been carefree or unproblematic. Whilst retention rates are excellent, recruiting the target group has been difficult in some cases. Finding and equipping premises has not been easy. Creating a syllabus and materials has been a major task. Reconciling the need for 'hard' evaluative measures with the learning needs of parents and children has been problematic. When children are already in school there are competing demands on their time. On one programme the children clamoured to attend the joint session but their mother attended erratically. Taking the hard decision to turn the children away led to regular attendance by the mother. There have been very fruitful collaborations between adult and early years workers, but it is important not to underestimate the work that lies behind these. At a simple level the fact that in schools parents are always formally addressed by their surname and in basic skills first names are invariably used symbolises some of the ways in which staff have to reach understanding and respect for contrasting approaches. The workers on the programmes have been brought together by ALBSU for four residential seminars so that thought-provoking issues can be examined across all programmes.

Small Grants

Through the small grants programme, organisations are invited to bid to ALBSU for funding to support local family literacy work. It must involve parents with literacy and language needs, and their children, and must aim to enhance literacy. Beyond this the framework is deliberately open and bidders are invited to shape the work to suit their local context. All of the grants involve partnership and bring together different organisations which see family literacy as relevant to their priorities. Over 100 grants have already been approved, throughout England and Wales, aiming to work with over 5,000 parents and children.

They are very diverse, and reflect the expertise and imagination of those planning the work. For example, a college and local primary school in Gwynedd will focus upon book sharing through the medium of Welsh. In Rochdale, the LEA is working with a cluster of primary schools, all of which draw from families where the home language is not English. Libraries are partners in a number of grants, offering premises and orchestrating sessions with an emphasis on drama, storytelling and puppets as well as the staple of books. Some programmes involve home visits, or in the case of work in Birmingham with women in Purdah, home based sessions. On the Isle of Wight, a playbus is the travelling base for joint sessions with parents and children. In London, work with Barnados is with refugee families in temporary accommodation. In Sefton there is work alongside the major City Challenge programme.

Primary and nursery schools, often working with a local college, LEA or basic skills service, are the lead partners in many grants. Sometimes they are planning to add family literacy to an existing initiative such as Reading Recovery or a home/school reading scheme. There is variety in the methodological approaches, as well as the venues and the partners. Many grants plan to work for, say, two hours a week with parents and children separately and one hour together. Other formats include summer schools, intensive weeks of activity and short courses building in the use of computers. In all the work there is a lively interest in drawing in parents and looking at how to extend enjoyable, shared activities that foster literacy and language. A group of parents in a Swindon primary school has particular skills in handicrafts. The grant there involves making 'book bags'. Each bag contains a favourite story book, accompanied by models of the characters and an audio tape. These are the basis of sessions with parents which look at making story reading an animated, interactive process. And of course the bags go home.

Each grant will evaluate changes which take place, in parents and children. They will also be invited to comment on problems they met [and solutions they may have found] and ideas which are worth broadcasting more widely. In order to try and capture some of the lessons from this wide ranging array of work ALBSU is commissioning research which will look in more depth at a sample of contrasting grants and draw out findings.

Most of the grants begin work in September and it is therefore only possible to comment on the stage which has involved creating bids. What is striking about this is the enthusiasm of people in mainstream education but also in libraries, social and health services to become involved. They have frequently commented upon the value of the forums which have been established to draw together a bid. This should not suggest that such exploratory work is either simple or easy. A range of issues, from how to attract the intended target group, reach a shared vision between adult and early years workers or sustain funding remain as challenges.

Work with the BBC

The BBC has had a long-standing commitment to the promotion of literacy. In February 1995 it will make a major input to family literacy. This will include promotional 'shorts' [created by a PR company], a free orderline, an information/signposting/activity pack, a video for use by parents, and features across radio and television programmes. ALBSU is working closely with the BBC on all of these and is also preparing staff development programmes which will be shown on BBC Select.

Conclusion

Work with the BBC focuses on promotion. Many of ALBSU's other activities, including the production of posters, newsletters and materials to support teaching and learning, look towards the longer term when it will be necessary to try and ensure that the positive lessons from the development stage of family literacy are translated into widespread provision.

References

ALBSU (1992) *The ALBSU Standards for Basic Skills Students and Trainees* London: Adult Literacy and Basic Skills Unit

ALBSU (1993a) *Family Literacy — Getting Started* London: Adult Literacy and Basic Skills Unit

ALBSU (1993b) *Parents and their Children* London: Adult Literacy and Basic Skills Unit

ALBSU (1993c) *Viewpoints — Family Literacy* London: Adult Literacy and Basic Skills Unit

Birmingham Community Education Department (1993) *Leading to Reading* Birmingham: BCED

Butler, D. and Clay, M. (1979) *Reading Begins at Home* London: Heinemann

Clay, M. (1987) *Writing Begins at Home* London: Heinemann

Dickinson, D. (1994) *Bridges to Literacy* Oxford: Blackwell

Ekinsmyth, C. and Bynner, J. (1994) *The Basic Skills of Young Adults* London: Adult Literacy and Basic Skills Unit

Hannon, P., Nutbrown, C. and Weinberger, J. (1991) *Ways of working with parents to promote early literacy development* Sheffield: University of Sheffield

Hannon, P., Weinberger, J. and Nutbrown, C. (1991) *A study of work with parents to promote early literacy development* Windsor: NFER Nelson

Littlefair, A. (1994) *Literacy for Life* Cheshire: United Kingdom Reading Association

Minns, H. (1990) *Read it to me now!* London: Virago

NFLC (1993) *Creating an Upward Spiral of Success* Louisville: National Family Literacy Centre

Nickse, R. (1989) *Family and Intergenerational Literacy Programs* Urbana, Ill: Educational Research and Information Clearinghouse

Sticht, T., Beeler, M. and McDonald, B. (1992) *The Intergenerational Transfer of Cognitive Skills* New Jersey: Ablex

St Pierre, R. and Swartz, J. (1993) *National Evaluation of the Even Start Family Literacy Program* Washington: US Department of Education

Taylor, D. (1983) *Family Literacy* New Hampshire: Heinemann

Tizard, B. and Hughes, M. (1984) *Young Children Learning* London: Fontana

Topping, K. and Wolfendale, S. (eds) (1985) *Parental Involvement in Children's Learning* Beckenham: Croom Helm

REFERENCES

Chapter 17

Hackney PACT, home reading programmes and family literacy

Roger Hancock
PACT Co-ordinator

The Origins of PACT

In 1979 The Pitfield Project was set up in Hackney with the aim of giving support to a small group of schools in order that they might more effectively help children with learning difficulties. The Project team included Alex Griffiths, an educational psychologist, and Dorothy Hamilton, an advisory teacher, and they were based at Pitfield Street Teachers' Centre in south Hackney. Alex and Dorothy were both committed to the benefits of involving parents in children's education and therefore included home reading as one of the range of support initiatives offered by the Pitfield Project.

Encouraged by the success of the Project and the publicity given to home reading projects in Haringey (Hewison and Tizard, 1980) and

Rochdale (Jackson and Hannon, 1981), the Pitfield team decided to set up a home reading initiative in one Hackney school, De Beauvoir Junior School. This involved what has become the classic home reading arrangement whereby children regularly take school books home to read with their parents and teachers and parents communicate about children's reading progress on reading record cards.

The term 'PACT' (Parents And Children and Teachers) arose out of the work of the Pitfield Project and was chosen by Dorothy Hamilton to represent the broad idea of parents and teachers working together for children's learning. Dorothy's experience as a psycho-therapist had put her in touch with the difficulties that children experience when they find themselves handling different sets of expectations from home and school respectively. This resulted in a deep commitment to the idea of home and school working closely together for the benefit of children's development and learning. More specifically, 'PACT' also came to stand for home reading and many teachers now refer to 'PACT schemes' and 'PACT programmes'.

PACT, both as a service and as home reading, attracted considerable interest in Hackney and in other Inner London Educational Authority boroughs. Francis Bacon considered time to be the greatest innovator and time was certainly right for the idea of home reading in Hackney in the early 1980s. So much so that the Project team became quite well-known personalities. They were sought after for their ideas and experience, they were invited to speak in staffrooms, at teachers' centres and conferences, and they produced materials to help those who wanted to replicate the home reading idea. In short, the PACT team were involved in the classic features of project dissemination. They focused on the range of activities that enables a project to become more 'visible' to potential adopters in the educational world, activities that would support the movement of an idea from the wings to the centre stage of educational practice.

The Spread of Home Reading Programmes

There is reason to think that the school take-up for 'PACT' (as home reading programmes) was quite rapid and wide-spread. For instance, in the mid 1980s, a telephone survey in Hackney showed that 43 out of the Borough's 73 primary schools were operating programmes (Hitchen, 1984). My own surveys in Brent (Hancock, 1988), in Tower Hamlets

(Hancock, 1991, 1992) and in Hackney (Hancock and Gale, 1992) similarly showed high levels of commitment by schools, both for the practice of sending home reading books with children and for operating formalised programmes with parent-teacher communication cards. From my more recent contact with many schools within inner London and further afield, I can conclude that there continues to be high professional regard for the idea of collaborating with parents to support children's reading and that the original 'PACT' idea has entered professional practice in a very substantial and pleasing way.

One therefore imagines that many children have benefited from this practice, not only in terms of their actual reading attainments, but also in terms of their love of books and their increased motivation to become life-long readers. PACT as home reading has to be seen as a success story for children's reading and for the development of home-school relations and I am pleased to be part of a profession that 'opened up' its practice in a key area of the curriculum.

The Translation of PACT into Educational Practice

When Dorothy and her colleagues started disseminating the ideas and learning associated with concept 'PACT', what came through for teachers (and children and parents) was the very specific practice of a home reading programme — PACT was interpreted only as this. The broader, more challenging message — that parents and teachers and children should work together in as many ways as possible and learn from each other — was, to a large extent, lost in the 'packaging' and 'selling' exercise. Dorothy identified a tension:

> The Pitfield Project was deliberately a narrowly based initiative to work with the teachers and children of a small group of schools. PACT as home reading was seen by us as an important way into the schools' practice. We recognised rightly, that if you don't give schools a fairly precise, a fairly tight agenda with objectives and practical points to follow which are carefully bounded, then nothing happens at all. The flip-side, of course, was a narrowness of interpretation of the idea of parental involvement in education. (Hamilton, 1994)

However, even though the broad idea of PACT had been 'lost' to home reading programmes, there was still a possibility that collaboration on children's reading would give rise to a two-way dialogue between parents and teachers and therefore closer home-school understanding.

Like all practical ideas in educational life, home reading can be set up well or otherwise. In the rush to implement a good idea in the busy context of school life, many teachers concentrated on integrating programmes into classroom practice but neglected to give sufficient time to the parent side of the arrangement. For instance, there was a need to consider existing parental activity in the area of literacy learning and to link creatively with such parent practices, skills and knowledge. There was also a need to give special support to those parents who were not confident or able to work with their children on the sorts of reading activities that were being suggested.

Generally, it was assumed that literacy learning begins once the child moves from home to school. There was a tendency to present home reading as a new professional idea being put forward by teachers, almost as though parental involvement in reading had suddenly been discovered by schools in the early 1980s! In Hackney, parents were offered stickers and badges saying 'Read With Your Child'. Some parents were offended by an imperative which, although clearly well meant, was disregarding of the long tradition of home involvement in children's language and literacy learning and overlooked the ongoing practices of many parents.

The main thrust of interpretation was therefore made by us teachers who invited parents to become involved in supporting children's reading by carefully following professional advice and the sorts of things we do to promote reading at school. The result was that parental involvement in children's reading was very much conceptualised and organised by us — there was a real lack of negotiation about the form that parental support might take. We assumed that the school's approach to teaching children to read could be moved into the home, that parents should simply do more of what we would do if we had the time. 'Schooled literacy' (Meek, 1991) was sent home.

As I have said, there was certainly value in this for children's reading progress but as someone who recognises the enormous educational sense of bringing home and school closer together, I feel it was a missed opportunity to learn about ongoing home literacy practices and to have formulated appropriate professional approaches in the light of this.

How can we explain what happened? First and foremost, I think it is important to remember the significance of what we did. Collectively, as a profession, we decided to let parents into a high status curriculum activity. It was a very significant development in our professional history. Hitherto, we had been 'possessive' about the teaching of reading and our various professional associations gave us full backing. In the early 1980s, the barriers came down, or maybe partially came down. However, home reading, as an experimental initiative, had to be defined by us at that point in time. We needed to bed it into our practice and feel confident and safe about the collaboration we were setting up with parents. We needed to be in control of the new development and the related new relationship — we would have been a very unusual profession if this had not been so.

What is there to learn about literacy in the home?

Every parent instinctively makes a contribution to the development of the 'language ground' which is crucial if children are to make sense of reading and writing at school. From early babyhood, parents help their children to use and understand a variety of linguistic 'registers' that are linked to the various functions that language can perform and are therefore very relevant to literacy learning.

In addition, many parents do much to promote their children's actual reading and writing skills so that by the time they start school, a substantial number of children are, in fact, readers, writers and spellers — albeit at a beginning level. However, parents don't stop giving this natural, informal support once children begin school. They still want to continue doing as much for children's literacy development as possible — with or without the school's knowledge or guidance. Evidence of the occurrence of this sort of parental support for children's literacy development is considerable and goes back a long way (e.g. DES, 1967; Newson et al, 1977; Hewison and Tizard, 1980; Tizard and Hughes, 1984; Minns, 1990; Hannon and James, 1990). Such studies not only reveal the considerable extent of parental activity but also remind us of the way in which we, as professionals, continue to overlook what they are doing and generally fail to link with it.

We (the professionals) know quite a lot about literacy at school but we actually know very little about literacy in the home, particularly when we remember that families are highly individual groups of adults and children with differing social class, religious and cultural affiliations. Some writers, however, have begun to give us illuminating glimpses of the sort of family practices that are supportive of children's literacy learning (e.g. Bissex, 1980; Taylor, 1983; Tizard and Hughes, 1984; Goelman and Oberg, 1984; Minns, 1993). What seems to be coming out of such studies is the message that there is considerable literacy learning in the home but it tends to be embedded in the social processes and cultural traditions of family life. For instance Taylor, in her study of six white, middle class, American families, writes:

> Within the context of the family, the transmission of literary styles and values is a diffuse experience, often occurring at the margins of awareness. Even when parents quite consciously introduced their children to print, the words were locked into the context of the situation. The label on the shampoo bottle, the recipe for carrot bread, and the neon signs in the street were not constructed to specifically teach reading; they were part of the child's world, and the child learned of their purpose as well as their meaning. (Taylor, 1983:20)

Taylor introduces the notion that literacy in the family is often inextricably bound up with family life and interests. Families 'mediate' literacy through a wide variety of social situations and environmental contexts. It is actually a complex and difficult phenomenon for a researcher to study because it can be subtly integrated into the web of family interactions which not only involve parents, other adults and children but also the many private, unobserved interactions between siblings. Literacy in the family can be momentary and, like a lot of human learning, it can be difficult to 'see', difficult for an observer to capture (Hancock, 1995). Indeed, Taylor found in her study that the parents themselves were often unaware of the way in which literacy learning was being supported in their own homes.

Minns (1990) picks up this analysis and moves it on when she examines the pre-school literacy histories of five children in the north-east of Coventry — two from 'white' families, two Asian and one African-Caribbean. She charts the uniquely rich family, cultural and religious 'literacies' of each of the five children. Her study underlines the wealth of literacy experiences and learning that is generated by families. She thus helps us to recognise what family literacy (in the home and community) actually looks like.

Defining and interpreting PACT in the 1990s

PACT (as a Hackney service) is now involved in a wide range of initiatives and projects that aim to enable home and school to work closely together for the benefit of children's learning. Indeed, there is almost no end to the curriculum and organisational contexts in which the concept 'PACT' can be realised. For instance, over the past year, PACT has been involved in projects which involve parents, children and teachers in school policy making about behaviour and discipline, in home and community activities related to various school-industry links, and in shared maths homework (IMPACT).

These are important and exciting focuses for home-school collaboration and, although literacy is not specifically mentioned, they all involve a lot of language and literacy learning for children (and parents). It is, however, important to stand back and consider the value of such 'PACT' activities in terms of a general backcloth of bringing the institutions of home and school closer together. Apart from being interesting and sometimes novel ideas, I like to see them as potential 'points of entry' for relationship making. They all require that teachers and parents talk to each other and share ideas about children and their learning. They all enable parents and teachers to get to know each other better, to reveal their respective skills and understandings and thus to express more clearly what is it that each partner wants for children's development and education. They all offer the possibility of home having an influence on school and school influencing home. They inhibit the development of a split between home and school (Dyne, 1993).

In addition to these sorts of additional PACT activities, PACT (the service) has continued to work with schools to extend and develop the idea of home reading programmes so that parents are more actively involved as collaborators than they were some ten years ago. As I have indicated, in our enthusiasm to get a good home-school idea going, we did tend to take over and dominate the relationship. To a large extent, this can be put down to our general lack of experience of working closely with parents — we were an 'inexperienced' profession moving in a new direction and we needed time to get it right. In Hackney today, there is much to suggest that many schools are more sensitive to parents' needs, more in touch with their ideas about reading and more confident at negotiating a reading partnership which shows respect and equality.

A key message is the need to relax from our earlier tight professional definition of what should happen when we work with parents on reading and to be better at setting up a dialogue with them about what they are already doing or feel they would like to do in order to support their children's literacy learning. This is particularly important when working closely with parents who have their own traditional ideas about how reading is best taught and what children should be reading. PACT is encouraging of a range of parent practices which can support children's literacy development and give them access to the home and community literacies that are to be found in a multicultural area like Hackney. There is thus a sense in which home reading programmes are professionally very valuable because they can serve to put teachers in touch with family literacy.

This looser, more creative, interpretation of home reading programmes involves being a 'listening professional' who overcomes the temptation to take control when meeting parents (see Hancock, 1994). It involves gaining an insight into what is already happening with regard to literacy in children's homes, establishing what ideas parents have about reading and writing and then working with them to develop the most meaningful and effective home practice. Sometimes, this can simply involve accepting that their existing practice is very sound. On the other hand, it often involves drawing upon our professional insights to suggest how 'natural' forms of home and community support can be made more effective and extended to dovetail with the more formal educational focuses of school. Clearly, this involves a lot of learning for us as teachers, because as already indicated, we don't really know very much about literacy in our children's homes. I have highlighted some of the writers who can point us in the right direction but in terms of our own localised and particular classroom practice there is no substitute for proper engagement with the individual parents of the children we teach.

In Hackney, this engagement can put us into some very challenging situations because not only do many parents experience a lack of confidence to speak openly and freely when they enter a school but also a substantial number speak and read very little English. An additional professional problem is the lack of official time that our contracts give us for unhurried consultations with parents. At a time when our obligation to parents as 'consumers' is being stressed, this must surely be seen as a strange and very unsatisfactory historical anomaly. However, despite these impediments, there remains a high level of commitment from Hackney teachers to the notion of closer home-school understanding and this serves to give energy and ingenuity to overcome many of the difficulties.

Family Literacy programmes and models

The idea of 'family literacy' has been around in education for some time. In Hackney, for example, the Haggerston Family Literacy Group was launched in 1991 (Wallace, 1993). Recently, however, the notion has received increased attention due to the way in which it has been developed in the United States. There, two themes have provided a driving force. Firstly, the wish to break into the cycle of educational underachievement and literacy difficulties in adults, and secondly, the idea of doing this through a family context in which adults and children learn to be literate together. In Britain, central government has embraced the idea of family literacy and encouraged its practical formulation through a Family Literacy Small Grants Programme administered by ALBSU (Adult Literacy and Basic Skills Unit).

The notion of 'family literacy' carries a certain immediate attraction — it has a high 'feel good' quality that few would want to challenge. However, the idea is not straightforward. At face value, it is referring to the literacy learning that takes place in a family setting, away from the more formal educational settings — the sort of natural home literacy learning that I briefly discussed earlier. However, current discourse from America, the DfE and ALBSU refers to family literacy 'programmes'. It seems that certain ingredients of 'natural' family literacy (viz. parents and other family adults learning together with children) are being selected and then incorporated into formalised educational programmes which are set up in suitable locations outside the home. Alan Wells, ALBSU's Director, has indicated that the aim of the Small Grants Programme for family literacy funding is to:

> '. . . encourage a great deal of diversity and experiment.' (Wells, 1993)

This sounds very promising indeed. However, he has also said:

> '. . . we're very clear that it (a family literacy programme) needs to be sharply targeted and sharply focused with very clear aims and objectives.' (Wells, *op.cit.*)

Although I recognise there is some value in specifying aims and objectives in certain teaching and training situations, I am concerned that we should be encouraged to emphasise this at the start of a programme, before we have had the time to get to know parents and children and consult with them about their ideas and wishes. From my experience of working with family groups, this essential period of consultation cannot be rushed. It depends upon building a climate of trust and security and it can take months before parents and children feel able to reveal their real literacy needs.

Alan Wells has also suggested that the role of the demonstration programmes is to find a model of working that maximises the effectiveness of the family literacy idea. As professional educators, it is understandable that we should be looking for a model to guide our practice — education is very much about formally organising and arranging teaching to promote certain sorts of learning and understanding. However, again I feel concern that the search for a model could dominate our thinking at too early a stage and cause us overlook the need to liaise and consult fully with the families attending the 'programme'.

Conclusion

In the early 1980s, PACT became involved in the dissemination of home reading programmes. There was considerable local interest in this practice and much that was good in terms of the relaxation of professional boundaries, in terms of teachers and parents beginning to work together and in terms of the consequent extra support for children's reading. However, there is reason to think that this innovation was mainly defined and organised by schools and that parents were not generally given an opportunity to contribute in any substantial way to the formulation of what took place. To some extent, therefore, it was a lost professional opportunity to learn about ongoing home and community support for reading and literacy, and a lost opportunity to set up a genuine dialogue for the benefit of children's learning and development.

I welcome the recent focus on the notion of 'family literacy' as it can be seen as a broader, potentially richer concept than 'home reading'. However, an early emphasis on finding an effective model concerns me because, as with home reading programmes, there is a risk that family literacy could be tightly defined and owned only by professionals.

As one who is very committed to closer home-school understanding, I feel great excitement about interpreting the notion of family literacy. I believe there is a chance that family practices, insights and materials will figure more strongly than they did with home reading in the early 1980s. If we can now work with families to create stimulating literacy learning contexts which not only incorporate the meaningfulness, relevance and subtlety of literacy in the home but also benefit from our professional insights with regard to the teaching of literacy we will indeed have a very powerful family literacy model.

References

Bissex, G. L. (1980) *GYNS AT WORK: a child learns to write and read* Cambridge: Harvard University Press

Department of Education and Science (1967) *Children and their Primary Schools* The Plowden Report Vol 1 London: Her Majesty's Stationery Office

Dyne, D. (1993) 'Who's kidding whom?' in Merttens, R., Mayers, D., Brown, A. and Vass, J. (eds) *Ruling the Margins: Problematising Parental Involvement* London: University of North London Press

Goelman, H., Oberg, A and Smith, F. (eds) (1984) *Awakening to Literacy* London: Heinemann

Hamilton, D. (1994) Personal communication, 22nd May 1994

Hancock, R. (1988) 'Parental Involvement in children's reading: results of a survey of Brent primary school headteachers' *Reading* 22, 3, 169-174

Hancock, R. (1991) 'Parental Involvement in Children's Reading in Tower Hamlets'. *Reading* 25, 1, 4-6

Hancock, R. (1992) 'Parental Involvement in Children's Education in Tower Hamlets' *Learning by Design* London: Tower Hamlets Professional Development Centre

Hancock, R. (1994) 'Professional language, literacy and parents', *Language Matters* 3 16-19

Hancock, R. (1995) 'Family Literacy — a French Connection.' *Primary Teaching Studies* 9, 1

Hancock, R. and Gale, S. (1992) *The 1991 PACT Survey* London: PACT

Hannon, P. and James, S. (1990) 'Parents' and teachers' perspectives on preschool literacy development, *British Educational Research Journal* 16, 3, 259-272

Hitchen, A. (1984) The results of this telephone survey of Hackney schools were reported on 21st December 1984 during a conference at the London Institute of Education

Hewison, J. and Tizard, J. (1980) 'Parental involvement and reading attainment' *British Journal of Educational Psychology* 50, 209-215

Jackson, A. and Hannon, P. (1981) *The Belfield Reading Project* Rochdale: Belfield Community Council

Meek, M. (1991) *On Being Literate* London: The Bodley Head

Minns, H. (1993) ''Don't tell them daddy taught you': the place of parents or putting parents in their place?' *Cambridge Journal of Education* 23, 1, 25-32

Minns, H. (1990) *Read It To Me Now!* London: Virago Press

Newson, J., Newson, E. and Barnes, P. (1977) *Perspectives on School at 7 Years Old* London: George Allen and Unwin

Taylor, D. (1983) *Family Literacy: Young Children Learning to Read and Write* New Hampshire: Heinemann Educational Books

Tizard, B. and Hughes, M. (1984) *Young Children Learning: Talking and Thinking at Home and School* London: Fontana

Wallace, W. (1993) 'Mum's the word for reading skills' *Times Educational Supplement* January 11: 8

Wells, A. (1993) Address at ALBSU's 'Developing Family Literacy Conference', Queen Elizabeth II Conference Centre, London, 13th October 1993

Chapter 18

The '99 by 99' Campaign: the pledge for literacy

Charlie Griffiths

'99 by 99' Project Director

Every year, about 100,000 or 16% of youngsters leave school with poor literacy. Many of them are unable to do essential everyday tasks such as taking down a message, filling in a form, reading simple instructions, making an appointment, or even checking what's on television. This situation is nothing new, however. Britain has always had a literacy problem. That figure of 16% has remained constant for over 50 years no matter which method of teaching has been in vogue or which government has been in power. It is not that standards are falling; rather that the literacy demands of society have increased dramatically. Every job requires an application form; every job requires some degree of literacy; the majority of employers need people who can take on new skills and adapt to the ever-changing world in which we live; and in these days of self-service, you can no longer rely on someone else to give you what you need — you have to be literate enough to read labels, prices, contents, instructions, everything, yourself. Today, those with poor literacy are more disadvantaged than ever before. It is surely unacceptable for a child to be allowed to enter this fast-moving, intolerant, adult world without the skills to survive in it.

It was this last belief that prompted representatives of some 50 organisations — including all the Teachers' Unions — to meet, 4 years ago, and discuss setting a target of 99% literacy for school-leavers. We believe this target is vital, not only because it gives us all something to aim for, nor because it gives parents and teachers a lever when trying to obtain extra support for a child, although both are valid enough. The 99% target is necessary because children respond to our expectations of them. If we expect them to fail, they will have no belief in their abilities; if we expect them to achieve, then they will strive for success. The formal adoption of the target would mean that, as a country, we accepted and recognised that the vast majority of children can learn to read, write and spell adequately, given the right help at the right time with the right resources.

The group decided that the best way forward was to form a new organisation, the '99 by 99' Association, with an executive committee elected from and by the original 50 organisations which would then work specifically for the 99% target. For the next two years, the interim executive continued to meet and in February 1992 it ran a very successful conference at which Dame Marie Clay was the keynote speaker. However, it was not until September 1992, when School Book Fairs stepped in and generously offered to cover the daily running costs of the newly named National Literacy Association that we were finally able to get the idea of the '99 by 99' campaign off the ground.

With the views and opinions of so many organisations to consider, our original aims and objectives ran into five or six pages — all important but '99 by 99' couldn't possibly address them all! So in consultation with the member organisations and with teachers out in the field, we selected three main aims which, if achieved, would have a significant impact on children's literacy: to give greater support and encouragement to parents and other adult carers with helping children with reading, writing and spelling; to ensure that children have greater access to books and other reading material at school and in the home; to give greater emphasis to the teaching of literacy skills at teacher training level and to give on-going support to all teachers.

We felt there were two main issues to address. Firstly, we needed to make people aware of the extent of our literacy problems and the implications for those with poor literacy. Secondly, we wanted to generate the feeling that literacy should be the concern of everyone; that each of us has a responsibility to ensure that every child has the right to be literate and that we can all do our 'bit' to help. At the same time, we wanted to popularise the whole thing and make it fun without at all diminishing the seriousness of our message. We needed to take '99 by 99' to places not normally associated with books or education or academia. We certainly wanted the support and involvement of such places — libraries, book shops and so on — but, if '99 by 99' were to reach a wider audience, then we needed to find a different kind of outlet. As far as we were concerned, there was only one high-street name which met all these requirements: we were thrilled when McDonald's Restaurants gave their wholehearted support to the campaign and agreed to act as our National Information Point.

We launched '99 by 99', built around *The Pledge for Literacy,* in July 1993 at the Shakespeare Globe Theatre Museum. Signing *The Pledge* is a means for people to demonstrate their support of the 99% target and to make their personal pledge or commitment to do something, however small it may seem, to help towards it. We suggested a range of activities to which different sectors of the community could 'pledge' themselves. For parents, it might be something as simple as pledging to share a book with their child each day or pledging to take their child to the library on a regular basis; for employers, it might be to support their local school for the purchase of books or to encourage their workforce to volunteer to help with children's reading at the local school; for teachers, it might be to devote a staff meeting to discussing literacy initiatives in the school; for those in national and local politics, we asked them to call for 99% literacy for school-leavers to be set as a national target.

The Pledge has been used by libraries, schools, book shops and parent groups. It has been translated into Welsh and even used by groups and organisations as far afield as Canada and Kuwait. McDonald's has hosted *Pledge* signings all around the country and supported local initiatives under '99 by 99' as well as the national campaign. For example, they funded a literacy corner at Somerford School in Christchurch, supported a reading scheme at Queensbury School in Bradford, held a champagne lunch to launch '99 by 99' in Birmingham, organised by the Federation of Children's Book Groups, sponsored a creative writing competition organised by Ann Coffey MP for primary schools in Stockport, provided books for mother and toddler groups meeting in their restaurants; the list goes on. Nationally and locally, *The Pledge* has been signed by representatives from all sectors of the community, including employers, the media, education and health professionals, and those working in national and local politics. In fact, our launch in London saw the general secretaries of three teachers' unions — Doug McAvoy, Nigel de Gruchy and Peter Smith — sharing a patform with Ann Taylor MP and Don Foster MP — a rare feat indeed! The support and commitment of all these groups and individuals is vital to the success of the campaign, but the pledge of 8-year-old Amel Patel to read his football mags instead of just taking out the posters is equally important!

Since our launch just over a year ago, '99 by 99' has maintained an unceasing level of activity. Every McDonald's Restaurant in the country, more than 500 outlets, displayed *The Pledge* together with our other two campaign posters — Have You Shared a Book Today? and Right Said Fred; we printed and distributed 250,000 *I've Signed The Pledge* leaflets; circulated 100,000 copies of *The Literacy Times for Schools*; distributed 20,000 *Literacy Times for Employers*; launched an annual nation-wide competition organised by the publishers, Child's Play, to encourage children's literacy; in July 1994, we printed and distributed 320,000 copies of *Read Hot!* a newspaper for children designed to stimulate interest in literacy (this project was so successful that *Read Hot!* will now be an annual publication aiming to reach every primary age child in the country); and in October '94, we ran a '99 by 99' Fun Day at London Zoo attended by some 1,500 children. On a political level, we haven't been idle either. We have held fringe meetings at the main party conferences; had an Early Day Motion tabled in the House of Commons calling for support of the 99% target; had a meeting with Baroness Blatch to discuss the work of '99 by 99'; contributed to the Reading Manifesto for Government and had the target of 99% literacy for school-leavers officially endorsed in the Labour Party's Policy on Education.

In everything we have done, '99 by 99' has sought to co-operate; to highlight the need for involvement from all sectors of the community in raising levels of literacy. We need government and those in positions of influence to take the lead but each one of us, as individuals, has a role to play; collectively, we have the power to create lasting change, to ensure that the 99% target becomes a reality.